MY LIFE IN THE NEWS

From Village Fete to the Front Line

MICHAEL CLAYTON

Merlin Unwin Books

First published in Great Britain by Merlin Unwin Books Ltd 2022

Merlin Unwin Books Ltd
Palmers House
Corve Street
Ludlow
Shropshire SY8 1DB
UK

www.merlinunwin.co.uk

The author asserts his moral right to be identified with this work.
ISBN 978 1 913159 51 1
Typeset in 12pt Adobe Caslon Pro by Merlin Unwin Books
Printed by CPI Group (UK) Ltd., Croydon

CONTENTS

To Marilyn
who made this book possible

INTRODUCTION

I have endeavoured to describe my life in this memoir of 20th century journalism because every field in which I worked has been changed profoundly by the digital revolution. War is a recurrent theme in my story; it intruded on my childhood during WW2, during my teens as a National Serviceman, and it dominated my years as a news reporter for the BBC.

The whiff of printing ink in a newspaper office, a press reporter's desperate search for a telephone box, and a television crew sending filmed reports home in tins, are among so many features of journalistic life which have disappeared. Perhaps the 'romance of journalism' was always a myth, but I certainly believed in it when I set out.

I started my career by calling on local paper offices on my bicycle. After many miles of pedalling far from my home in Bournemouth, I gained an apprenticeship as a reporter on an excellent weekly paper, the *New Milton Advertiser* and its sister paper, the *Lymington Times*. They were owned by the Curry family who worked apprentices hard, and paid them little, but to whom I owe immense gratitude for the thorough training I received.

It was a route to reporting in Fleet Street, and then to BBC national and international reporting in radio and television. I began reporting flower shows and local courts, and progressed to the Vietnam War, and conflicts in the Middle East and the Indian sub-continent, plus Iceland's 'Cod War' and disasters ranging from Aberfan to rail and air crashes.

My former colleague, and now justifiably an eminence in BBC news, John Simpson, referred to my performance as a war zone reporter in his book *We Chose to Speak of War and Strife*.

Simpson says Michael Clayton was a 'tall, elegant, idiosyncratic figure .... who first won fame in Britain by having the courage to show how scared he was during the various firefights he got himself into. At that stage viewers were still used to the clipped, impersonal style of the Second World War, and a man who insisted on thrusting himself in the way of danger while being clearly scared stiff was something altogether new and distinctly admirable'.

Simpson, a distinguished author as well as broadcasting legend, was generous in his assessment. I think it was borne out of my coverage of the Cambodian War which produced a very high casualty rate among journalists. I had the closest shaves of my career in Cambodia, causing me on one occasion to perform a notably fearful report lying down after our car had been shot up by North Vietnamese. The trauma of an exceptionally narrow escape caused my veteran cameraman to suddenly abandon me and return to London, soon to be replaced by another crew to work with me in further Cambodian scrapes.

Perhaps I made some contribution to news bulletins' depictions of war correspondents under fire, but it was entirely spontaneous, and it seemed to earn the sympathy of many viewers who wrote to me. On the whole I took the view that the news bulletin was not a theatre to show the correspondent performing feats of courage, but should concentrate on telling the story. I suspect brave World War 2 reporters winced under fire too, but they were reporting for radio only and could not be seen at moment of danger.

I admire today's media reporters covering the appalling Russian invasion of neighbouring Ukraine. They are all at grave risk, and they are often working in conditions of considerable discomfort and difficulty. I am glad the role of the war reporter is far better recognised in TV offices than it was in my day. They often have local interpreters, production back up teams, protective helmets and flak jackets, and far better communications than we enjoyed.

Nevertheless they are working in peril of their lives, and they are continuing the vital tradition of telling the world in words and pictures what is happening on battle fronts.

I followed a path to the top in TV war reporting which is virtually impossible today without the university or college education which I lacked. The internet and digital technology have cut costs and speeded up the transmission of news. But is it fair to ask whether higher educational and technological standards have vastly improved the quality of writing in the press, or level of reporting on television and radio?

My 'university', as an apprentice reporter on an excellent local newspaper, taught me first-hand a great deal about the law, local government, and politics. My 'exams' occurred every time my reports were published. Disgruntled readers did not only write letters to their local newspaper, but called in at only too accessible offices in New Milton. 'Get it right!' was the message drummed into me day after day. I still quake when I recall referring to a local family as Mr and Mrs Softer, when the use of a phonetic check would have established their name was in fact Foster. I owe the Editor a deep debt for not firing me over that one!

Those who warmly welcomed the digital revolution in journalism, did not foresee that it would soon imperil newspaper in print form, and broadcasting news. Many younger people nowadays do not buy newspapers. They rely on social media on the internet for their news, which is too often wildly inaccurate. They peer at their smart phones instead of reading a printed page.

Newspaper circulations have fallen, hitting hard the local and national press, while the BBC and other main TV outlets are under considerable pressure from streaming services provided by Netflix, Amazon and others. Licence fee income is under threat.

TV news bulletins today rely heavily on a battery of correspondents described as 'editors' specialising in different subjects. Much of the news film is streamed in from sources all over the world. It still calls for courageous reporters in battlefields. But it is fair to question whether the bulletins are more entertaining and informative than in the past?

The machine-like 24-hour rolling news bulletins run by the BBC, ITV and Sky, can produce a turn-off effect for viewers. Attempts are made by the TV giants to produce feature material as well, but they have to compete with current affair programmes on the main channels.

Whether or not you believe journalistic standards are higher since the digital world hit the press and media, I can assure you that the old-time Fleet Street and broadcasting outlets were far more fun for the reporter. There was a buccaneering element in a newsman's life which is eroded by today's need to spend hours staring at screens in on-line research for a news story.

I am sure there is still fun to be had in journalism, but the special flavour of reporting in Britain's earlier postwar years is worth recalling and recording.

When I entered Fleet Street, newspapers were kings of the printed world. Circulations were soaring; most railway commuters buried their heads in evening papers on their way home from work. *The London Evening News* where I worked, proudly proclaimed it had the world's largest evening paper circulation, well over a million copies. The competing *Evening Standard* and *Star* papers provided widely varied alternatives.

The Fleet Street reporter, having received a chit from the news desk, called out to the copy boys who ran round the office with pieces of news copy: 'Boy get me a tenner!' Armed with this cash advance on expenses, the newshound could rush out of the office to his car, or hail a taxi, and race to the scene of a breaking news story. There were few parking regulations, no security cameras, and no mobile phones. Getting the story back to the office meant dictating from a phone box, or paying a shopkeeper to use his phone.

Most morning and evening papers were centred around Fleet Street, and each paper's staff gathered in their own favourite pub. London was greyer, grimier, and more full of street crime, hold-ups and bank raids, than today when money is transported on-line.

Of course it all had to go, but I have sought to document one journalist's turbulent life in newspapers, magazines and broadcasting in an era which has disappeared, and will never return.

Chapter One

DESERT DRAMA

I am standing in a desert. It is uncomfortably hot, although it is a dry heat which is doing my sinuses some good. Everything else in my environment threatens to do me a great deal of harm.

I am not alone, and any minute I fear I shall be shot or taken prisoner: King Hussein of Jordan's armoured vehicles and tanks form a wide outer ring of vehicles facing inwards, with guns trained on the centre. Shimmering in the heat haze in the centre are two large passenger aircraft: a Pan American Boeing 747 and a Swissair Douglas DC-8.

These aircraft, carrying nearly 300 passengers and 30 crew between them, have been hijacked by members of the Popular Front for the Liberation of Palestine.

I can see some of the PFLP commandos roaring across the desert in a couple of jeeps. Some of the hijackers are standing up, with their head-dresses streaming, and all brandish rifles or machine guns.

At such a moment it is commonplace that one's entire life flashes before you. I am not getting the full-life treatment, but certainly my career as a reporter is recalled in a fraction of a second. I marvel that recording local events on a weekly newspaper in Hampshire has so quickly resulted in my attempt to report this potentially lethal drama for the rest of the world.

My best asset is that I am accompanied by the best BBC TV news crew in the business: cameraman Bernard Hesketh and his young, and equally brave sound recordist, Barry Lanchester.

As if filming a traffic incident at home, Bernard says calmly: 'Better get on with it. I don't think we've got a lot of time. Keep talking and I'll pan off you to get in as much of the scene as I can; we'll try to do it all in one take.'

So I stand with my back to the aircraft, and the imminent threat of the commandos approaching, and begin declaiming a piece to camera with as much passion, and as many facts, as I can muster.

Sometimes I am talking to the camera; other times I seem to be hovering above, looking down at myself performing this ridiculous charade, and wondering how I can keep it going...

'I think that's it. They're probably coming to get us,' says Bernard conversationally, stopping his camera, and peering over my shoulder.

He is such a professional that he insisted we brought two taxis from Amman. He unclips his roll of film, hands it to Barry who jumps into a taxi and promises the driver a big tip to get to Amman airport at top speed.

Bernard methodically folds his large wooden tripod and packs his camera gear, while I turn to face the dust cloud of the commando jeeps now heading our way.

*****

The Palestinian aircraft hijacking drama on 6 September, 1970, was the closest I got to a world-wide TV news scoop in my eight years with the BBC. By sheer chance I happened to be the only British TV reporter with a crew in Amman at the time. I was attempting to report growing civil strife between the Jordanians and Palestinians occupying huge refugee camps since leaving the Israeli occupied West Bank of the Jordan River after the Six Day War in 1967.

ITN as usual had arrived in Amman first: their reporter Gerald Seymour had produced reports already broadcast, and ITN decided it was safe for him to go home on the day I arrived. Gerry Seymour used his TV reporting life as fodder for his hugely successful second career as a thriller writer.

For once, the BBC's slow decision-making process on the foreign desk paid dividends, because soon the hijackings were underway, and I was jolting in a taxi across the desert to Dawson's Field, a former RAF desert airstrip. We gained a tip from the British Embassy that this could be the hijack scene.

I had only assimilated a few facts from my short-wave radio before we left Amman: the PFLP planted explosives under the aircraft after their armed hijackers on board had forced the pilots to land during the night in the desert, using flares and vehicle headlights to light the strip.

They were demanding the release of Palestinian prisoners from the West in exchange for the bewildered airline passengers now perilously held hostage in sweltering desert heat.

After our film was more or less safely on its way to Amman with Barry Lanchester in the second taxi, Bernard Hesketh and I waited for the arrival of the Palestinian commandos, speeding towards us in a cloud of dust in two small armoured cars. Their head-dresses swirled in the wind; they waved their rifles in the air as they approached. Hesketh stood there as calmly as if waiting for a number eleven bus in London; I took my cue from him, and tried to show similar outward calm, although my stomach was churning wildly; it seemed likely I had made my last ever piece to camera.

The PFLP boys screeched to a halt, and ordered us to follow them in our taxi. I was surprised to see several uniformed air hostesses in the vehicle with the hijackers, apparently laughing and joking. Was this a brave attempt to create a relationship with the hijackers which might ward off mass murder, I wondered?

The armoured cars led us right up to the boarding steps of one of the hijacked aircraft.

'So which TV company are you from?' asked a bland, young man in a fawn suit and sunglasses, speaking in perfect English.

When I explained, he replied: 'Ah, Michael Clayton of the BBC? Yes, I heard you the other night on the World Service from Amman, a bit confusing, but not bad, not bad at all.'

I thanked him for his mixed compliment, but our cordial chat was interrupted by two heavily scarfed hijackers who demanded in heavily accented English that we hand over our film and cameras. They poked automatic weapons in our chest to emphasise the point. Hesketh went through a pantomime of emptying his camera of a roll of unused film, handing it over gravely.

I was left to wander about, and walked to the foot of the landing steps to see an air stewardess looking down from the plane's open door.

'We're from the BBC,' I shouted. 'Are you OK?'

'It's getting very hot, but we're OK so far,' she shouted back. Then she ducked back inside, apparently at the order of a hijacker.

After a further chat with the sunglass smoothie, Hesketh and I were graciously advised we could go, and our empty camera was returned. We gave humble thanks and sped off in our taxi, exulting that thanks to Hesketh and Lanchester, and good editing in London, my lengthy stand-upper in the desert was the BBC exclusive lead story in the UK bulletins that night, also used by NBC in the US, and widely distributed throughout the world.

Our end of the story was temporarily eclipsed when the Palestinians tried hijacking an Israeli El Al flight from Amsterdam to London, only to be foiled by armed stewards and belligerent passengers. One hijacker was shot dead, but his partner, female terrorist Leila Khaled was taken prisoner and turned over to police in London.

Jordan became top of the news again when the Palestinians succeeded in hijacking a BOAC VC-10 flight on its way from Bahrain to London. Airport security checking was virtually non-existent in those days, and no-one thought to clamp down extra security after the first hijackings, although another Pan Am flight had been hijacked, then landed in Cairo and blown up after the passengers were released.

The arrival of a British plane in Jordan brought Fleet Street's finest, and some BBC 'reinforcements' to the Intercontinental Hotel in Amman where the crew and I were staying. Michael Blakey arrived for BBC TV, and Michael Elkins for radio, plus the hasty appearance of my friend and rival in Cambodia and other hot-spots, Michael Nicholson, desperately keen to 'catch up' for ITN; a plethora of Michaels. I was not overjoyed to see them on 'my' story.

Nicholson, the most forceful of the TV war groupies, made his presence felt literally next morning when we were among a large, excitable group of hacks at a bizarre press conference called by the hijackers at Dawson's Field. The Palestinian bosses had a keen sense of theatre: they scratched lines in the desert sand, made the press keep behind one line, and members of the hijacked plane crews and selected passengers keep some distance behind another line, with the planes in the background.

We shouted questions across the gap, and they replied on a loud hailer. A PFLP officer gave us a stentorian speech on the Palestinian cause, which he claimed justified risking the lives of several hundred innocent men, women and children passengers.

It was splendid television, and it was not long before the demarcation lines became blurred, as TV crews surged forward to nab individuals for 'exclusive' interviews. Nicholson was interviewing a pilot when I pushed in with my crew, and he responded by some judicious kicks to my shins below camera level while I interjected with BBC questions.

Fearless, enterprising and a genuine believer that what he was doing actually mattered, Nicholson has made a distinguished life-time career out of war reporting, and I much admire his skills and fortitude. But I remonstrated with him after Dawson's Field that proper war correspondents worthy of the name did not kick the shins of colleagues just to get a few more minutes on the telly.

Nicholson laughed it off, and he was to be a good companion in further adventures, notably crossing wildest Tanzania to the Ugandan border when Idi Amin was in power.

As I said in a BBC 2 *Timewatch* reconstruction of the Jordan hijackings, broadcast in 2007, I especially admired the coolness of the British pilot of the BOAC flight. Despite the stress and danger of landing his airliner safely in the desert in the dark, he behaved at the press conference like a middle-aged Englishman merely irritated at being interrupted while gardening.

I was pleased to learn later that good old BBC radio had fully used a spare sound tape I had included in our package in which I had been able to indulge in descriptive comment. It was a link with my former journalistic life as a 'words man' which I still found more compelling than scribbling terse TV scripts confined to those aspects of the story for which we had the pictures.

The Jordan hijackings story developed a plot worthy of a fiction thriller: most passengers were released, but arrived at the Intercontinental Hotel just before Jordan's King Hussein launched his army in a bitter struggle with the Palestinians. The PFLP kept some male passengers as bargain hostages at another venue in Amman.

The press and most passengers, including the women and children, were all trapped at the Intercontinental while shot and shell raged in the streets outside, sometimes holing the hotel and smashing its windows. My bedroom acquired a jagged port-hole, fortunately when I was elsewhere, and I slept thereafter on the floor in the corridor for a few hours each night, using a spare mattress as a token barrier against further gunfire.

All the hijacked passengers in the hotel were flown out in a Red Cross-arranged truce, amazed that the press and TV hacks voluntarily remained behind in the shattered hotel. By then I was extremely tired of living on cold scratch meals from the Intercontinental's kitchen bereft of fresh food and power, and not only was I missing my family, but the early foxhunting season was now in full swing at home. I had undertaken to write regular hunting reports for *The Field* in the season ahead, and I learned later that, tongue in cheek, that august sporting magazine published a short piece apologising to its readers for the absence of its hunting correspondent who was currently 'trapped under gunfire in war torn Amman'.

Now operating among a competitive mob of 'colleagues', I concentrated on surviving a situation which seemed to promise the further excitement of a direct hit on the beleaguered press.

American, French, German and British TV crews amused themselves concocting stirring pieces to camera in the hotel lobby while the Army provided plenty of gunfire a few yards from the doors. Soon we were all running out of film, and increasingly frustrated by our inability to send anything home.

Press reporters typed away on the portables in the corridors, but they could not dictate their stories: Amman's phone land lines were down, and radio telephones were in the future.

One afternoon the Jordanian Army operated a brief truce, and I was among several reporters who walked out of the hotel grounds into streets littered with cartridge cases, amid empty buildings with gaping windows and holed walls. Hussein's army had been ruthless in driving from the capital the Palestinian guests who had presumptuously sought to take over the country which had given them sanctuary from the West Bank, albeit in the squalor of crowded, insanitary camps which had been for too long tolerated by the world in general.

I was talking to a group of soldiers outside the hotel when I heard that all-too-familiar pop-pop of incoming AK47 rifle fire, and I dropped to the ground with the same instinct I had developed in a gruelling tour in Vietnam that spring.

The incoming fire continued, apparently from a sniper in an upper window opposite. I jumped over an ornamental bush and ran on all fours to the hotel lobby, where I flung myself behind a pillar. I hardly cared that my knees and hands were bleeding from glass splinters all over the hotel's bullet shattered frontage.

Although there were joint operations to save water, and share the Intercontinental's shrinking supply of tinned foods, the media mob could not maintain solidarity for long.

A French TV crew achieved a deal through their Amman embassy to leave the city, and drive down to the Gulf of Aqaba to escape the country – and scoop the world with their film.

They left amid grim silence from the remaining press and TV crews, but only 24 hours later there was a storm of ribald laughter and applause as the dejected three-man French crew returned with a Jordanian military escort.

They had been turned back on the road to the Gulf, and refused exit.

Meanwhile, we had arranged a mass media escape from Amman, operating through the American, British and other embassies.

Amusingly, the French were not included in this arrangement, and we were even more entertained as they protested loudly to various diplomatic and Red Cross staff who arrived with one khaki-coloured bus to take us to the airport. Eventually the French were allowed on board too, and the bus set off through a burning, shattered Amman which we were sternly forbidden to film.

A Jordanian Army officer warned us we could come under fire at any time, and I was among those not ashamed to shelter behind my typewriter case held against the windows.

We reached a deserted terminal building in Amman airport to be told there was no chance of a plane arriving until next day. Palestinian commandos were said to be intermittently mortaring the far end of the runway area.

A few Arab embassy children were in our escape group, and several of us used this as an excuse to break into the terminal's small buffet kitchen, raiding its meagre stock, and boiling up pots of soup on electric stoves which were working. With chocolate forced from slot machines we produced a 'feast' for everyone, and then spent a desperately uncomfortable night trying to sleep on wooden slatted seats in the terminal's austere waiting area.

A Jordanian passenger plane braved the airport's possible hazards to arrive next morning, and amid cheers we took off for Beirut airport where I was surprised to find the BBC operating with unusual efficiency. A back-up team of news staff organised a runway switch to a London plane just about to take off, and there was a special reception at Heathrow to whisk me to Television Centre, although I found time to give a radio interview to my old friends in Broadcasting House before I left the airport.

In those days editing yards of film and laying a sound track was a laborious process. The film editors did a magnificently swift 'pull together' of the film in what appeared to be a logical order, and on the 6pm news I gave an unscripted introduction, unshaven and in the same filthy shirt and slacks I had been wearing for days, before producing a live commentary under the film report. I am glad to say they gave full credit in the bulletin to Bernard Hesketh and Barry Lanchester, who produced marvellous footage. Bernard played a great part in helping the film editors achieve some sort of chronology and priority of shots chosen.

It was rough and ready editing, but it had genuine news immediacy, and it filled virtually all the bulletin. Perhaps in a small, clumsy way it contributed something to the growing trend towards 'live' coverage from the heart of the action, which satellite technology would soon make far more possible.

Afterwards I was expecting to be asked to produce a more polished job for the main nine o'clock news, but they had recorded the whole item on video-tape and the editors liked the rough version enough to reproduce it in full again that night, although I remained in full desert kit to read a more updated introductory script.

Despite imbibing frequent cups of terrible BBC coffee, I was visibly wilting by then. The Editor of TV News, Desmond Wilcox, a decent man but often a somewhat remote figure, thanked me for the work, and bestowed his own chauffeur-driven car for my trip home to Blackheath where my wife was waiting with our infant daughter and son. The home news was that son Marcus had a nasty cold which had prevented the family coming to the airport to join other BBC families. We were awoken from exhausted sleep soon after midnight by continuous ringing of our phone. A pert Canadian lady apologised, but said she had my number from her BBC colleagues, and would I mind giving an interview down the line to CBC? I asked grumpily how much they were paying.

'It's a reciprocal arrangement with the BBC', she said.

'Of course,' I replied. 'What a joy to be a BBC staff man.'

I gave the interview, sitting in the dark on the edge of the bed, while the rest of the family waited for the so often absent husband and father to finish the latest unprofitable aberration demanded by his ridiculous job.

I received a modest BBC bonus of £250 – for the Amman stint – some of which I spent on a badly-needed new hunter. I named this apparently workmanlike gelding Hijack.

Unfortunately, I was 'had': Hijack was not a sound horse, incapable of turning out regularly in the hunting field. Fortunately I had insured him to the hilt. When he was put down I received full recompense which enabled me to buy one of the most exciting horses I ever had the privilege of riding – the great Foxford who was to be instrumental in totally changing my life.

Chapter Two

CHILD OF WAR

Although the stresses and strains on our parents and their friends grew grievously, the Second World War was mostly an exciting, stimulating time for young boyhood if you were sublimely lucky enough to be brought up in a suburb of Bournemouth, one of Hitler's lowest priority targets in the world.

Aged five when it started, I enjoyed a 'good war', until one afternoon in a news cinema in 1944 I experienced a devastating revelation of what the horror of Nazi domination had meant on the European continent only 30 miles or so across the Channel from Bournemouth's tranquil but fenced-off sea-front. The images remain crystal clear today, reinforced by the Holocaust films I have seen since. My childhood illusion that I lived in a world of reason was shattered beyond repair. No matter how shocking, nothing I experienced later as a reporter in Vietnam and the Middle East was of any surprise, having absorbed the deepest, darkest horror of the Holocaust at the age of ten.

In the red-brick classrooms of Hillview Road Primary School, most of us welcomed the excitements of lessons being interrupted for instruction in donning gas-masks. I can still smell the rubber, and recall giggling helplessly as my vision was blotted out by my breath causing the Perspex window to be misted up.

It was possible to make very rude noises by blowing on the rubber of the gas-mask, much to the annoyance of our teacher, Miss Wilkinson, a tall slim maiden lady who taught us to read and write with admirable dedication and skill amid wartime difficulties.

There were further interruptions while we were shepherded to newly-built air-raid shelters, erected in the playgrounds in white brick lined with sandbags. We took for granted the immense effort of grown-ups in throwing up such defences all around us.

Outside school I played war games endlessly with my best friend, Geoffrey Northover, who lived in a house with a garden adjoining the far end of ours. We became such friends that our fathers made a small gate in the garden fence, and thereafter I achieved the company of Geoffrey, his sister Ann and groups of friends who played endlessly in the Northovers' garden, amid increasing areas of home-grown vegetables. 'Dig for Victory' was the first of a welter of war-time slogans which all helped to make life even more interesting.

At the bottom of our garden my father, and Geoffrey Northover's father, a Post Officer worker named Dick, dug a home-made shelter. It was a six feet deep, rectangular hole in the ground, covered with cast iron sheets laid on struts. It had seats of planks, and a small cupboard containing water bottles and packets of crisps. We children thought it was heavenly, and we were dying to use it in a real air-raid. The shelter would have been useless in a direct hit, but would have been some defence against 'blast' we were told by our parents. I longed to experience 'blast', but it never seemed to arrive in our garden.

We heard sirens soon after war's outbreak, but the phoney war period was somewhat disappointing for us. We were kitted out in toy tin hats, carried rudimentary home-made wooden rifles, and spent much of our playtime running about the garden, pointing these at the sky shouting 'ah-ah-ah-ah-ah....' to simulate the sound of automatic weapons.

Soon we were shouting at real German airplanes. The Battle of Britain, fought over the south coast skies, produced occasional dog-fights over the Bournemouth suburbs and the surrounding Dorset countryside.

For six and seven-year-old boys it was wonderful because the aerial combat took place in daylight.

On one occasion Geoffrey and I were trapped in his house, while his parents were out, and with not slightest thought for our own safety we gazed delightedly from an upper window at RAF fighters diving from the sky in combat with Germans. We heard the planes firing as they dived.

'Look, look, there's a Nazi!' we screamed with excitement, as we saw, or thought we saw, a plane bearing the German cross on its wings.

News of such encounters was either ignored, or only vaguely referred to in press and radio, bound by the requirements of war-time security, but word of mouth 'news' about the war on the home front spread rapidly, despite the new posters warning that 'careless talk costs lives'. We were aware, but blithely unconcerned, about the increasing government poster campaigns.

I wondered about the latter slogan for some time, and failed to understand it until I heard on the radio about the risk of talking to spies, or even more mysteriously 'fifth columnists'. It seemed to mean that anything remotely German was to be abhorred. My mother found a 'Made in Germany' label on a mechanical toy in a Bournemouth department store, and took it to an assistant who hastily apologised for selling such appalling pre-war stock.

Somehow we heard of planes brought down locally after the Battle of Britain aerial dog-fights. One morning we cycled several miles westwards into the green Dorset countryside which lapped our estate.

Near the village of Kinson small, excited groups of people were pointing down one lane. We rounded a bend and to our intense excitement we saw a German Messerschmidt lodged in a cottage front garden, its nose buried in the lawn, and its tail sticking high in the air.

There were no police or Air Raid Wardens present, and we joined other little boys collecting fragments of grey metal broken off the crashed plane. We took them home and kept them in precious caches of souvenirs in our bedrooms, alongside models of Spitfires,

Hurricanes, Blenheim bombers, and German aircraft which were especially popular for swapping in the school playground. I recall gaining a battered model of a Messerschmidt in return for a huge pile of conkers I had carefully collected for several days.

Kinson boys told us lurid, and possibly fictitious, stories that the pilot had parachuted down nearby, and had been captured by local farm workers armed with pitch-forks. However, such dramas did take place, and we were frequently reminded that someone 'over there' was trying to kill us in our own home town.

Bournemouth suffered far less than nearby Southampton and Portsmouth from enemy air-raids, but when Hitler's bombing campaign changed after the Battle of Britain, Bournemouth suffered sporadic night-time raids. One night I awoke when our bungalow shook alarmingly after a German land mine was dropped in Winton, largely destroying a local school – a pity it was not mine, I reflected wryly. There were one or two bomb sites in Bournemouth by the end of the war, but nothing compared with the devastation of London and many of our industrial cities.

'They drop bombs here when they've got a few left on their way back to Germany after trying to hit the factories inland,' my mother told me. She made me an 'air raid suit', a warm, brown garment of trousers, top and a pointed hood, with a long zip down the front. Thus attired I was rushed down the garden path to the new air-raid shelter, sometimes having to be dragged down the steps because I wanted to see the new night-time phenomenon of search-lights piercing the skies. It was especially exciting when I heard the drone of bombers somewhere over-head.

In the shelter we would meet the Northover family, and join in night-time picnics which were jolly for the children, but must have been tiring and stressful for our parents. My luck held out because my father, as a qualified electrician, was drafted into a 'reserved occupation', ship-building work in Southampton. He cycled from home six days a week, usually before dawn, to join train-loads of workers travelling 30 miles each way from Bournemouth station to Southampton docks. In winter he would return after dark, tired out, and often facing an interrupted night caused by the air-raids which I was enjoying so much.

Often his daily rail journey was delayed by the effects of overnight bombing on the docks, and sometimes the train was stopped in the New Forest by enemy air-raids, the men spilling out onto the track and into the heathland until the all-clear.

Once my mother took us to Southampton to join my father for a midday 'dinner' in a local café, a rare alternative to sandwiches packed by my mother. We waited outside metal gates at the docks until the workers appeared on the other side, penned in a mass against the gate. A whistle sounded, the gates swung open, and the mass of men and women poured out. My father, grimy in overalls and smelling vaguely of machinery and oil, emerged from the crowd, and joined us for a deplorable greasy spoon meal in the crowded café. I was not too young to realise with a pang that his war was no fun at all. He said very little about his work in Southampton, but I heard him quietly remark to my mother that the complicated wiring in the submarines they were fitting out was 'absolute hell'.

At home my father served as an Air Raid Warden, and for a while had to pound along Western Avenue during winter nights. He was supposed to shout the famous slogan 'Put that bloody light out' if a chink showed in the blackout, but I never heard him raise his voice.

One Sunday morning I accompanied him to a hilarious session learning to use stirrup pumps to put out incendiary bombs. It was conducted by my school headmaster, Mr Eaton, whose manner and diction was remarkably similar to Captain Mainwaring in Dad's Army.

I recall that the simulated incendiary bomb burnt down a small shed completely because the stirrup pumps were not employed effectively by my father and other men. Mr Eaton, tall, bespectacled and loud voiced, grew redder and redder, and nearly collapsed with indignation. I thought it was the best live comedy show I had seen for a long time.

Whatever his discomforts and stresses, my father was with us throughout the war, and did not undergo the rigours and risks of battle. I knew that most of my friends' fathers were in the Forces, away from home. Some never came back, or returned shattered, but a significant number undoubtedly had a 'good war,' and returned with new vigour to start businesses and careers.

My father, with his undemonstrative, non-ambitious attitude to work and life, endured his war-time routine stoically. It did not widen his horizons noticeably; he was only too glad to return to a peace-time job in Bournemouth at the end of the war, similar to his pre-war role.

My mother, with a far more highly strung nature, increasingly found the war irksome and wearing. She worked before marriage as a highly proficient shorthand-typist; now she was drafted to a dreary war ministry office in Boscombe, and later in the war when released she undertook temporary work cleaning a local public house to help our meagre budget. In the grim winter of 1943 she succumbed to a near fatal bout of pneumonia. With hospital beds full, she was nursed at home by daily visits from our excellent veteran family doctor, and a health visitor. As usual I was shielded from the worst news, but it was the most worrying event so far in my childhood, and I was deeply relieved when my mother rallied and recovered, despite the absence of penicillin and other drugs.

Soon after the war she worked for some years as a telephonist for the 'Blower', the bookmaking fraternity's private information service, conveying by phone the betting prices from tic-tac men on racecourses to off-racecourse bookies. It was a hectic afternoon's work against the clock, but my mother enjoyed the company of her 'Blower' team in a Bournemouth office, and made friends among local bookmakers who were sometimes remarkably generous in seasonal presents of Christmas fare which were highly welcome during postwar austerity.

We became a family of four at the start of war as my father's immediate elder brother, Oliver Clayton, was divorced from his wife Molly – a comparatively rare event in the 1940s – and his daughter, Nina, came to live with us permanently.

Only two years older than myself, Nina was a welcome addition to the household, although I did not see it that way at first. My place in the sun as a threesome with my parents was imperiled, but my mother dismissed my whining complaint brusquely and firmly. On this occasion corporal punishment was not employed, but I knew that Nina's arrival was non-negotiable. Cruelly, I referred to her inaccurately for a few days as our 'bossy evacuee', but this earned a stinging 'clip on the ear' from my mother's right hand, and I faced reality.

Rightly, my mother felt my only-child status badly needed changing, and she welcomed the virtual adoption of a daughter of whom she became very fond.

Her new life in our family was far more traumatically unsettling for Nina than perhaps we suspected, but she adapted remarkably well.

The arrival of evacuees from 1940 was another glimpse of war's reality in peaceful Western Avenue. As a six-year-old I was shaken when we opened our front door one evening to find a large tweedy lady with a weary small boy in tow, clutching paper bags, a small case and gas mask box. He was wearing an identifying brown paper tag, with a name scribbled on it, like a parcel hastily packed. While London and so many other centres were being heavily bombed, the risks of suddenly dumping children in unchecked new homes were irrelevant. Even as a six-year-old I felt a stab of pity for the new breed of evacuees from far away London.

'Can you take him in?' the Evacuation Officer gabbled as soon as the door was opened. My mother explained we had only two bedrooms, and both were occupied, but if Nina had not arrived I am sure the little boy would have moved in that night. I went to bed reflecting for a few minutes before sleep on my mother's reminder that I was 'one of the lucky little boys who did not have to be an evacuee'. One of our neighbours, an elderly, childless widow, Mrs Ruddle, took in the boy evacuee that night; he stayed for the rest of the war, and returned frequently as a teenager. My mother said he had done a lot to give Molly Ruddle 'a new lease of life'; she loved the boy and was very kind to him.

War intruded more dramatically in our bungalow when suddenly one Sunday lunch-time there arrived four British soldiers in uniform. They were among the thousands rescued across the Channel in the evacuation of Dunkirk at the end of May 1940.

It was typical of the war-time English that we heard few harrowing details of Dunkirk from these soldiers who had just escaped from the horrors of aerial bombardment on the beach, and a hazardous cross-Channel journey in one of the hastily assembled armada of 'little ships', some from Poole and other ports near Bournemouth. They chatted away politely throughout lunch before returning to rejoin shattered units to re-make Britain's Army.

The following Sunday a group of French soldiers who had escaped from the Dunkirk beaches arrived for lunch, and again it was a relaxed social occasion, amazingly unclouded by the blackening threat of Hitler's invasion of Britain.

My parents and their friends, in the presence of their children, never discussed the likelihood of Britain losing the war. I was of the generation brought up firmly to believe that we lived in the best country in the world, that we were invincible, and that it was only a matter of time before we beat all our foes.

One evening in June 1941 we heard on the BBC Home Service news that Russia had been invaded by Germany. My father said immediately with remarkable prescience: 'That's it then. We're alright now. Hitler will never beat Russia.'

Soon we were giving pennies to war-aid collections to help send munitions and other aid in perilous convoys to 'Uncle Joe Stalin'. We were sublimely unaware of Uncle Joe's appalling CV. I recall his friendly smiling face pictured in the *News Chronicle*, and I felt much reassured that this dear old man in Russia was on our side. The horrors of the Russian campaign remained completely unknown to me and my friends throughout the war. We knew very little about the Japanese war, although gradually the Far East campaign began to seep into the news occasionally.

The only war we understood was the one we were waging with the arch devil Hitler who lived somewhere the other side of the Channel. Thanks to him we could not even swim from our beaches any more, and it was entirely his fault we could not buy an ice cream, a fond and distant memory for a child of five at war's outbreak.

While at play with our wooden guns my friends and I regularly sang our anthem, to the Disney tune:

> *'Whistle while you work;*
> *Hitler is a twerp;*
> *Goring's barmy, so's his Army,*
> *Whistle while you work.'*

Such sentiments were reinforced constantly by the truly brilliant propaganda campaign waged by the war-time government headed by Winston Churchill. The cinemas soon re-opened after a brief closure early in the war, and I became an ardent fan of the superb war films which came to our screens.

I believed implicitly in the honour and rightness of our cause, as expressed by films carefully aimed at boosting war morale. My friends and I re-enacted incidents from such epics in our games among the furze bushes on Redhill Common.

There was no fantasy about a German aircraft raid I experienced while sailing my boat on the Bourne stream on a sunny Saturday afternoon in Bournemouth's sedate Lower Pleasure Gardens. With my father's help I was pushing my wind-up motor boat into the stream. Scores of other families were enjoying the same treat.

Suddenly we heard screams from further up the stream, and the roar of an airplane. It roared towards us, flying very low, and suddenly we heard the chatter of its guns. Everyone by the stream panicked and ran into bushes and woodland in the park. My father scooped me up and scrambled into some rhododendron bushes clothing a slope below the bandstand. It was a good move: the German fighter pilot made a turn, and embarked on another low-level attack on the civilians in the park, firing all the time, before making his exit over the nearby coastline.

Little or nothing was published or broadcast about the raid, presumably meant to dent civilian morale, but there were several fatalities, and one boy attending my school had his foot blown off. If we needed confirmation, the rending of the peace of Bournemouth's Pleasure Gardens was a reminder of how close we were to the war. Another daytime air raid hit a local hotel and killed several hundred servicemen, many of them Canadians about to sit down to lunch.

BBC radio was the greatest influence throughout my entire childhood. During a series of desperately cold winters we sat in our small living room in the evenings, by an inadequate coal fire, often smoking horribly, under one overhead electric light bulb which frequently flickered and reduced its glow. Power cuts were increasing, and were to get even worse soon after the war as Britain's ruined economy struggled to 'win the peace'.

We listened, and we roared at Tommy Handley's sublime Itma show – I could mimic nearly every voice – and the BBC's other wonderful war-time comedians such as Rob Wilton who started his monologues with the words: 'The day war broke out, my wife said to me....' There was a wealth of other programmes which I enjoyed enormously on BBC radio, and whatever shortcomings there were in my formal education, there were riches to be gained from imbibing Lord Reith's educational brand of broadcasting, and a home where reading was a major recreation. Very early in life I could speak in standard BBC announcer's English, differentiating clearly between that and local Dorset or Hampshire dialects which I could adopt at will.

In Bournemouth boys called each other 'moosh', and if we wished to be aggressive we would threaten to 'knock your block off...', or 'give you a good 'iding.'

My mother was immensely strict about 'bad language' and I never heard four letter words until in my teens, and never used them until I was a National Serviceman.

We listened of course to Churchill's historic rallying broadcasts, and as a child listener I was impressed not by the content but the rolling, confident manner in which he spoke.

I recall one evening when my father, despite my mother's protests, tuned in to one of the regular pro-Hitler broadcasts from Germany of the traitorous Englishman William Joyce, known derisively to us as 'Lord Haw Haw'.

I was fascinated, and slightly horrified, to hear him promise that 'Swaythling in Southampton is on our list of targets...'

My much-loved Auntie Bess, sister of my maternal grandmother, lived in the suburb Swaythling. I was much perturbed when the oily traitor described Swaythling's Town Hall clock and promised it would all be demolished. How did he know of the clock? There really must be spies about, I surmised.

It was the only occasion I heard the reverse side of the relentless pro-Allies propaganda we imbibed throughout the war, contributing to the extraordinary national ambience of cheerful, matey togetherness, no matter what our foes could hurl at us.

It was a Britain never to be experienced again, and modern society is firmly divided between those who lived through the war, and those born later. I cannot imagine what the reaction of our war-time contemporaries would have been to a forecast that later in the 20th century the British would avidly buy cars and many forms of technology made in a Germany and Japan who would prove they could make them better and cheaper than our own industries.

We were a white, indigenous society containing many virtues of care and voluntary service, but there were long established social injustices and avoidable inequalities. The best, and strongest element in war-time society was still the nuclear family, although orphans and others who slipped through the safety net of family and friends were still likely to face a rough fate. Working conditions for many were harsh and badly paid, but the war produced a host of new jobs for those who had long been unemployed in the 'thirties. A shamefully large number of working men given their medicals on joining the Army at the outbreak of war were found to be suffering from malnutrition.

Food rationing was a severe penance for many urban working class families, but most rural families were spared the worst effects of shortages. My mother's attempts to keep chickens were hopeless; she simply was not an animal person.

A generation of Britons developed an exceptionally sweet tooth because we queued relentlessly for our full ration of chocolates and sweets.

We knew nothing of obesity as a problem; we never lacked exercise because we walked or cycled endlessly; and we learned to value small gifts and rare luxuries. Above all, we liked each other's company.

The Warren family, a wonderfully cheerful brood of Dorset people who lived next door to us, ran an informal entertainments centre for servicemen in their bungalow throughout the war. Miraculously they boarded large parties of men in their small rooms, and every evening was a party.

My mother, and my father when available, joined evenings of mild drinking, sing songs and dancing with young servicemen who were to include increasing numbers of American troops arriving in Britain before the Normandy landings. I thought some were dangerously attractive, and noted that my mother and other local wives seemed to like them tremendously.

'They were just kids,' my mother would recall sadly. 'A lot of them never survived D-Day, and at least they had just a bit of fun in Bournemouth, but looking back it really wasn't up to much. We gave them what we could, but we didn't have much to give, and they were very well-behaved.

I was thrilled when the Americans brought delicacies we had forgotten such as tinned fruit and cream, and I learned to join the children's chorus of 'Any gum, chum?' when a US soldier approached on a Bournemouth street.

The end of the second world war, called V-J day (victory over Japan) was marked in Bournemouth in 1945 with an open air night-time party in Westover Road, still the smartest street in the town. I went with my mother and several of her friends. We were caught up in a huge communal sigh of relief and relaxation. Bournemouth did its best to behave like a holiday town. Music boomed into the street, and we linked arms with strangers to dance congas and the Palais Glide, which I performed inexpertly but with gusto. Perhaps because of my height, and the darkness, quite a lot of ladies of all ages kissed me rapturously, which I rather liked, although I detected some were less than sober.

Then suddenly, I knew the war was really over: the dark bulk of a concrete structure in front of the Pavilion suddenly exploded into a delight of splashing colour. Bournemouth's huge fountain, pride of the 1930s, was switched on again – and its huge plumes of water were illuminated brightly in constantly changing colours. The fact that the fountain still worked after a wartime of inaction seemed the best miracle of the victory night.

The black-out which had attended most of my childhood years was over.

There was a future of colour and delight. The fountain said it all. We gazed at it in wonder and delight.

That night in Westover Road we were ignorant of the prospect that Britain was about to enter more years of dire austerity, with economic depression, social deference, and food rationing still firmly in place.

The fountain lit the way far beyond. Although a gauche teenager I knew I was lucky to be alive, and it was just possible I could leave Bournemouth and explore a far more exciting world beyond.

Chapter Three

IMAGES OF HORROR

Throughout my childhood, until the age of 11, I partook of religion in my two inherited ordinations. Nearly every Sunday for five or six years my parents took me and my cousin Nina to the Bournemouth Meeting House in the centre of the town, for the Quaker form of 'religion without ritual'.

The Friends sat in silence on wooden chairs in their austere, bare walled meeting room. The Clerk of the Meeting sat facing them at a top table, but no-one conducted any sort of formal service.

After a while one of the Quakers would be moved by the spirit to stand and address the meeting on their religious thoughts, perhaps touching on some of the topics of the day with their relevance to Christian faith.

I found it difficult, if not impossible, to understand most of these contributions, but I was thrilled when on rare occasions my grandfather stood up and spoke.

I thought he was an excellent speaker, and I paid special attention, but I cannot recall a word he said. My mother, staunchly Church of England, used to say: 'You Quakers have all got the gift of the gab through all that spouting in Meeting every Sunday.'

This was a little unkind to my father who was far too shy to engage in oration. I must have taken after my grandfather and his generation, because I have never found public speaking daunting, and have engaged in it most of my life. Nowadays I suspect my words share the same fate with my former listeners as my grandfather's.

After about 25 minutes we younger children were allowed to leave the Meeting and were taken upstairs to engage in drawings with crayons, supervised by a delightful young lady who I noticed became quite volatile once she had left the meeting downstairs.

After the service all the Quakers broke their silence with animated chat in the vestibule when they emerged from their service. Some of them seemed relatively affluent, since Quakerism has never been a bar to success in business, demonstrated by the Cadbury and Fry families who built up their chocolate empires.

My mother responded on behalf of her religion by encouraging me to enrol in the choir at the little church, St Thomas's, at the top end of Western Avenue. Geoffrey Northover clinched it by assuring me the choir were given top-class outings every summer, and special treats at Christmas.

So I donned a stiff celluloid collar with a black bow tie, a cassock and surplice and trooped into St Thomas's with the other boys. I understood the sonorous sermons from the Vicar rather better, although they were strictly non-controversial. Sometimes I enjoyed the hymn singing, although singing psalms always seemed to me gobbledegook. Special services such as Harvest Festival and Christmas were fun, but sometimes I tired of religion with ritual, and volunteered to stay behind the scenes helping to pull a wooden lever which pumped air into the church organ.

As a Quaker I was never confirmed in the Church of England, and my mother did not urge this step. By the age of ten I had already decided to remain a birthright Quaker, and was contemplating registering as a conscientious objector to avoid any form of military service that came my way.

Then in the third week in April, 1945, I suffered a huge shock which has influenced the rest of my life far more profoundly than my family or friends have ever known.

One of my favourite treats was to visit Bournemouth's small, cramped Newsreel cinema in the Albert Road, often going on my own on a Saturday afternoon to buy a junior ticket for sixpence. I was fascinated by the Gaumont British and Pathe newsreels, with their formalised, gung-ho commentaries by Leslie Bridgemont and others.

The war news was mainly designed to keep up civilian morale. 'Our boys' waved and gave thumbs up signs to the camera as they trooped on and off ships, either completing a victory over 'the Hun' or on their way to another. I was bored by female fashion news, but I liked the newsreel feature stories about clever dogs or zoo animals.

My greatest joy was the accompanying Disney cartoons, and the comedy shorts provided by Laurel and Hardy, Buster Keaton, or my greatest screen hero, Charlie Chaplin.

On this occasion I settled in my seat for an innocent afternoon's entertainment without suspicion that anything was different. At ten I was already growing tall, and perhaps the ticket office lady was not paying attention when I walked in.

Within a few minutes I was riveted by the extended, single topic newsreel which consumed most of the afternoon programmes. There were no cartoons, nor any other 'funny' films. They would have been highly inappropriate.

We were watching a special report, filmed only the previous week, of the British Army's relief of the Bergen-Belsen concentration camp, starting on 15 April.

I can recall as vividly now, as I saw it then, the monochrome scenes of the hideous suffering of Belsen's starved, skeletal inmates still just about alive, and obscene mountains of human bodies of hundreds of others being carried into pits by former guards. Typhoid was rampant in the camp, and the troops were burning buildings and bedding.

Much later I learned that Belsen alone had killed 50,000 civilian prisoners, mostly Jewish, and 20,000 prisoners-of-war, mainly from Eastern Europe.

The horrific pictures, the bleak commentary, and some halting interviews with Allied soldiers overcome by the horrors they had discovered, impressed on me for a life-time the real nature of the Nazi rule we had been combating with our relentlessly brave and jolly 'people's war'. I reflected, shuddering, on the incomparable good fortune that Hitler's troops had not crossed the Channel and marched into the centre of Bournemouth.

We had known virtually nothing in our corner of the Home Front of the Holocaust taking place on the other side of the Channel, which persecuted and killed 20 million people with industrial efficiency and hideous cruelty, involving the specific murder of over five million Jews. There was a strong Jewish community in Bournemouth, and some of my school-friends were Jewish. I realised at last what the war had meant to their families and their relatives on the continent.

No wonder a Jewish friend of mine, surname Silver, had bravely stood up during a history class to protest against some anti-Semitic remarks made by our ancient History Master, Mr Arrowsmith, in connection with the establishment of the state of Israel. Arrowsmith stood silent, goggled-eyed in front of the class, as young Silver made his protest in a piping voice, and then walked out. I admired him enormously, and was most impressed that Arrowsmith had not dared to give him a detention punishment.

Ever since the impact of the Belsen film I have always abhorred antisemitism, and other forms of racism and tribalism. It is alive and flourishing in today's world, including we must admit, a few nasty corners of the English psyche, although we are vastly more tolerant than many other societies where I have seen and reported some of its worst excesses.

My mother had previously shielded me from the sparse news of war-time atrocities which had seeped into newspapers, and had been reported on the radio, including the superb eyewitness piece on the release of Belsen by Richard Dimbleby which became a classic BBC archive.

I left the Bournemouth newsreel feeling shattered, among a totally silent group of adults who stumbled into the daylight with grim faces. There appeared to be no other children in the audience. When I reached home I said little about what I had seen, but enough to cause my mother great indignation that they had allowed me to enter the cinema.

Despite the trauma I do not regret having suffered the experience, and count it as a necessary understanding of the true nature of a war which for me had been heavily laced with innocent jingoism, and ho-ho songs about naughty old Hitler.

I awoke several times that night with nightmares of the Belsen horrors, and they recurred for several weeks, and intermittently for years when I felt low. They have remained ever since among my private demons, all too easy to recall in ghastly, acute detail. Modern TV comedians milking laughter out of 'funny' impersonations of Hitler and his SS bullies merely make me feel sick.

My father was understanding, and quietly discussed what I had seen. He agreed that it made no sense, but confirmed what I had now discovered: there were virtually no depths of evil and depravity to which human beings could not descend, even if they looked outwardly just like the ordinary decent people I met every day.

I was not too young to vow that I would never espouse pacifism.

The Belsen film report taught me that the entire war, and every sacrifice made, had alone been justified to terminate the Holocaust, as well as the liberation of all German and Japanese-occupied countries.

I have to admit that horrific newsreel pictures of the carnage caused by nuclear war on Japan did not have anything like the same impact on me, nor the community in which I lived. My generation understood immediately that the nuclear bomb had saved many more thousands of lives than it cost, by avoiding US forces having to invade the Japanese mainland. I reported some of the largest anti-nuclear demonstrations in the 1960s, but I never shared the enthusiasms of the nuclear disarmament movement.

The reality for adults in 1945 was that it took at least another decade before a far less grey, restricted society emerged. Much has been written about the disappointments of postwar Austerity Britain. A family living on about £3.50 a week at war's outbreak was generally managing on about £6.50 a week at the end of the war. Liberating forms of social welfare, the Beveridge Plan and the Butler Education Act had arrived, but continuing shortages and restrictions contributed to Labour's inability to hold power for more than one term.

Although many families were reunited, the growing Cold War with Russia offered a chilling background of appalling new threats. My parents, still in the wage sector struggling on tight budgets, were well aware that we were still a long way from 'the sunlit uplands' which Churchill had promised in his great war-time speech. We were still eating dried eggs, and eking out our clothing coupons.

We admired Churchill as a war leader, but my grandfather and my father had no hesitation in voting Labour in the '45 election that returned Attlee's government. They wanted above all to avoid a return to a 1930s Britain of grim unemployment and social deprivation.

For myself and my school friends none of these post-war dark clouds mattered a jot. Youth is nothing if not resilient; we were still a bicycling community with sparse spending power, but we picked up joyfully every scrap of fun peace-time Bournemouth could offer, including ice-creams and the re-opening the beaches.

I thoroughly enjoyed my teens, although life was still to be shadowed by a threat of war which would eventually force me to become a reluctant National Serviceman. Uncle Joe had lost his friendly smile in the newspaper cartoons, although the *News Chronicle's* great cartoonist Vicky had never been reluctant to mock all the world leaders in their attempts to reorganise the world.

In my teens I drifted away from organised religion into agnosticism, whether Quakerism or Cof E, and developed cynicism about the Christian claim that man is made in the image of God. The Holocaust did not become an overwhelming obsession for me, but I read as widely as possible about the scale of the Nazis' genocide, learning of the ultimate evils of Auschwitz, Treblinka and so many more concentration camps.

I went on to take up a journalistic career bringing eye-witness experience of many horrors, but none ever made on me the degree of impact of my afternoon's viewing of the Belsen film report in that Bournemouth newsreel.

Over 30 years later, during a trip to a German horse trials on Luneberg Heath, I took my son Marcus and daughter Maxine, barely in their teens, to the Belsen-Bergen camp memorial. None of the camp buildings remain, just a clearing in a pine forest, with a simple memorial accompanied by some pictures and text. My children noted the extraordinary silence of the site, read the texts under small photographs of the original camp and its desperate inmates, and said little. They were spared the shock I had suffered because they had already learned something of the Holocaust in schools, but I am glad they had seen some of the remaining tangible evidence.

The Holocaust should remain a permanent feature of education syllabuses, along with searing reminders of the subject on national TV. I hope such documentaries continue to be broadcast on appropriate anniversaries, so that future generations will never forget the ultimate dangers of totalitarian rule by evil regimes.

I still believe my early exposure to man's inhumanity in its most extreme form was a factor in my mid-life decision to relinquish a career in journalism devoted to covering the 'bad news'.

Chapter Four

WEEKLY CHALLENGE

The arch Tory politician Norman Tebbitt is famous for recounting his father's solution to joblessness between the wars: he 'got on his bike' and went out to get a job.

I did exactly the same in the summer of 1951, but I claim no shred of Tebbitt resolve and initiative. I went on my bicycle because my mother ordered me out on to the streets.

She was alarmed that for the first fortnight after leaving school I had spent nearly every day on Bournemouth beach. The August weather was perfect, and lying flat on the sands after a delightful swim seemed the best position in which to contemplate my forthcoming career in journalism.

I had written a couple of letters to the local newspapers, and was awaiting replies – which never came.

My mother was nowadays no taller than my shoulder, but she still packed a hefty punch, and I meekly agreed to her firm instruction to cycle to local newspaper offices and demand interviews. Demand? My stomach heaved at the thought; it was to do the same countless times later when news editors ordered me to take on hopeless missions.

My first trips produced several hours of tedious waiting in the outer lobbies of the evening paper, the *Bournemouth Echo*, and the weekly, the *Bournemouth Times*. I was able to cycle home after tired looking grey men in shirtsleeves, well below Editor rank, emerged briefly into the waiting rooms to advise me to 'come back when you have some experience'. They did not proffer advice on how such experience was to be gained.

'Well cycle further tomorrow, and keep trying,' my mother ordered sternly, with a fierce glint in her eye as she lit up another Craven A cigarette before grasping the handle of her much hated, manually operated, clothes wringer.

I had read somewhere that the great BBC journalist Richard Dimbleby had started his career in Lymington, about 25 miles eastwards along the coast. Perhaps there was a newspaper office in Lymington? After a tedious crawl from north Bournemouth in a head-wind I pedalled my black upright bike through the narrow streets of Christchurch, totally missing the offices of the *Christchurch Times*, and continued through suburban Highcliffe to the outskirts of New Milton, a small, retirement town which had mushroomed before the war.

By now I was bored and weary, and would have accepted a job to sweep the road if it meant I could stop pedalling the damned bike. I turned left into Old Milton Road which would take me into the town, and onward to Lymington. Pedalling much more slowly I noticed I was passing on my left a sort of garage, or large shed, set back from the road. It bore a faded sign proclaiming *'New Milton Advertiser* and *Lymington Times'*.

Gratefully I swung into the gravel forecourt, propped the bike against the front wall, and walked into an empty, concrete-floored hallway. Through the glass window of a door ahead I was awed to see men in overalls leaning over frames of lead type; there was a clack of lino-types beyond, and a smell of paper and printing ink.

A trim youth in shirtsleeves, carrying sheaves of paper, dashed from the works, and gave me a friendly grin.

Ian Wooldridge would be acclaimed for over 40 years by Fleet Street as the 'greatest sports writer of his generation'. In that moment he gave me my first experience of the inimitable Wooldridge charm and bonhomie which he famously bestowed on his vast readership until a sad group of us gathered in New Milton in March 2007 to mourn his untimely death.

'Want to see the Editor? You want a job? Well, I think you've arrived at just the right time. His name's Mr Curry; we call him 'the Old Boy', and you're in luck – he's right here. Everything will be fine; don't worry.'

Wooldridge threw open a rickety side-door and ushered me into a long, narrow office, crammed with desks, shelves, paper, and antique typewriters. A smartly dressed middle-aged lady with a charming smile sat at a desk in the middle; Mrs Paddy Salt took advertisements, small or large, in the same room used by the editorial staff.

This meant we were always likely to be confronted face-to-face by people who called to place advertisements – and register comments or complaints about last week's issue. It was the most fearsome weapon in establishing accuracy I ever encountered in a lifetime in journalism.

Wooldridge smilingly swiftly introduced me to a small man in a brown suit, and smoking a malodorous pipe, who swung round to see me from a large roll top desk facing the end wall. Charles Townley Curry MBE was the only Editor/proprietor I ever worked for, and no matter how ramshackle his office and printing works, he exuded a confidence I never saw exceeded in the most exalted towers of Fleet Street. He ran the most independent publication ever to give me employment.

A Cornishman, son of an editor, with a lifetime's experience in provincial and national newspapers, Curry was a shrewd news man who had hauled himself up by his bootstraps to own the newspaper he edited since the year of my birth. He bought the paper with a partner who failed to come up with the money, and the Curry family mortgaged a house to raise the slim capital needed.

By now Curry was fighting acute bronchial trouble which made him cough and spit, but did not deter him from lighting up his pipe, puffing away while he scribbled away over reams of page proofs.

I soon learned his greatest passions were playing bowls, and lambasting Lymington Borough Council in thundering editorials. He scourged them in his editorial columns for daring to propose building a new town hall at a time of austerity. He campaigned with all the verve of Lord Beaverbrook for whom Curry had worked on the Sunday Express. The Old Boy seemed pleased I had cycled from Bournemouth to get a job; questioned me very briefly about my school and my availability to start work.

'I could start right away,' I croaked.

Between his clouds of pipe smoke, and awesome coughing, I discerned in a daze that Curry was offering me a job as a trainee-reporter immediately, with a view to becoming an articled apprentice at a wage of two pounds per week, rising by ten shillings per year for a five year term.

I gabbled that I was pleased to accept, and groped in my old blazer pocket for my O level Certificates.

'Don't show me those things!' the Editor ordered gruffly, waving away the prized results of my painfully won scholarship.

'We'll soon see what you're made of! Drummer will show you the ropes.'

[In his youth Ian Wooldridge was known to everyone in his home town as 'Drummer', possibly due to playing drums in a cadet band.]

'Am I on trial?' I quavered. 'Of course you are – always,' the reply rapped from the editorial chair before it swivelled back to the desk where the Old Boy buried his head in the page proofs.

My mother received the news of my first job with little surprise; she seemed to think it was an inevitable result of a cycle ride. I knew it was sheer luck rather than enterprise, but felt I deserved some congratulation, if only for the pedalling.

Much later I realised the full extent of the good fortune for which I am forever indebted to the Curry family. They taught me that proper journalism is not a job, but a vocation where 'working to hours' is irrelevant; that news must be scrupulously accurate, and comment fearless. The Old Boy's elder son, Charles Curry junior, has continued the family's ownership of the *Advertiser* and *Times*, taking over as Editor in 1996, remaining in office until the age of 86 with a mind as sharp and active as ever, and an acute sense of humour. He telephoned me sometimes, until not long before his death in 2019 at the age of 98, and we discussed news stories past and present with much relish. I always liked Charles junior enormously; his sense of ironic humour was one of the few qualities his father lacked.

Charles Curry's remarkable record as Britain's oldest and longest-serving Editor says much about the therapeutic effects of never retiring, and keeping abreast of current news.

I loved my job from the start, but my euphoria was jolted on Friday morning at the end of the my first week as a trainee reporter. I was ordered to join Drummer Wooldridge at the printing press, housed in an echoing tin barn two blocks up the street. Crammed inside was a huge rotary press which had been tucked away in the countryside by one of the national newspapers to be used in an emergency if their London press was bombed. It was the special pride of Charles Curry junior who has always adored 'mucking about' with old cars and printing equipment.

Drummer took his jacket off, rolled up his sleeves, and introduced me to Tom Selby, a cheerful oil-smeared engineer, with carrot coloured hair, who alone could conjure twelve thousand somewhat smudgy copies of the newspaper once a week off the historic press. He seemed to spend much of his time inside its tiers of black levers and wires, attaching semi-circular casts of type onto the press drums. Otherwise he was engaged in coaxing the sleeping giant to shuddering, deafening life. It was a dark, underworld version of a giant funfair machine, and its magic was to print, cut and produce the copies with exciting speed from the newsprint spiralling its mysterious routes through the machinery.

I was horrified to see Drummer crouch down on his knees at the end of a short conveyor belt where batches of the newspapers were spewing out. He collected them in bundles, heaped them on to a box, tied up each one with string and wrapping paper, and stuck on a delivery label.

'Come on!' he gestured, since speech was impossible above the fierce roar of the rotary which was at its most intense at this level.

I threw off my jacket and joined in the task. If my friends could see me now! I could certainly claim I was getting printing ink into my system, I reflected wryly. The chore passed quickly before we donned our jackets and returned to the reporters' office, smelling of sweat, oil and the all-pervading stink of ink.

Thereafter I accepted the weekly immersion in the printing process as a badge of pride. It taught me the stark lesson that journalism, whatever its pretensions to be a profession, is inextricably trapped between harsh commerce and light engineering, and cannot survive without either. No matter what ambitions and illusions we harboured about our role as reporters, the Friday morning job ensured there was never any danger of Wooldridge and I acquiring journalistic airs and graces.

Ian cheerfully told me his close links with the printing staff enabled him to call into the printing shed late on a Thursday night to retrieve an early copy for his father, Edmund Wooldridge. He thereby gained early access to the classified advertisements where he sought items for the used furniture shop he ran at Old Milton.

The task of ensuring basic journalistic techniques were implanted into the paper's junior reporters was mainly undertaken by a large, slow-moving man I had barely noticed on my first visit to the Advertiser office. Roy Instrell was chief sub-editor and deserved the cliché of 'backbone of the editorial staff', having worked there since boyhood. His service had been broken only by war-time in the RAF, which had taken him to East Africa, an experience from which he reamed countless anecdotes, told in slow, monotonous tones, but always with a good punch-line, if you could keep awake until then.

Reaching for yet another cigarette with nicotine-stained fingers, he sat all day at a desk wedged under a ladder with a rope hand-rail, leading up to an attic ambitiously known as the 'accounts department' where Charles Curry's younger son, Teddy, operated with part-time accountancy help.

I spent hours up there with Teddy, reading copy aloud while we took turns correcting the long, flapping galley proofs which emerged from the tiny, cramped lino-type room where three or four operatives slogged away at the keyboards from early morning to late evenings. I was not surprised they tended to be crotchety at times; it was my first experience of factory conditions and I wondered how the human frame withstood the constant noise, the heat, and the lack of fresh air and exercise. I resolved I would strive to be 'an outside man' for the whole of my newspaper career, if there was to be such.

In contrast the young men working as compositors in the 'stone room' were a jokey group who larked about as well as working hard, making up pages of type in frames on metal table tops, the 'stones' of ancient printers' jargon.

One of the money-saving procedures of the Curry empire and its 'rival' newspapers was regular news copy exchange.

The *Lymington Times* had no staff resident in Lymington, and was a slip-edition of the *New Milton Advertiser*, containing the same advertisements, but with adjustments of local news content. The provision of news from Lymington cost virtually nothing because most of the copy from that area arrived free from a delightful double act, George Eynon and Leslie Lowe, staff correspondents respectively of the *Western Gazette* and the *Echo* evening group operating in Southampton, Bournemouth and Weymouth. The great TV presenter and reporter Richard Dimbleby was Leslie Lowe's predecessor before the war.

George and Leslie received copies of all our New Milton and district news copy, some of which they used in their papers. Roy Instrell transformed the free copy into stories with new headings in our pages, plus lifting late stories from the *Echo* evening papers. His moon-like face, shyness and slow speech were contrasted by a sharp intelligence, and a kindly personality with a keen sense of humour. He was a stickler for accuracy and proper journalistic style in news coverage, and we younger members of staff owed him much.

I failed badly at an early assignment: interviewing by telephone a young lady on her overseas holiday experience. It wasn't a bad piece, although not much more than a schoolboy essay, and I was inordinately proud when it appeared as one of my first published reports. Next Monday morning Teddy Curry gave me a justified verbal tongue-lashing in the office because my story repeatedly referred to the young lady as a 'Miss Softer', whereas her name was of course 'Miss Foster'.

The Old Boy never mentioned it, and nor did Roy Instrell. I wondered fearfully whether I would be making my last cycle ride back to Bournemouth at the end of the week, but no more was said. Phonetic spelling of names on the phone became automatic for the rest of my life.

For a few weeks I commuted six days a week from Bournemouth Central station by train to and from New Milton, which is on the main line to London, but the stern demands of the *New Milton Advertiser* involved frequent evening work for the reporters.

Roy Instrell, in his kindly ponderous manner, advised me I could get excellent 'digs' with his neighbours, Bob and Ethel Gates in Barton Lane, a couple of miles away.

It proved to be another slice of luck, but the weekly bill for bed, breakfast, lunch and a high tea was two pounds and ten shillings.

My mother showed her true metal by providing the ten shillings above my starting wage, and giving me some pocket money, although I had little time to spend much, and the bike remained my main form of transport.

She had always intended to support me after leaving school, provided I was 'in work', but it meant that she continued to work hard herself to scrape up the extra cash, and it contributed more stress to a life already burdened by having lost one eye in a childhood accident of which she would never talk.

She coped remarkably well, and her brunette good looks were hardly affected, but in later life she became increasingly temperamental, suffered deteriorating health in her fifties, and died at 63 after an agonising 18 months of cancer at a time when treatment was limited, leaving my father a widower from 65 until his death 19 years later. I was deeply fond of both my parents, kept closely in touch with them throughout their lives, and as an only son their deaths were personal crises I found hard to bear, and still recall with pain.

As a grammar school day boy, New Milton was my first experience of living away from home, and I was lucky to bask in the warmth and kindness of the Gates household where there was a freckled, schoolboy son, Vernon who I liked.

Sometimes I would cycle to the office alongside Roy Instrell, and it was an office joke that Roy cycled more slowly than anyone could achieve without actually falling off. Keeping at his speed as we trundled into a head-wind required cycling skills I had not used since I had ridden 'no-hands on the handle-bars' as a gymnastic junior schoolboy.

I liked most of the evening work: annual meetings of local societies, occasional dinners such as the National Farmers' Union where the West Country ex-farmer author and broadcaster A.G. Street was the speaker, much to my delight; and an increasing diet of reviewing amateur theatrical productions which I especially relished. I had virtually no interest in sports reporting, but was expected to cover soccer matches on Saturday afternoons in the winter. At the annual general meeting of New Milton Football Club I was shaken when a disgruntled member explained they had lost a key match through the goalkeeper letting in a goal: 'because he was distracted by the *New Milton Advertiser* reporter talking to his girl-friend on the touch-line.'

Drummer Wooldridge had started at the *Advertiser* and *Times* even one rung lower than mine: a boy helping the printers at ten shillings per week. He was soon promoted to 'trainee' reporter, and as everyone on the paper immediately recognised, he was truly a born journalist, and appeared to need little training; news sense, a distinct style, and an ability to entertain as well as inform the reader all came naturally.

Drummer had performed all the hatch-match-and-dispatch tasks of local newspaper work before I arrived, aided by considerable local knowledge of his home town, and a host of relatives and friends.

But after I began to share these jobs, his talent increasingly flowered into articles marked by his own distinctive style.

He was one of those fortunate people who at an early age have a sharp focus on their future career, and know they possess the talent to make it possible.

Wooldridge adored sports reporting, and regarded working in Fleet Street as inevitable. None of us doubted this from his earliest days on the *Advertiser,* and it was of no surprise to me that he became a renowned *Daily Mail* columnist for 40 years, hailed by his buddies in the sports writing fraternity in the obituaries after his death in March 2007 as 'the greatest sports writer of his era'.

It was always a treat for me when George Eynon and Leslie Lowe appeared at the same functions, or made rare visits to our office. They were real, grown-up reporters, who I much admired, and they treated me with mateyness, as if I was something near an equal. They seemed to enjoy life, always cracking jokes, and after one lengthy evening of tedious after-dinner speeches, when we were all well laced with cheap wine, they came to my office to write their speeches and tactfully asked advice in deciphering shorthand outlines. I glowed with pleasure on joining the local big boys of the newspaper world.

George, with a West Country burr, protruding front teeth and floppy blonde hair, had an extrovert personality, and a fund of off-colour stories; he was a prodigious worker, generating many columns of copy from his far flung patch for the *Western Gazette,* then a genuinely rural weekly paper with tomb-stone make-up, and classified advertisements all over its front page. I had read it since boyhood, and much enjoyed its extensive equestrian advertising, and its regular Hunt reports.

Leslie Lowe, ex-Army Major, was slim, dark and more intense. He once gave me a marvellous practical lesson in journalistic ethics: we were covering a Sunday morning Conservative party local conference in New Milton when a pompous visiting speaker turned to the press desk, and said patronisingly: 'Don't publish the next bit. I'm going to speak off the record.'

Leslie stood up, banged his notebook shut, put it in his brief case and addressed the stunned delegates loudly and precisely: 'I was invited here to report this meeting; I am not here to be told what I can and cannot report. That's my judgement; not yours. So goodbye.'

When he turned to leave, the speaker was like a collapsed balloon, made a grovelling apology and begged Leslie to stay. Grudgingly, Major Lowe re-opened his notebook, and sat down, remarking to me in a loud stage-whisper which reverberated through the hall: 'I don't know what makes the bugger think he's said anything worth publishing anyway.'

From the start, the Curry family treated my journalistic training seriously: I was instructed to make a long bus journey into Bournemouth two evenings a week to learn shorthand and touch-typing; a very pleasant exercise, surrounded by a class of comely Bournemouth girls. I also passed basic examinations in the law of libel and the British constitution under an external training scheme. Aided by extra coaching, I reached a maximum of 140 words per minute in Pitman's shorthand, and thereafter relished reporting meetings and court work.

I was so proud when an angry Lymington Councillor attacked the *Lymington Times* during a major debate in which the new Town Hall project was abandoned.

'Charles Curry is kicking this Council around like a football!' declaimed the furious Councillor. I took down reams of verbatim copy, including the abuse of my Editor. As I expected, he was thrilled when he read it, scrupulously publishing every word in the news columns – and answering it with another broadside in his editorial column called 'Notes and News' by 'Townsman'.

I was given my own 'patch' to cover: the village of Highcliffe, already sprawling into a retirement suburb, and the more rural hamlet of Hinton Admiral on the New Forest border. Every Monday I would cycle round my domain, calling on the policeman, the vicar, the old folk's home, and the gents' barber who was the most potent source of exclusives, some of them sexual scandals which were non-publishable until they reached Christchurch Magistrates' Court which I covered regularly.

I would make regular attendance at a magistrates' court compulsory for teenagers today. No matter what depths of depravity I was to report in the lurid sphere of Fleet Street, it carried no surprise for me after my early induction into human weakness in an ordinary magistrates' court. At first I was amazed when a smartly dressed senior RAF officer appeared on a charge of exposing his genitals to young females.

The outer reaches of human perversity were reached in a Lymington court case where a New Forest man was charged with bestiality, endeavouring to have sexual relations with one of the pigs turned out on the forest every autumn.

George Eynon and I rocked with laughter afterwards as we recalled the shocked magistrate asking: 'But how on earth could you make the animal stand still?'

The defendant looked furtively at the Bench and muttered: 'Well sir, you throw down some of them acorns....'

Local journalism anywhere can be suddenly enlivened by dramas, some which plunge the area into headline news.

I spent some bleak but exciting days and night-times on the shingle beaches of the Milford-on-Sea coastline covering shipwrecks, one of them a three-masted sailing ship.

In January 1952 I was endeavouring to stay interested in reporting a New Milton Rugby Club match, always a problem because as a schoolboy soccer-player I was hazy about the rules of rugby. Suddenly play stopped while everyone stared at the sky.

We saw a huge jet-plane soaring down in an arc, with crimson flames bursting from one wing; then several crew members ejected in a flutter of parachutes.

I cycled to the nearest phone box, and rang the first tip-off to the news desks of half a dozen national Sunday newspapers, the Press Association and Ex-Tel agencies. I carried their numbers with me constantly in a pocket dictionary.

So-called 'linage payments' for stories Drummer and I sent to the national press were in the name of Roy Instrell. He never showed us the receipts, but some weeks later, after careful consideration, he would hand out some badly-needed banknotes and silver to the impecunious junior reporters who had produced the story, less a commission for himself, we suspected.

The production of copy for the nationals was a considerable fillip to the meagre incomes of provincial reporters. George Eynon would report with relish the profitability of sending yards of 'dirty stories' from the courts to the *New of the World* who published soberly reported scandalous cases at inordinate length for the titillation of the sex-starved 1950s readership. Before the modern age of celebrity, vicars or other pillars of society who erred sexually were especially popular with the 'Screws of the World' news desk.

Much delayed by the tip-off calls, I pedalled my trusty bike in the direction the plane had taken. I arrived at Bransgore amid dense tree plantations in late afternoon darkness, worn out and distinctly displeased to find Drummer Wooldridge had zoomed to the scene first from his soccer match coverage.

No pedalling for him: among his New Milton mates were members of the local voluntary fire service, and they broke all regulations by giving him a lift on the fire engine to the air crash scene. Drummer phoned the nationals colourful reports from the scene, and there was nothing much for me to do in writing up my first aircrash.

Weeks later, however, I had some satisfaction when Roy Instrell announced lugubriously that the nationals had paid by far the biggest lump sums for the first tip-off, and therefore my share of the riches was the greater, amounting nearly to a magnificent ten pounds, more than three times my weekly wage at the time. It was a big front-page lead story in the Sundays: the crashed plane was the Vickers Valiant, Britain's only atom bomber at the time. Paraffin had seeped into the back of one wing and ignited, and the plane nose-dived to disintegrate. Four crew survived the parachute jumps, but the second pilot was found dead in a field.

Later that year Drummer started his own two years' National Service, securing a rather special role as a Royal Navy coder, learning Russian to decipher Cold War messages. He embraced the role with his usual cheerful enthusiasm, and became a life-long advocate of the military in general, making some excellent TV films extolling the virtues of the British Army and Navy. My own impending National Service was to be far different.

As well as succeeding in his role as Number One Junior, for a while I inherited Ian Wooldridge's girlfriend: the attractive brunette Veronica Churcher, secretary in a local solicitors. Wooldridge, of course, ultimately 'got the girl': I was his best man in October 1957, when he was working on the *News Chronicle,* and returned to his home town to wed Veronica in Milton Parish Church.

I discovered that although my surplus income for entertaining females was virtually nil, I could rely on free tickets from the local cinema, the Waverley, by writing film previews for the paper. Veronica was one of several girls I took to the Waverley, followed by long walks or cycle rides to their homes in all weathers, thereby avoiding expenditure on such luxuries as bus tickets or cups of coffee.

During the next two years until my call-up in 1954, my scope as a local hack widened in coverage of local government, the courts, and inquests where I learned that suicide was far more prevalent than most people would care to admit in comfortable England.

With my shorthand and typing skills I tended to write most stories far too long and verbosely, but I aimed at maximum accuracy, and I learned to write succinctly and reasonably quickly when absolutely necessary. I had not yet acquired the knack of instant composition over the phone, an essential tool if I was to become a national reporter.

Over brown ales consumed in the local Unionist Club, where I pretended I could play snooker with Wooldridge, I assured him I would certainly follow his path to Fleet Street, although I would concentrate on what I considered, with the naivety of youth, to be my prowess in handling 'hard news'.

Attlee's 1945-51 government attempted a social revolution in healthcare and nationalised industries, but it left alone many traditional elements of English life.

When the Conservatives under Churchill took over in 1951 we still believed in our empire, upheld the penalty of hanging, maintained homosexuality as a crime, and the royal family was immensely popular, not yet afflicted by vulgar tabloid press intrusion, and protected by the Lord Chamberlain from mockery on stage and screen.

Deference to authority and class was still a major element in society, especially in the comfortable mono-culture in our corner of Hampshire where lifestyles were now showing much improvement after 1940s war and austerity.

It is difficult to exaggerate how shattering it was for conventional Middle England in the still inhibited climate of 1953 when Lord Montagu of Beaulieu became embroiled in a homosexual scandal which was to run and run.

It was smack in the middle of our circulation area, and nowhere was the fever of interest greater. Crowds of local people, silent, and some looking sheepishly embarrassed, lined both sides of the main street in Lymington when Montagu and his co-defendant Kenneth Hume walked into the cramped Town Hall where the prosecution's case was heard in detail by the local magistrates. In the Unionist club bar that evening some middle-aged men were asking me diffidently what exactly Montagu was alleged to have done.

Most of the press reporting in the climate of the 1950s referred only to 'an unnatural practice'. The 27-years-old peer was charged with this serious offence, and indecent assault, after allegations from two boy scouts who had been taken to a beach hut at Beaulieu for a swim by Montagu and a friend in August.

The prosecution evidence in court was lengthy and specific in describing homosexual intercourse; I scribbled away in my shorthand, trying to find new outlines for sexual acts I had never attempted to report in such detail previously. Good old Pitman's had not quite prepared me for this.

I was sitting at a press desk only a few feet away from Lord Montagu, a slim, pale-faced figure, who was sitting on a chair in the gangway of the council chamber.

As an 18-year-old junior reporter earning £3 ten shillings a week, I was the *Advertiser* and *Times's* sole reporter at the magistrates' hearings, and I stayed at a public house in Winchester to cover two Assize trials where Montagu appeared in sensational cases which attracted international press as well as the Fleet Street hordes.

Seeing national reporters and photographers in action at close quarters was a riveting aspect of the case for an 18-year-old junior reporter from a local weekly. I noted the non-existent shorthand of some London reporters, painfully making notes in longhand. Some hardly came into court, but seemed to rely on chats with policemen and barristers in the local bars for the heavy 'colour pieces' they were concocting for publication after the verdict.

Famous by-lines I knew well in national papers became faces, men with whom I drank in the pubs near the courts. They were usually charming and friendly, although I knew they were often pumping me for background 'local colour'.

I noted how the press box protected itself from embarrassment at the wealth of detailed homosexual evidence by swapping crude jokes and limericks based on the case.

The trials attracted major coverage in the quality broadsheet newspapers as well as the tabloids, and commentators of distinction as well as hack reporters sat in the cramped press boxes. If I had any doubts previously, I had none now that I had chosen a calling which could suddenly put me close to history in the making.

In the boy scout case, Montagu was acquitted at Winchester Assizes on the more serious charge of the 'unnatural offence', but the jury disagreed on the lesser charge of indecent assault. Montagu and Hume were to be tried again on that charge, but sensationally three weeks after the end of the first trial, fresh charges were made against the peer.

Montagu, his Dorset landowner cousin, Michael Pitt-Rivers and Peter Wildeblood, the *Daily Mail's* diplomatic correspondent, appeared before Lymington Magistrates on indecency charges involving two RAF men, McNally and Reynolds. These two men were allowed immunity from prosecution by turning Crown evidence against the others, and this time the prosecution prevailed: at the end of an eight day trial in Winchester's lofty Assize court, Pitt-Rivers and Wildeblood were sentenced to 18 months in prison, and Edward Montagu to 12 months.

I reported and typed more column inches on both cases for the information of the citizens of the New Forest and surrounding communities, than any other story I covered during my apprenticeship in the rough trade of news reporting. It had been highly educational in terms of journalism, and an unexpected window on the dark side of 1950s British 'justice'. Despite this, I was immensely glad to cease taking shorthand notes on the subject.

I found myself adopting the same armour of cynicism and detachment as the rest of the press box coterie in coping with the job of reporting the case, but I was increasingly aware of its wider implications for British society.

It was a relief after the verdict to read good examples of polemical journalism in the *Sunday Times,* the *New Statesman,* and elsewhere on the stench of hypocrisy surrounding the ruthless handling of the second trial, and the wider issues of society's attitude to consenting homosexuality. It was a healthy reminder that good journalism sought to change the world as well as record it.

Soon the Wolfenden committee was formed to consider the law on homosexuality; society slowly moved forward to today's tolerance of private consenting homosexuality which would have been inconceivable in the bad old days' of the 1950s.

I have never met Lord Montagu, but I admired his strength of character in not retreating into obscurity after his sentence, instead becoming a popular and much respected public figure, creating his marvellous motor museums and other attractions at Beaulieu, and making many other valuable contributions to the quality of life.

My first journalistic idyll at New Milton could easily have come to an abrupt end through a brush with the law in a comedy of errors.

It proved to be a thorough lesson in journalistic ethics which I never forgot.

Drummer Wooldridge, with all the charm of a Bertie Wooster, advised me one summer's day that he had evolved a 'marvellous wheeze' to make us some much-needed cash. I was especially hard up at the time; I had now acquired girlfriends in Bournemouth and Southampton and the bus fares were crippling. Even without the financial inducement, I was ready to follow his advice on any journalistic matter, so I agreed to his great plan. He was working for the *Advertiser* while on leave from his National Service.

We would go the cliff-top at Barton-on-Sea one Saturday morning with two friends armed with duelling swords. They would pretend to duel on the cliffs; one of them would fall over, but get up, and both would retire.

Then, Drummer promised with a gleam in his eye, he would phone a 'really topping colour story' to the Sunday papers, about a mystery duel. They would love it, he promised me. The linage payments would simply roll in: a very welcome bonus for all four of us. No-one would be any the wiser, he promised with his usual disarming confidence.

Sure enough, on a gleaming summer's morning we met two student friends of Wooldridge on the cliff overlooking a shining blue sea, with the Isle of Wight looming beyond, and enacted our little farce, with Drummer and I acting as seconds in a brief scenario worthy of a second rate costume drama.

It would add greatly to the veracity of the story, Drummer remarked afterwards, if we were to ask the New Milton police whether they had received any reports of a 'mystery duel'.

My stomach began to churn: I had established very good relationships with the coppers in the station virtually next door to our office. I liked them, and I was not comfortable about asking phoney questions. However, Drummer came with me and breezily asked for 'news' of the duel. It was received with mild amusement by the police, but they were a trifle puzzled when he could not name his informant. They had heard nothing and had far better things to do, they said.

Wooldridge had already written his story with his usual panache, and busily phoned it to the appropriate Fleet Street news desks.

I heard no more, but next morning while visiting my parents in Bournemouth my stomach lurched again as I read on the front page of a downmarket Sunday rag a half-column report of police investigating a 'mystery swords-for-two and coffee-for-one encounter' on the cliffs above the Solent. Good old Drummer's style was shining through as usual, I thought gloomily.

Next morning the atmosphere in the *Advertiser's* office would have suited a hangman's scaffold as I scuttled to my desk.

'It's all over; no more linage. The nationals will never use us again,' intoned Roy mournfully.

Then Teddy Curry waded in, for which I could not blame him, angrily telling me that Wooldridge and I could have been prosecuted for 'creating public mischief', and we should be thoroughly ashamed of ourselves. However, he and Charles junior had talked it over with the Old Boy and he had decided to take no action, provided we had 'learned our lesson.'

Of all my debts to the Curry family this was no doubt the greatest. A sacking for faking a story would have been a severe setback.

I went next door to the police station to apologise profusely to the station officer. He said with a weary smile: 'Wooldridge has already put us fully in the picture. Put it down to experience. We're not taking it further, although we could have done. We think you were just an accomplice, and you made a mistake. You can carry on dealing with us, but we're not taking any more press queries from that Drummer.'

I was not entirely pleased to be summed up as the dumb side-kick of the would-be master illusionist, but I was hugely relieved. Wooldridge had nobly taken all the blame himself I discovered later, which was typical of his generous nature. Fortunately, the Curry family knew his worth, and replacing me at short notice would no doubt have been inconvenient.

Drummer had been reporting a New Milton soccer match on the Saturday afternoon of the scam when two uniformed policemen tapped him on the shoulder, and said: 'Wooldridge, we know all about it. We want to talk to you.'

'Bloody funny, really,' he later told me.

'Fleet Street really liked our story. Apparently it was a slow news day, so several of the Sundays were sending down teams of reporters and cameramen to cover the 'mystery duel' in more detail. They bothered New Milton police with telephone inquiries, until the coppers thought they'd better look into it.

'Our big mistake was to go along as seconds. Every morning a Barton-on-Sea ex-Naval man surveys the sea and the cliffs on his blasted telescope.

'He recognised me immediately, and would you believe it, he told the police all about it, and named me.

'I phoned the Sunday paper news desks to say it had turned out to be a hoax. Said I was sorry, but do you know, they didn't mind a bit. Several thanked me for a 'jolly good story'.'

Wooldridge was indeed a born Fleet Street man, and could already talk confidently to his own kind in language they understood.

Absolutely nothing more was said in the office about the infamous hoax until several weeks later when Roy Instrell took me aside, and coughed.

'We did, in fact, get paid something for the duel story,' he said with a pallid smile.

'Er… here's your share. And I've paid Drummer something too. Nothing more needs to be said to anyone else.'

Chapter Five

GERMANY CALLING

'And how did you address the Editor on your newspaper?'

'Er, well I called him Sir …' I quavered.

'You haven't used the word Sir once in addressing us!'

The beady eyed RAF examiner on the officer recruitment board had me floored.

Quakerism, journalism, and my lack of service in the school cadet force were all equally frowned upon by the trio of examining officers, immaculate in their tailored uniforms, with wings, medal ribbons and umpteen rings indicating rank.

After my interview at the Air Ministry in London I felt I had about as much chance of a commission as I had of being allowed to fly an airplane in my conscripted service to my country. Someone with a sense of humour had put me down as a POM (potential officer material) during the initial six weeks square-bashing training, and I was sent to the Air Ministry in London for an interview. It was a one day escape from the monotony of square bashing, and that was all.

I was not at especially disappointed: the only option for a National Service officer at the time was to become a fighter-plotter which apparently involved hours watching radar screens and pushing counters about indoors in operations rooms. It seemed a terribly tedious way of spending the next two years.

I had indicated the RAF as my first choice when my National Service call-up came inexorably in the late autumn of 1954, but only for the puerile reason that it seemed a more comfortable option than the Army.

This seemed another major error of judgement when snow and fierce frosts afflicted the Staffordshire moorland throughout November and December when I engaged in such ridiculous tasks as 'guarding the coke compound' at three in the morning at RAF Hednesford where I was posted for 'square bashing'. Our sergeant seemed to have had acquired all his lines from Ealing comedies: 'If brains was dynamite you lot wouldn't 'ave enough to blow your 'ats orff!'

Most of the other new conscripts huddling round the coke stoves in my hut were excellent company, and had already developed high levels of cynicism about their value to the country as National Servicemen. The only young men who seemed to suffer were those who had 'never been away from home before' and were amazingly home-sick. The few public schoolboys among us did not suffer from this of course, and the value of a public school's diet of discomfort and poor food was evident in their ability to undergo the privations of square bashing in mid-winter without a qualm. Having had plenty of discomfort camping in the Sea Scouts, and living in digs for three years, I was not concerned about the practicalities of RAF life. My main worry at the outset was that I would be thoroughly bored for the next two years.

I had departed my life as a local reporter with the utmost reluctance, desperately bereaved of a job and lifestyle I felt I had thoroughly mastered. Additionally I was suffering pangs of unrequited love, and lust – I was still virginal – having acquired simultaneous attractive new girlfriends in Bournemouth and New Milton whose affections I deeply hoped would translate into something even more exciting. I wrote to them fervently for some months, but the heady delights of the south coast in summer ensured neither remained faithful to someone destined not to return for two long years, which was a blessing since I outgrew my feelings for them remarkably quickly once I discovered that my new lifestyle had much to offer.

My early personal relationships were much coloured by my mother's strict warnings against 'entanglements' (girls becoming pregnant), accompanied by the strict warning 'he travels the furthest who travels alone' (girls seeking husbands).

My temporary yearnings of the heart meant I had ticked an RAF form to indicate I wished serve my National Service in the United Kingdom. Fortunately the RAF totally ignored such nonsense, and in January 1955, I was crammed into the dark depths of a troopship across a heaving North Sea to Holland, and then to a newly-built, sprawling NATO airbase, RAF Laarbruch, set in sandy pine forests just across the Dutch border in Germany's North Rhine area.

My shorthand/typing skills ensured I was immediately promoted two minor ranks up to Leading Aircraftsman, and slotted into Laarbruch in a solo position as the 'C.O's Clerk', with my own office in Station Headquarters. My fellow clerical airmen cynically advised me I would be universally known as 'the C.O.'s bumboy', and I soon discerned a certain caution on everyone's part in not expressing flagrant criticism of the rulers of Laarbruch in my presence.

They need not have worried: I was secretly as subversive as any National Serviceman, but I had already discerned that military law was incredibly harsher than in civilian life. I firmly resolved not to spend a second longer in the RAF than conscripted, and certainly not in one of the military jails which in the 1950s were rumoured to be pits of hell.

The Clayton luck held marvellously: the Germans as part of their reparations had built Laarbruch's barracks, offices and air facilities to a far higher standard than most in the UK. My shorthand/typing qualifications meant that I began my service as an LAC, Leading Aircraftman, was soon promoted to Senior Aircraftman, and quickly uplifted to the giddy heights of Corporal. Now I had my own room, with modern central heating, excellent showers and lavatories. Every morning after our atrocious breakfasts, often striving to hide my amusement, I would assemble my little squad of Station Headquarters clerks outside our barracks. Our 'working blues' uniforms were soon faded and baggy, and more than a few of my men were bespectacled and bookish in mien.

'By the left, quick turn!' I would pipe, and they would shamble mutely along as a forlorn little band towards Station Headquarters where we would thankfully subside into our offices for our first cup of tea of the morning. My own sign of rebellion against the relentless regimentation of service life was to sport a bizarre cigarette holder to smoke Balkan Sobrani cigarettes.

It was of little surprise to me that the RAF had no plans for non-commissioned National Servicemen to take part in foxhunting. Germany, I knew, had banned hunting live quarry with hounds in the 1930s under Hitler's new Nazi regime. This became part of our propaganda in endeavouring to ward off abolition in the United Kingdom. The Nazis had banned hunting mainly because it was already apparent that rabies was spreading from eastern Europe through wild foxes, and the Hitler hierarchy were most concerned to preserve shooting as their major country sport. Goring was especially keen on shooting deer, wild boar and game.

The British Army Draghound pack run by the Royal Engineers at Osnabruck Garrison did hunt wild foxes until German sovereignty in 1955, when they had to switch to draghunting to conform with German game laws.

It was abundantly clear that hunting of any sort was an Army officer-class activity, took place far from our camp, and was infinitely beyond my means.

I was disappointed, however, that Laarbruch did not have a riding school, an amenity established at some other RAF bases in Germany. Then I heard that a local German farmer had offered riding on his horses to 'competent riders' on the base.

I cycled about a dozen miles to a farmhouse on the edge of one of the North Rhine's huge forestry areas. Although he spoke no English, the farmer was polite and welcoming, and my limited German sufficed. He showed me half a dozen upstanding, brown riding horses in a range of stables. He selected a light bay mare of about 16.3 hands, with a kind eye; she stood quietly while we tacked her up. Hatless, and wearing only flannels and rubber boots, I set off for a solo ride in the forest, with the confidence of youth that all would be well.

This proved to be correct: the mare was delightful, well schooled, willing to cooperate at all paces, and not at all inclined to spook or shy at anything strange we encountered on miles of forest tracks. It was marvellous to be in the saddle again, and I felt a sense of escape from the prison of National Service far greater than at any other time out of the camp.

I did not realise it, but it was my first experience of riding a German Warmblood, the sport horse which would dominate postwar competition fields in dressage and show jumping. The Germans are a great equestrian nation, and they exercise their traditional discipline in ensuring that pedigrees are properly maintained, and breeding decisions therefore produce good working stock, sound and with excellent temperaments.

To my amazement the farmer declined to take any payment on my return, saying he was glad to have help with exercising them. We spent the afternoon looking at his other horses turned out in the fields, and we chatted happily about them.

I rode his horses intermittently for the next six months, but sadly he told me he was moving them to a new yard in a business shared with others, and he could offer me riding no longer. Although friendly, he never invited me into his house, and with the thoughtlessness of youth I did not make enough effort to establish a lasting relationship. Riding in Dorset and the New Forest was one more reason I longed for the day when my National Service ended.

*****

As the C.O.'s Clerk I was inevitably regarded by most of the other airmen on the station as doing a job which a burly Corporal in the Transport Wing described as 'something a WAAF would do better, and would be a bloody sight easier on the eye'.

This repartee occurred in the Corporals' Club with its own bar and lounge rooms, although not as munificent as the Sergeants' Club and Officers' Mess. The station's dreadful food become a source of major trouble for the Admin Wing in which I languished, and indeed for the Commanding Officer and his acolytes. When the Air Officer Commanding, a god-like creature with much scrambled egg on his cap, made his first annual inspection of the station, a momentous occasion in Service life comparable with the Second Coming, I trooped my pitiful squad into the huge airmen's mess for the midday meal only to find it empty, although a far more sumptuous spread than usual was set out.

The great man appeared with my C.O. and other senior officers, all looking harassed.

'Where is everybody?' they demanded.

'I simply can't imagine,' I quavered from my squad's short table, the only one occupied in the vast acres usually filled with hungry airmen.

It appeared that because of our proximity to the rulers, the Station Headquarters clerks had been left out of a secret plan by all 'other ranks' to stage a boycott of the airmen's mess, in protest about the dire food, much of which was tinned stock of World War 2 vintage.

The protest was a huge success. I thought we would all be shipped off in lorries to prison camps, but instead the great inspection was immediately abandoned. The Catering Officer was given a tremendous grilling by the scrambled egg toffs, and the airmen's complaints were backed by pilots in Flying Wing who were concerned about their men's welfare.

We were hugely impressed when for the next month senior officers attended all airmen's meals, constantly asking us if the food was OK. It seemed remarkably humiliating for the station's luminaries who had never actually appeared amid the din and horror of airmen's mealtimes before. There were major changes in the kitchens, and for the first time fresh vegetables, meat and fruit were bought from nearby bountiful farms.

What a good story it would have made for Fleet Street, I sighed, but did not have the courage to send it to Wooldridge as linage. I feared gravely that conviction for a breach of confidentiality by the Station Officer's Bum Boy would entail a hideously long jail stretch in the Cold War climate of the 1950s.

For some weeks I had given secretarial assistance to a Wing Commander from the RAF legal department, prosecuting in several courts martial in 2nd TAF, and I was horrified by the swiftness of military justice and the punishments meted out. One pathetic airman, clearly in need of clinical therapy, was given two years in a military gaol for a first offence of exposing himself in a wood to some Service wives. I knew he would have had a much more merciful reception in Christchurch Magistrates Court, and it reinforced my longing to get away from the dire threats of Queen's Rules and Regulations.

After the catering debacle I was even more aware that the 'real' National Service airmen on the station were in the Flying Wing. I was much impressed by the engineering skills of the National Service squads who maintained the Canberras and Meteors, and had warm, mutually appreciative relationships with the officer pilots whose lives depended on their planes being properly serviced.

During exercises the engineers worked long night shifts without complaining; they appeared to enjoy their work immensely, and some would leave the RAF at the end of their two years with a bright future in the aviation industry. The C.O. for whom I worked, Group Captain George Petre, was a fine example of the RAF at its best.

He had been a distinguished wartime pilot, awarded a DFC and AFC, was courteous and friendly to those who worked under him, and might have stepped straight out of the WW2 Battle of Britain films I had watched endlessly during childhood. I liked him and respected him from the start, although I wondered whether he was as good a natural administrator as he was a pilot.

To keep up his flying hours, and his allowances, Petre made regular solo flights as a pilot, but as he was not 'converted to jets' he flew a small propeller-driven plane which, in lumbering into the air, required a ludicrously short length of Laarbruch's vast main runway, normally used by a couple of squadrons of Canberra twin engined jet bombers, and Meteor jet fighters.

The station's air operations halted while the C.O.'s plane climbed off the centre of the runway for his jaunt which was clearly one of the highlights of his week.

One of my perks was to accompany him sometimes, occupying a narrow, cramped cockpit seat behind the pilot. I struggled into parachute harness, painfully conscious I had no training in parachute jumping if I should need to use the thing. After take-off I strived to hear what the hell the C.O. occasionally barked laconically into my headphones.

It was highly alarming to discover rudimentary navigation was delegated to me.

'Just keep your eye on the river below us, Clayton,' he ordered.

'We'll go up the river, and back down it again. Tell me if you think we're wandering away from it because otherwise we probably can't find our way back.'

Really? It seemed a good idea to go home now, but I was trapped in my first-ever flight of any kind, and was surrealistically expected to help the pilot.

Such was my ignorance and lack of interest in aviation that I never bothered to check exactly what make of plane we were flying, but it seemed very similar to the large fighter aircraft I had so often seen crashing in flames on the screen of the Waverley cinema.

I had arrived at Laarbruch with a secret load of resentment at having to 'waste my precious time' for the next couple of years in the 2nd Tactical Airforce, a view much encouraged by the general view of regular RAF men that National Servicemen were just a pain.

The resentment gradually disappeared while I typed the C.O.'s classified material, and read some of his 'Top Secret' files. Laarbruch was a first line air base in a Cold War which was at a high level of tension in the mid-1950s, a state of affairs which seemed to have escaped the attention of my readers in New Milton.

I heard RAF flying crew laconically refer to East Germany as 'just up the road' in flying terms. I soon understood Russia's rockets and bomber bases in Eastern Europe were lethally within range of the heart of the UK. Although tightly constrained by the Official Secrets Act, and absolutely terrified of breaching it, I began to acquire an all round picture of Laarbruch's role as a first line photo-reconnaissance base, linked with both sides' abilities to fling nuclear bombs all over Europe, and especially at the England I loved.

I reflected sadly that I could have earned a lot of linage by adding colourful facts to the Cold War reporting I read with intense interest in the London newspapers which were, thankfully, fully available on the station. It was clear the Allied forces still in Germany were part of a much-needed shield against Russian aggression from the East European states she dominated.

Unfortunately I was also required to spend time working on boring administration for the Adjutant, Flight Lieutenant Albert Tauwhare, a rare example of a New Zealand Maori in the postwar RAF, far less charming, and much more ambitious than any of the native Maoris I met later in their native land.

He was inclined to pile mountains of routine work on to me, but his letters and memos were easy to type on the brand new electric typewriter they provided, far quicker than the antique machines I used in New Milton.

All the senior officers in the Headquarters seemed genuinely surprised to have at their disposal an airman who could take verbatim shorthand, and type it back fast, discreetly correcting their grammar where necessary. It was a piece of cake after Lymington council, and I dashed through the work

My other duty was to maintain the personal records of all the station's officers, and they came to my office to check their allowances. I particularly liked the cheerful pilots in a Dutch fighter squadron on the station who frequently seemed to 'prang their kites'. I was reminded that flying was the sharp end of the RAF when I dealt with the paperwork after air crew fatalities in several air crashes and collisions during exercises in the next two years.

I discovered that National Service gave me for the first time since I left school an opportunity to develop interests outside journalism, although I contributed regular articles to RAF news letters.

I extended my book reading, bought the *Observer* and other 'heavy' newspapers, learned basic German in classes on the station, and produced an updated guide to 'Dusseldorf after Dark' where I liked to think I had become a man-about-Germany.

I was fascinated by the clubs and bars of Dusseldorf, which were often seedy but far less sordid than Hamburg's, and I enjoyed dancing with normal German girls who were prepared for a chaste friendship of short duration if you could engage in basic conversation. I developed a taste for rum and coke, and was intrigued by Germanic novelties such as dance floors with mirror surfaces.

Dusseldorf was a handsome city only ten years after the war, looking far more affluent and sophisticated than 1950s Britain. We were amazed at the wealth of expensive goods in the shops, and the excellent range of restaurants and pubs.

'It makes you wonder who did win the bloody war,' my friends and I would gloomily reflect as we munched our way through Dusseldorf steaks and chips far more delicious than anything available to us in the gastronomic nightmare of the early postwar years at home.

We were under orders to wear civilian clothes outside the station because Germany regained its sovereignty in 1955, and we were warned local populations still had grim memories of RAF bombing. In comparison British soldiers in Germany received a far better reception from German civilians.

One night in the Klamotte club in Dusseldorf where I was listening to an excellent jazz group, an RAF sergeant/pilot, much the worse for drink, stood swaying in front of the bar and shouted: 'I used to come over 'ere and bomb this place night after night!!'

Clearly there were plenty of English speakers present. A huge German in a long green leather coat landed a massive punch on the pilot's jaw, knocking him backwards over the bar where he subsided in a shattered heap of glasses and bottles. The band played on, and it really did resemble many a cowboy film I had enjoyed. I laughed until several of the RAF men's friends joined in a tremendous punch-up with a group of Germans, probably ex-members of Hitler's Army. I edged to the door, and made my way up a shady hall to the exit when to my horror a group of 'Snowdrops', RAF policemen with white topped caps, surged in.

They looked at my blazer and RAF tie, and asked respectfully: 'Where is it happening, sir?'

'Just down there chaps. Hurry up,' I barked, and made my exit swiftly, but with as much decorum as I could summon. The bar was off-limits to 'other ranks', and 'posing as an officer' was an offence with consequences I quaked to imagine. I went over the Dutch border for the next few weekends, exploring the delights of Amsterdam and Arnhem where the RAF's wartime exploits could earn even the most callow National Serviceman a certain amount of undeserved popularity.

On the whole though I much preferred Dusseldorf to Amsterdam where the only way of meeting an unattached female seemed to be in the city's famous red-light area where the girls sit in windows, of interest to me as a gawping tourist, but I wanted a friendly female relationship, however brief, not a shopping trip in the sex industry.

With a friend who had bought a cheap German car, I toured much of the British zone, and made a memorable visit to the Belsen concentration camp site which had horrified me on the newsreel. It was a now just a wire fenced clearing in a pine forest, bare of buildings except for an exhibition of terrible photographs. We all experienced a dread atmosphere, but reflected afterwards that it was 'all in the mind'.

At Laarbruch I filled my ample spare time by developing a stand-up comedy act which I performed in the station cinema and various bars, and became a keen member of the station's dramatic society led by the splendidly histrionic station padre, the Rev. Gordon Bennett who gave me a lead role in several farces.

In the stand-up act I doffed a duffle coat on stage and then shot it with blanks from a pistol, whereupon it was supposed to run off stage on the end of a thread, but somehow it fell over the footlights into the imperturbable Station Commander's lap which proved even more popular.

'Good show, Clayton. At least you can say you fired a gun once during National Service,' he said next morning.

These appearances led to my first taste of broadcasting, in a British Forces Network radio play broadcast from their station in Cologne, and my stand-up act was broadcast as part of an RAF variety show. We went on tour to other RAF stations, and I learned to deal with heckling as well as laughter and applause.

I was somewhat alarmed after I said on air in an ad lib that 'RAF Laarbruch, set in a forest of trees, is the favourite posting – for RAF police dogs'. Received with roars of approval from the airmen, it seemed dangerously near the sort of humour routinely punished by the Station Warrant Officer as a 'breach of good order and discipline'.

Denis Scuse, the BFN producer, and broadcaster in 'Two Way Family Favourites', encouraged me to think about a career in entertainment. The amateur band which accompanied our station variety show suggested I accompany them on a summer season to Jersey after my demob.

It could have been a major career change, but I rejected the offer. Although the RAF was leaving a far better taste in my mouth than I expected, I was yearning to return to newspapers. Although I felt the allure of the stage, I did not want to spend the rest of my life speaking 'someone else's lines' at the behest of dictatorial producers.

Without a shred of hesitation I turned down instantly a Laarbruch recommendation to apply for a regular RAF commission, but it was good to get reversal of the original 'Potential Officer Material' rejection.

Service bureaucracy insisted we travelled laboriously to a UK base to be demobilised. They were adamant we left the station to go home in uniform, but I changed into civvies in a railway station lavatory, and never again wore any part of the uniform, except the black tie.

I was still cynical about society's view that 'National Service is good for you,' (I would have preferred two years in a university), but I had returned with useful experience of continental Europe, and had discovered I might have other talents than reporting. My knowledge of the military was to be of use in future stints of war reporting. I knew I was only at the edge of a life-time of attempts at self-education, and there was much to be learned.

I came of age during my National Service. Perhaps the most significant change wrought by two years in the Queen's service was that I had discovered I was not prepared to be 'pushed around' beyond certain strict limits for the rest of my life.

Chapter Six

THE PACE QUICKENS

'Kick on' means accelerate in horseman's language. After two years away in National Service I 'kicked on' more rapidly than at any other time of my life.

I rushed from one newspaper job to the next, with Fleet Street as my goal. With hindsight it was not a wise policy, but there were so many jobs available for trained young journalists in a fast expanding newspaper industry that my applications proved timely, no matter how meagre my skills and experience.

The Curry family wanted me to return to New Milton, but in my post-National Service bolshy mood, I objected to their proposal to start me at the same three pounds weekly wage I had been earning when I left.

They had replaced me with an excellent trainee reporter, Brian Freemantle from Southampton, who was failed medically for National Service. He propelled himself from New Milton to the *Daily Mail* where he became Foreign Editor, then transforming himself into a phenomenally successful thriller writer, especially known for his Charlie Muffin detective series.

I elected to join Ian Wooldridge who was now sports reporting at the weekly *Bournemouth Times* and its slip edition, the *Poole and Dorset Herald*. They had no immediate reporting vacancies but I accepted a post as sub-editor at £8 per week. It was a chance to live at home with parents in Bournemouth for a while.

In the *Bournemouth Times* office near Branksome, four sub-editors laboured long hours under the leadership of the laconic, highly talented Bert Barham to turn mundane material into lively journalism, with snappy headlines and 'bright' make-up in two editions a week.

The *Times and Herald* sought to offer a more entertaining weekly alternative to the local evening papers in the *Echo* group which were somewhat dull at that time, but Bournemouth readers did not appear ready for anything more exciting in the 1950s.

When we dared in our columns to mock the standard of amenities in the Pavilion complex, our circulation showed no sign of rising, and the Town Hall temporarily withdrew its advertising which the paper could ill afford. So much for the local authority's interest in the freedom of the press!

Wooldridge had formed a jolly group of friends who re-introduced me to the hedonistic delights of Bournemouth in winter-time. Much of the fun was generated by Gordon Williams a young reporter from Paisley who introduced us to a brand of iconoclastic Scottish humour similar to that which later made Billy Connolly a huge success. Williams was out to shock 'the South Coast smoothies', and would tell us: 'No-one wore a bloody kilt in Paisley. If we ever saw a man wearing one we'd know he was a queer, and we'd kick him to death.'

He emerged in the 1960s and '70s as one of the most gifted UK novelists of his generation. He drew on his time as a *Poole and Dorset Herald* reporter in his novel *The Upper Pleasure Garden* which claimed to bring 'a powerful, if sceptical eye to bear on the claustrophobic intensity of English small town life.' It was not exactly the Poole and Bournemouth I knew, but I still enjoy the book as a memoir of one of the most original personalities I met in newspapers.

Williams gained most acclaim, and money, with his brilliant thriller novel *The Siege of Trencher's Farm* set in rural Devon where he lived briefly with his second wife Clarewen; the book was filmed by Sam Peckinpah as the *The Straw Dogs*, probably his most violent and controversial production.

Gordon, who liked to project himself as an Angry Young Scotsman, hard drinking and suffering intense mood swings, came to London to astonish us by securing a job producing the Boy Scout magazine before switching to full-time writing. He shared flats with Wooldridge and me, and was a friend we valued greatly until our paths diverged widely, and we lost touch.

I appreciated the novelty of living with my parents again in Bournemouth, but although the subbing experience was useful, I was fretting for a return to the great outdoors world of reporting.

The following spring I successfully applied for a reporter's role in the Chichester office of the *Portsmouth Evening News*, and said goodbye to the prospect of a comfortable career in Bournemouth.

Working under the genial Paddy Welsh, an excellent journalist who remained reporting happily in the area for the rest of his life, I found a lifestyle in Chichester which I enjoyed, but recognised as another temporary training slot.

The *Portsmouth News* was then a routine but efficient evening paper, with several local editions, and I was pleased to find I could cope easily with its tighter deadlines. I lived comfortably in digs, with the Turner family of ex-boarding house keepers, in Chichester's historic South Street.

As in Bournemouth, I was reporting for another well-upholstered south coast community, and despite its ancient respectability, Chichester had excellent pubs and several new jazz clubs which I visited as much in pursuit of female company as in musical appreciation.

The coastline at Selsey, and the beautiful hinterland of Goodwood and the South Downs, appealed to me enormously. I joined the new scooter craze, bought a blue Vesta on hire purchase, and zoomed about the area sporting L plates. Through crass over-confidence I failed my first driving test as a scooter rider, but rashly abandoned my L plates thereafter, and never re-took the test. Girlfriends were intrepid enough to ride pillion, and I have happy memories of trips to the sand dunes at East Wittering.

I hired mediocre horses for strictly limited hour-long hacks near Chichester, but I could not afford the hiring and transport of a hunter, plus a £2 cap per day to ride with the local Hunt, the Cowdray, based at Midhurst.

I followed a few Cowdray fixtures on the scooter, but longed to be in the mounted field. My best equestrian experiences were visits to Fontwell Park and Goodwood racecourses on press tickets. At Goodwood's just re-opened motor racing track one afternoon I met an immaculately suited Fleet Street reporter, Ken Howells of the *London Evening News.*

During an amiable chat Ken advised me there was a vacancy on the reporting staff in London and advised me to apply. It seemed a leap too far too soon, but my delectable Chichester girlfriend Fenella kindly typed a beautifully-presented letter to the News Editor, and I was shocked to receive a positive, terse reply by return from a gentleman with the Dickensian name of Mr Samuel Jackett.

My life changed utterly. However hum-drum its appearance, Fleet Street was to me the famed Street of Adventure, and I was utterly thrilled to be walking its pavements to the red-brick fortress of Carmelite House where Northcliffe had ruled his *Daily Mail* empire.

The *Mail* was now produced at a newer, uglier building further up Carmelite Street, but the *News* remained in the Northcliffe eyrie which by now resembled a working museum.

I travelled up to the newsroom in a creaking black metal cage lift, with noisy sliding doors. The newsroom was narrow and high ceilinged, crammed with old wooden desks in dark fumed oak, set in two rows facing each other. At their head were two large desks side by side, where sat the News Editor, his Deputy, and two secretaries. At the side of the room male copy-takers, wearing telephone earphones, sat at ancient manual typewriters, clacking away incessantly. Copy boys in their late teens trotted between the desks constantly banging down sheafs of paper into trays.

A couple of venerable ticker-tape machines, in polished wood cases, whirred away. Telephones abounded on every desk, and buzzed incessantly.

No-one actually wore an eye-shade, but for a young provincial newcomer it was a daunting scene to match all my visions of Fleet Street conjured up in cinema dramas. I learned later that one desk bore the initials of the great thriller writer Edgar Wallace who served his time as an *Evening News* reporter.

Despite the atmosphere of purposeful haste, several male reporters sat at their desks calmly reading editions of the paper. The *News* still maintained the anachronism of a separate 'Lady Reporters' room', occupied by just two females. Unlike the vast open-plan media layouts of today, Carmelite House contained a mysterious warren of cubby holes for photographers, feature writers, and specialists all contributing to the daily miracle of multiple editions. In three years on the paper I visited very few of them.

Fleet Street was still the home of most national newspapers. It was a busy, grey street in the 1950s, with people walking briskly to work in the newspaper offices located in adjoining narrow streets and alleys. Lorries delivered rolls of newsprint and cans of ink, and print staff in stained overalls stood on pavements outside the presses on the ground floor of the great newspaper offices, chatting and joking between editions.

However mundane, it was what I had yearned for since I left school, and I fully intended it to be my base for the rest of my life. Neither my original ambition, nor Fleet Street itself, would last over long, but it was a head-spinning thrill to win a place there at the age of 23.

The Rothermere group's broadsheet *London Evening News*, sister of the *Daily Mail*, boasted the world's largest evening paper circulation of well over a million. It competed with two tabloid evening papers of vastly contrasting styles: the *Star* sold about 700,000, an excellent middle-brow paper owned by the Cadbury family in concert with the *News Chronicle*; while the *Evening Standard*, owned by Beaverbrook, then sold well under half a million. The *Standard* could claim to be the most upmarket evening paper, aimed mainly at the West End and City.

Sam Jackett was a distinguished-looking, silver haired figure, wearing a well tailored suit with lots of white shirt cuff. A

Cornishman long absorbed in metropolitan life, he had been leading crime reporter for the *News*. As News Editor he was nearing the end of his career in a role which I soon recognised was unrelentingly stressful. He was succeeded by his Deputy, Percy Trumble, a dumpy Londoner with a trim moustache, who had risen from the ranks of copy takers, and was as decent and likeable a man as ever gave me orders.

Jackett interviewed me for about 20 minutes, amid the din of the News Room, seemed pleased by my 'experience' as a reporter, and did not ask for any written qualifications, although I had my crumpled O level certificates in a pocket.

I was whisked briefly into the office of the Editor, Reg Willis, another West Countryman adorned in an expensive suit. Reg was *par excellence* a top-class evening paper sub-editor; during high pressure peaks in the afternoons he would doff his jacket, roll up his sleeves, sit next to the chief-sub, and peer through his heavy horn-rims at incoming copy, tersely ordering re-makes and re-jigs of front pages. We respected him as a real professional, although he did not seem to take much interest in the reporting staff.

My appointment was eerily similar to my arrival on the *New Milton Advertiser* because Jackett soon offered me a job. He asked casually if £18 per week would be 'OK for starters', and I heard myself gulp, and stupidly ask the same question I had asked the Old Boy: 'Am I on trial?' I received almost exactly the same answer, barked out curtly: 'You're always on bloody trial here.'

It did not bother me; I had more than doubled my wage, and I had secured the job of my dreams.

I was single, and with not the slightest knowledge nor interest in mortgages and income tax. I knew neither how to save, nor to spend wisely. Although in those days before credit cards and massive loan offers, it never occurred to me to spend a penny more than was in my brand new bank account opened with the Fleet Street branch of the Midland Bank, then a solidly English institution.

The reality of my new life became starkly apparent immediately I started work in Carmelite House: in my first few days at the *Evening*

News I had grave doubts I would survive long. I could take fast shorthand, and type quickly, but I soon learned the most important requirement was to compose readable, accurate copy swiftly on your feet out on the streets, dictating it down a telephone line to the office copy takers. It could be printed in the next edition even before you could get back to the office. The subs were marvellous, but the pressure on the reporter to 'get it right' was immense. The thought of perpetrating a huge libel action through crass incompetence haunted me for my first few weeks in London, and then dissolved like a morning mist.

The *News* usually produced seven or eight editions a day, but when late stories were running big, and could sell extra copies in the West End, the paper would rise up like an old ship meeting an awesome wave, to produce at least ten editions by early evening.

The sub-editors' room was the heart of the editorial department: shirt-sleeved men, mostly middle-aged, sat either side of a long table, subbing copy paper from the agencies or staff reporters which was rushed by copy boys to the composing rooms. Features were subbed separately, but they too were often changed rapidly during the day.

All day the stone subs, the chief sub and assistants, climbed up and down a metal circular staircase to the composing room on the floor above, where hot metal type and photo plates were made up with deft speed.

In the subs' room below you could hear the thrum of rollers when they produced the paper-mache moulds to make the plates of type for the batteries of rotary presses down in the engine room of our editorial ship.

There was a legendary story that an *Evening News* sub-editor slumped forward over his desk during preparation of a vital edition; no-one paid any attention until the edition was away, when they found he was dead. Observing these grey men beavering away with heads down in concentrated effort to convert our copy into readable copy with pictures, I could well believe it. They seldom mixed with the reporting staff in the pub, preferring to rush home in the commuter traffic as soon as their gruelling shifts were over.

I was unfailingly thrilled when I was in the street outside in late afternoon while the *Evening News* fleets of yellow vans with black rubber front mudguards, trundled in line into the bay of Carmelite House print works, to receive bundles of West End final editions bearing the famous red sun setting over an outline of London's skyline. At the same time men with glue brushes slapped paper headlines on the billboards carried on top of each van.

It was a costly form of distribution, immensely heavy in labour, and would help spell the end of old-style evening paper competition in London, but it was an impressive example of team work and effort, going back to the intense manual labour used by the Victorians in their creation of the mass popular press.

I was surprised at first to find out how often the *News* required me to write cute, 'colour' stories in a style which could be dreadfully arch. I found myself able to mimic the dreadful stuff all to easily, evolving such stories as an ill-behaved peacock's annoying neighbours (Downfall of the Peecock's Peacock), a Chelsea house decorated bizarrely ('It's Pink, It's Daring and Some Say It's Dreadful').' Many evenings I would return to Earls Court to the sardonic laughter of Gordon Williams after reading the latest Clayton tosh.

Fortunately, the *Evening News* required its reporters to change rapidly into a far higher gear. Violent crime, major fires, and rail or air crashes were frequent in the 1950s in a war-battered London desperately in need of investment in rebuilding transport structures, and adequate security. Cash had to be transported manually, and bank vehicle raids by armed gangs were common. The war produced a huge surplus of guns and men who knew how to use them. The Met police seemed to me to be under-staffed and ill-equipped.

I soon discovered to my relief that on the *Evening News* the legendary ruthlessness of Fleet Street was virtually absent when it came to dealing with staff, although a reporter or sub who could not cope with the pace consistently would not last long.

Sam Jackett usually overlooked reporting disappointments while giving gruff praise to successes. The traditional instruction from the

News Desk after we had hastily phoned over our story was: 'Eat and come back', or blissfully 'Eat and go home.'

Our shifts began at 7 am in the office, and ranged in half hour gaps up to 9 am, so there were always reporters in the office up to 6 pm. It was possible to get up before dawn and work a 14 hour day if your story needed updating through to the final editions.

I had to learn to cope with languid hours of doing very little, contrasted by frenetic activity amid intense competition. I erected mental barriers and an outwardly calm exterior, but my stomach churned in protest, and I understood why Fleet Street had a reputation for heavy drinking, ulcers and broken marriages.

At least we usually had our evenings free, while the morning paper staffs laboured long into the night. If you were out of town on a running story it was essential to keep in touch with it late into the night so that by 8 am next morning you could phone an up-to-date story for the first edition which went on the streets around 9 am.

I would not have survived without the Cockney kindness of the older copy-takers who would helpfully coax me along as I stumbled through dictation, nor the example and advice of senior reporters, led by the marvellous Dickie Herd, an East End crime reporter with black hair like patent leather, and rimless spectacles. He it was who returned my first attempt at filling in an expenses claim.

'No, no, no, dear boy....not like that,' he murmured, taking me into a corner of the News Room to coach me in the levels of 'expenditure' which would be acceptable, with plentiful use of euphemisms as 'subsistence', or 'hospitality'.

I learned quickly that Fleet Street reporters, and indeed some of their managers, expected to receive a significant, untaxed addition to their income through 'exes'. This produced years of subsidised romping on the lower slopes of the Fleet Street mountain, but too many old hands suffered when they reached thinner air higher up, and retired on low salaries which earned them paltry pensions.

I suffered a few terrible experiences desperately scribbling reports in tattered notebooks in London cafes before dictating them to the office, only to find I was 'late on the story'; reports had already arrived on the agency tapes, or worst of all, staff reports were in earlier editions of the rival evening papers.

Taking a deep breath I leapt into composing my reports from my notes while I dictated them. To my relief, the technique came naturally, and it became more sophisticated: I could compose 'colour' stories off the cuff as well as factual reports. The danger of such work is the reporter becoming reliant on similar strings of clichés to cover any happening.

I was glad to be given feature stories as well, involving research for a lengthy piece in the next day's early editions.

My *Evening News* colleagues were a remarkably matey bunch: I never detected the slightest sign of jealousy, nor bitching.

The worst aspect of metropolitan reporting was sitting at a news room desk, like a taxi cab on the rank, awaiting the News Editor's call to cover a story. One could sit for several days without work, I discovered with alarm.

It was no wonder Fleet Street reporters tended to spend long hours in their favourite pubs. Each newspaper had its own pub: the *Daily Mail's* was the White Swan, known as the 'Mucky Duck', and ours was the Harrow, a smaller establishment which we treated as an exclusive club, all of us known by name to the publican and his staff, and allowed credit in buying drinks, with a telephone used by the news room to call up reserves of reporting strength in the event of a major story breaking.

Perhaps due to my Quaker inhibitions, I have never been a heavy drinker, but I learned to enjoy pub life in Fleet Street more than at any other time of my life; the pub was a better place to snatch a quick meal than the mass of greasy spoon cafes abounding before the arrival of high class fast food.

I was camping chaotically in a crowded Earls Court flat with Wooldridge and other bachelor friends, eating random meals outside, and never relaxing indoors in the evenings; the Harrow provided the nearest equivalent to a sense of family, and the bachelor reporters would linger there for hours after work before returning to our austere bolt-holes before tomorrow's early start.

There was a sense of camaraderie, such as I never experienced anywhere else in journalism, and nowadays I deeply regret leaving it all too soon. George Hollingberry, another former copy-taker, was a warm, friendly example of Londoners at their best; and there were admirable colleagues with much talent, most notably the ex-Barnardo boy Leslie Thomas who was to become one of the most successful postwar novelists after his autobiographical account of his far more exciting National Service in Singapore *The Virgin Soldiers*. Leslie's great talent as a descriptive writer was soon recognised at the *Evening News,* and none of us begrudged him his share of the bigger stories, including his account of the trial of the Holocaust criminal Adolf Eichmann in Israel.

It was from the Harrow early on the evening of 4 December, 1957 that a group of us from the *Evening News* rushed to Lewisham in south London to cover an appalling rail crash of commuter trains in dense fog. An express steam train rammed into the back of an electric train, carriages reared in the air, and the railway bridge at St John's Station collapsed, magnifying the chaos and carnage.

I trundled there on my scooter, and spent much of the night at a desperate scene where rescuers hacked their way through to the dead and dying.

At dawn next morning, after a night without sleep, I was back in the office and sent immediately by Sam Jackett to the Southern Region press room at Waterloo, to relay each new official statement instantly to the office. The senior reporters continued to report dreadful rescue scenes which continued for several days, and I admired their professionalism and hard work over long hours.

It was my first disaster story, followed by many others during the next 20 years, but I found far more wearing the 'staking out' of doorways to snatch interviews, or wait for official statements. Another challenge were the smogs. London before the compulsory use of smokeless fuels suffered intense winter smogs which stifled all of us, and killed the weak and elderly. It was not without physical challenge even for a young reporter. An evening paper reporter was inevitably a leg-man, and it was the feet which suffered most on London's hard pavements.

Park Lane, Mayfair and the main railway station areas were thronged with prostitutes, some of the younger ones remarkably attractive illegal immigrants from the continent.

They would cheerful proposition me in mid-morning outside the Palladian frontage of Bow Street Magistrates Court, where the 'girls' had appeared to pay their statutory £20 fines. I was amused, but not at all tempted, since I was usually rushing to an ill smelling red phone box, fumbling for pennies to achieve reverse charge phone calls for my report of a sensational case, later to be heard in full at the Old Bailey. Sometimes you needed a strong shoulder to keep the phone box door shut while ponces and others of a criminal ilk tried to interrupt your lengthy call. I learned to pay newspaper shops a ten shilling note to use their phones without interruption, but acquiring quick use of a phone was always an evening paper reporter's challenge in the rush of heartless London's working day.

Well known people revealed to be sex perverts, or City fraudsters were favourite evening paper front-pagers from Bow Street for the midday editions, and woe betide the reporter who missed them.

The West End's first stop for miscreants since 1740, Bow Street inside was a cramped theatre of justice in dismal fumed oak and black iron railings, constructed to convey society's disapproval of the drunks, misfits and far worse who peered from its dismal dock at the bench. Despite the oppressive setting I observed London's stipendiary magistrates dispensing remarkably fair and accurate verdicts and penalties, or summarily committing them to the higher court. We could at that time report all the prosecution evidence in detail from the preliminary hearing, while the defence had to wait until a full trial before their case hit the press.

However exciting, our breathless reports from the leading London magistrates' courts could not compete with our readers' approval for the most popular column in the *Evening News*, 'Courts Day by Day by J.A.J.', cloaking the writer Jimmy Jones whose gentle wit and descriptive style produced a daily miracle of style from central London's minor cases of petty theft, prostitution or drunkenness. He had been producing his charming column reflecting London's nether regions for nearly 30 years when I joined the paper, and I noted with a pang that *Time* magazine called it 'the best read feature in the otherwise undistinguished *London Evening News*'. What did not those Yankee bastards know of our challenging ten editions a day?

My biggest court challenge was evening paper 'mob-handed' reporting of major cases at the Old Bailey. We sent a squad of three or four reporters, each departing the press box with a 'take' of evidence, to be phoned over immediately from the notebook, which meant summarising and composing as you dictated.

The perils of such speed were illustrated one day when an Old Bailey judge just after lunch sternly ordered a *Star* reporter to come before him. The judge sternly pointed out the *Star* had reported proceedings in court while the jury had been sent out, an error made by one of their squad rushing in to take his turn without noticing the jury box was empty.

The Judge warned of committal to prison for contempt of court for any reporter repeating this heinous offence in his court, and I continued note-taking with a somewhat shaky hand.

I was in the Old Bailey for the awesome moment on 25 September, 1959, when Mr Justice Edmund Davies put on the black cap over his wig, leaned forward and informed Guenther Podola he would be hanged by the neck until he be dead, the last man in Britain executed for murdering a policeman.

I had covered much of the story from the day Podola had shot a London police detective in South Kensington, his dramatic arrest by the Flying Squad in a local hotel, and a first court appearance with head injuries said to have been caused in a 'scuffle' during arrest, followed by his Old Bailey trials.

A few liberal journals fussed about this, but no-one on the *Evening News* thought it was at all questionable: shooting a copper naturally meant someone would get roughed up 'resisting arrest' before they inevitably got 'topped', they said over their beers in the Harrow.

Podola's defence tried his claim of 'loss of memory' as a tactic, but there was abundant evidence of guilt, and the jury took only half an hour to consider the case. He had an appalling criminal past record.

I was sent to the gates of Wandsworth Prison in the early hours of 5 November to write whatever I could about the execution inside. Old hands among the press squad advised me a faint banging noise was other prisoners crashing metal plates on their cell doors just before the hanging, which was the sort of copy the 1950s public expected to read on these occasions, including the wording of the execution notice posted outside the jail.

I am not in favour of a return to capital punishment in modern Britain, but I would not have objected if British society had retained the death penalty for the very limited number of cast-iron guilty killers today incarcerated for the rest of their lives, without any remission. The awful reality of endless incarceration without redemption surely cannot make us feel we have found a genuinely compassionate alternative to execution?

Having reported some of the worst of Northern Ireland's excesses, I would have additionally supported execution by shooting squads for terrorist killers from both sides. Ulster and Southern Irish society would have understood the equation perfectly. Of course they would have produced martyrs, but one side or the other did so relentlessly, every time a gunman was jailed.

UK society was no less compassionate in the 1950s than today, but it had recently emerged from close involvement in a world war, and thoroughly understood the consequences of taking life. Murders were reported in huge detail in the 1950s and '60s, not solely through prurient interest to stimulate press sales, but there was huge concern for victims.

Anyone who believes the modern British state is far beyond taking life in pursuit of its policies, should look again at the estimates of civilian casualty figures in Iraq. British society likes to think it cares today, but it suffers immense 'compassion fatigue' from TV rolling news coverage of violence and suffering, so remote from the comfortable armchairs of most viewers.

News coverage became less grim at the *News* when I was given a far more varied diet of stories. Sam Jackett kindly loaned me to the John Carpenter gossip column to cover West End overnight stories such as a first night at the swish Colony nightclub by Hutch, the coloured singer and pianist with a deep velvet voice. He entranced my current girlfriend, a young barrister, by joining us at our table for drinks, but it was our last date before she switched her affection from the press to more affluent members of the Bar.

Better still, my avowed interest and knowledge of horses was recognised by assigning me to write preview stories of major Turf occasions for the early racing editions.

My orders were to spice up the sober coverage of the racing staff with news stories and colour previews. The *News* turf team, led by Tom Webster were polite, but barely tolerated my intrusion on their territory, and never invited me into the official racing scribes' press box. I did not care: I tended to cover the inconvenient news the race reporters usually avoided.

Much to my surprise, and through sheer luck rather than expertise, I pulled off a minor coup when reporting the eve of the 1960 Epsom Derby early morning exercise gallops on the famous Downs. As a horseman myself, I surmised that a horse suddenly pulled up from a canter by its jockey was staggering with a heart attack. I ran from Tattenham Corner nearly to the finish where the animal was now lying down, and a vet arrived swiftly confirm it was dead.

I was warmly grateful to the *Express* group's Peter O'Sullevan and Clive Graham who courteously told me the animal's name and connections, completely unconcerned that I was from the rival group. The horse was Exchange Student, nominally entered as trained by Phonsie O'Brien, brother of the famous Vincent O'Brien who had temporarily lost his licence. I phoned through a speedy story to capture the *News's* first edition front page lead, scooping the other evening papers and agencies.

From now on my news gateway to the turf was wide open: I covered the first Flat race of the season, the 1960 Lincolnshire Handicap, then held on Lincoln's own delightful course. The same week I drove over the Pennines in my tiny Austin saloon to my first visit to Aintree where the mercurial Mrs Mirabelle Topham was in charge of the crumbling shambles of her late husband's race course, fighting for the survival of a Grand National meeting desperately in need of investment, although it made millions for the world's bookmakers.

This delightful, formidable lady chatted away amiably, although I doubt she liked my report of bushes growing out of the bricks on the grandstand, and sagging racetrack rails in need of repair and painting.

Neville Crump's ex-hunter from the Scottish Borders, Merryman II won the 1960 National, ridden by Gerry Scott. It was the first to be televised, watched by a ten million audience, and the last National before the great perpendicular fences were sloped back, not at that time for 'safety' reasons, but mainly to bring more top-class 'chasers back to Aintree, in which it partly succeeded. Television was increasing public interest in racing, and my role as a news reporter on course seemed established at the big fixtures.

The *London Evening News* offered me yet another permanent job and a way of life with increasing opportunities. I still had much to learn but I had become accepted as a reasonably useful member of the reporting team, and I was being given a better share of the big stories. There was every chance of specialising in politics; I enjoyed reporting by-elections and covered a Liberal Party Conference in Torquay where my 'opposite number' from the *Evening Standard* was the ebullient Randolph Churchill, son of Winston. Randolph, notwithstanding a reputation for drink and temperament, treated me as if I were a senior political scribe, rather than a callow youth, living on snatched bacon sandwiches and large cups of tea in London's greasy spoon cafes, resulting in my increasingly skeletal appearance.

During a genial chat in the bar later we were both amused by the way leading Liberal delegates sycophantically fawned all over Randolph at a reception.

They were rewarded in the *Evening Standard* by a searing indictment of their chances of ever gaining power from the robust Churchill pen, after which he left Torquay without ever entering their conference hall. We had convivial times later at several by-elections, and although Randolph generally gets a bad press as Churchill's son, I can only register that as an evening paper scribe he was a good companion, never pompous, and always behaving like a fellow professional.

On the last morning of the conference the Liberals went into 'secret' session, but they forgot to dismantle the live sound feed to the press room. So we sat around taking notes from the debate booming from the loudspeakers. Some of us ungenerously noted in our reports that it was not a good example of the Liberals' capability in running anything.

My days at the *Evening News* were numbered one afternoon when I offered a cigarette to a comely, blonde New Zealand feature writer, Mary Watson and later we were married in St. Bride's Church, Fleet Street.

The *Evening News* editorial 'family' was strongly supportive, often employing us in a joint role at the big race meetings. Mary covered social scenes at Royal Ascot meetings while I prowled about in search of racing 'stories'.

We worked together at Epsom for the 1960 Derby, one of the most hectic days ever on the historic Epsom course, ending darkly. I phoned one report after another report to the *Evening News* which they re-made on the front page for every edition, each one more sensational.

Winston Churchill's horse was suddenly withdrawn after injuring itself in its box; a signal man fainted in the heat on the line to Epsom Downs station, and the royal train was held up, bringing the Queen late to the course.

The Derby favourite was the French-trained colt, Angers, ridden by Gerard Thiboeuf. Coming down the hill to Tattenham Corner Angers' near foreleg snapped; he was suddenly out of the race, and had to be put down by a vet on the course. It was an amazing coincidence: I had already reported the tragedy of Exchange Student breaking a leg exercising the previous morning.

The race was won by St Paddy, ridden by Lester Piggott and trained by Noel Murless.

I was somewhat hot and bothered by the time I phoned through my account of the Derby itself.

'Don't worry,' said the copytaker in London. 'You drew St Paddy in the Press Club sweepstake; you've won hundreds!'

In fact I had won about £250, a huge sum in 1960, and we used the cash to help finance a voyage I had been dreading, but had agreed to make almost as part of the marriage vows: to visit New Zealand to meet my wife's family.

I agreed to a year's sabbatical, with a worrying possibility of staying there forever 'if I liked it'. I still recall my mother's tears as we bade her farewell in her Bournemouth bungalow. She bravely asserted: 'We'll come out to New Zealand too, if you're going to stay there.'

We journeyed across Europe by train, sailed from the port of Pireaus on a Greek liner via the Suez Canal to Sydney, then flew across the Tasman to Wellington where my father-in-law, Claude Watson, was the strict and somewhat feared Editor of the morning paper, *The Dominion*, although he was always charming to me.

The round-the-world trip, including camel rides to the Sphinx in Egypt while our ship went through the Suez Canal, was a mind-stretching experience. My past life seemed to be slipping away inexorably; not for the first time I wondered if I would ever regain it. When we berthed in Sydney the press interviewed my wife, and reported with awe 'She meets royalty'; Australian attitudes to a monarchy were still somewhat primitive.

The Kiwis were kind and welcoming, although over-anxious to get a good opinion of their country from the visitor as soon as he landed.

I stepped into a reporting role on Auckland's morning paper, the *Herald*, where another satisfying journalistic career could have been forged for a life-time.

I was immediately appointed Maori Affairs Reporter, perhaps because I could guarantee total impartiality, due to my ignorant

Pommy status, but I suspect that at the time no-one else wanted the job.

It seemed the Maoris were becoming far less sanguine about their marginal role in politics, and I wrote stories about their growing demands for a greater say in the running of the country they had handed over to the 'pakeha', the whites. This has rumbled on as a story ever since.

I found that 'right little, tight little New Zealand' was suffering from outbreaks of teenage violence, quaintly called 'larrikinism', one of many throw-backs to the Victorian language the early settlers brought with them. There was much concern about hooliganism by the young at something called the Hastings Flower Festival, which seemed unlikely but true.

I soon decided that any form of Kiwi hooliganism was due to complete and utter boredom by many of the young, no matter how beautiful their environment.

I travelled to Maori gatherings around delectable Lake Taupo and New Zealand's two islands have breathtakingly beautiful countryside and coasts. I enjoyed my sabbatical, and I appreciated the lengthy news-features which were coming my way, plus such roles as cinema reviewing. The *Herald* was a solid, workmanlike paper under its genial Editor, Mr Budge Hintz, who was a devoted angler.

After Fleet Street's 'roar of grease-paint and smell of the crowds' New Zealand at the beginning of the 1960s offered a wonderful future for anyone who wanted to enjoy an outdoors life to the full.

I still hankered for horses and foxhunting, but I was not ready for the remoteness of New Zealand society and politics at that time. Its post-war socialist governments were trying to create a welfare state offering absolute security from cradle to grave. It was highly bureaucratic: there were said to be more government departments than existed in the USA Federal government, and the country could not afford it. New cars for example, were heavily taxed luxury imports for a few. Socially, the country badly needed a much wider mix of immigrant to leaven the 19th and early 20th century influx of land-starved Scottish farmers.

The licensing laws were ridiculous, with pubs open all day, but closed at 6pm when all sales of alcohol were forbidden, a hangover from New Zealand's stern Presbyterian past. We worked a terrible 'split shift' at the *Herald*, starting at midday; then at the end of the afternoon the reporters and other staff would repair to the pubs, and hastily drink ice-cold beer, sprayed into glasses with hoses as they were lined up on the counter.

The ritual, known as the 'Six O'clock Swill' resulted in more drunkenness on the streets of Auckland than I had seen in London since V for Victory Day. The ridiculous licensing laws produced far more heavy drinking at home, and surreptitious use of hip-flasks in restaurants, than I had seen anywhere. Home brewed beer was a favourite hobby, to be consumed during lengthy hours sea fishing, or on the superb beaches where most New Zealanders repaired in the summer, staying in their own wooden holiday homes called 'baches' for long weekends which left the towns and cities emptied as if suffering from a nuclear attack.

We journalists would return from the pub somewhat groggily for a late shift at the *Herald* where I failed to enjoy scribbling and typing amid Auckland's summer humidity and mosquitoes. Far better were some marvellous out-of-town assignments where I often flew in 'Captain Ladd's flying-boats' over Auckland's remarkably beautiful harbour, landing in the sea and gliding up beaches to step out on to white or black volcanic sand.

London's growth into the Swinging Sixties liberalism, and intellectual curiosity, was notably absent in New Zealand's small cities and towns which were happily jogging along at least 40 years behind.

Even my father-line-law advised me that much of the South Island was 'the land of Nod', and I should not ever seek to work there.

When George Bernard Shaw visited the Kiwi paradise between the wars the Wellington press asked him at the dockside: 'What does the average man-in-the-street in Britain think of New Zealand?'

Mr Shaw replied tersely: 'The average man-in-the-street in Britain does not think of New Zealand.'

I agreed fervently with Shaw, and understood why many New Zealand journalists were emigrating to London, and staying there.

My wife was working all day on the Auckland evening paper, so we were in a journalistic lifestyle where we 'met on the stairs', but we had some marvellous trips exploring the countryside. I was already planning a return to London within the next 12 months, and Mary seemed just as ready to make our life in the UK.

My stomach churned when I learned that Fleet Street was in turmoil: the *News Chronicle* and *Star* collapsed overnight, under the weight of restrictive practice and high labour costs in printing and distribution endemic throughout the London press.

They merged with the Rothermere's *Daily Mail* and *Evening News*, but it amounted to close-down, and hundreds of excellent staff were thrown on the streets.

We were already committed to returning to London, but I feared this time the Clayton luck would not be sufficient to guarantee a job. There were dire reports that further recruitment was virtually non-existent on the surviving Fleet Street papers after they had taken on board as many survivors as possible of the *Chronicle* group debacle in which the Cadbury family proprietors, of Quaker origins, were much criticised by axed journalists for the suddenness of the collapse with insufficient safeguards for staff. It was somewhat unjust because no-one has yet devised a 'gentle' method of closing a national newspaper. It's like the theatre; a play which does not pay just comes off suddenly.

All this was much in my mind during a horrendous sea trip from Auckland to Sydney, beset with tremendous gales throughout, causing the death of several racehorses on board, and the departure overboard of cars lashed to the deck. I discovered I was virtually immune to sea-sickness, and continued eating boiled eggs in a deserted restaurant when sea-water roared down the companion ways and swirled about my ankles at the breakfast table.

Chapter Seven

THE BEAVERBROOK WAY

'For heaven's sake, it's only a murder. Just keep calm, and do something...'

The advice was drawled in my ear at a moment of crisis by one of the most formidable newspapermen in the history of Fleet Street. I was amazed, and somewhat dubious, to find myself sitting alongside him as his deputy.

Ronnie Hyde was News Editor of the *Evening Standard* for 32 years, and became a legend long before his retirement in 1972.

He had the most commanding presence of anyone I ever worked for, with the ability to reduce even the most hardened senior reporter to jelly.

Immediately I returned to London from New Zealand, I applied to rejoin the *Evening News,* but with, I think, genuine regret Reg Willis said he could take no more staff because he had taken on many after the recent closure of the *Star.*

Virtually penniless, I trotted round the Fleet Street pubs to meet former colleagues, and one murmured to me that I should apply immediately to the *Standard* where there had been a 'sudden vacancy'.

Ronnie Hyde appointed me as a reporter after a brief, incisive interview, and I soon relished working for one of Britain's finest newspapers at that time, edited by Charles Wintour who was in office from 1959-76, and again from '78-80.

'Chilly Charlie', or 'Mid-Wintour' as he was variously known to us, had great talents, and earned the respect of his staff, but not their universal liking. He was inherently shy, and used his coldness of manner as a weapon. One feature writer who became 'a sudden vacancy' ordered by Wintour, described the Editor's mouth as a 'surgical incision'.

He was much less chilly in his dealings with attractive, intelligent female journalists, and could force himself to show warmth when dealing with the coterie of top-class feature writers he collected and nurtured at the *Standard*. Ann Sharpley, Jean Campbell, a granddaughter of Beaverbrook, were brilliant descriptive writers, and Wintour would call on such talents as Malcolm Muggeridge to provide wit and intellectual weight. The great Vicky was the paper's superb political cartoonist, with Jak providing comedy cartoons better than most morning papers could produce.

Wintour was of a patrician military family and came down to the journalistic trenches of Beaverbrook's Express group via Oundle, Cambridge and distinguished war service in which he collected the Croix de Guerre. I have never been surprised that his daughter Anna Wintour has shown exceptional talent, plus a legendary ability to awe her staff, as a top-flight magazine Editor.

Charles Wintour was distantly polite to reporters, but gave the impression they were definitely 'other ranks', and Ronnie Hyde was delegated implacable power to keep them toiling.

Hyde, who read English at Cambridge, was far more sophisticated than any other news editor I encountered. Tall and imposing, with a shock of swept-back silver hair, and hooded eyes under bushy eyebrows, he ran the *Standard* news desk with firm paternalism, and judicious pressure, not to say bullying, on those he considered needed to work harder and faster.

Hyde was famous within Fleet Street for such bon mots as his exchange with a flustered reporter who, after dictating his story, said on the phone: 'I'm just on my way in, Mr Hyde.'

The News Editor drawled: 'On the contrary, dear boy. You're on your way out.' (In fact, he was anything but a quick hire-and-fire boss.)

I recall an experienced morning paper reporter joining our staff. On his first morning he leaned over the News Editor's desk and said conversationally: 'Hello, Ronnie. What would you like me to do?'

Hyde rapped out: 'First, call me sir! Then get off my desk, and take your hand out of your pocket. You can sit over there, and wait 'til I call you.'

The formidable News Editor seemed to like me from the start, and my admiration for him grew: he had perfected an elaborate act which worked well for him in controlling a highly varied and temperamental staff, but underneath was a good mind, a keen sense of humour, and a firm loyalty to his staff.

Most reporters stayed with him for the rest of their career, and he assembled the most effective group of evening paper staff you could find anywhere. Most were devoted to him, trusted his judgement entirely, tolerated his pseudo-arrogant style, and cherished his rare praise, since it came from a master of his craft.

John Miller and John Ponder were remarkable crime correspondents, although difficult men to control at times. Hyde would engage in lengthy altercations with either of them over his first morning coffee. You might have imagined he was about to sack them, but it was merely a ritualistic game which I suspect they all enjoyed.

Permanently based at Scotland Yard's press room for the *Standard* was 'Sully', short for Horatio Nelson Sullivan. He had become a reporter by sheer accident. Working as a copy boy, he had answered the phone late one afternoon when the caller was the proprietor, Lord Beaverbrook, a more important communication than one from the Holy Ghost.

The Beaver, in his Canadian twang, fired several questions about late share prices, which Sully answered promptly and accurately. Next day Beaverbrook congratulated the News Editor on his bright young reporter, and asked his name.

Hyde realised with concern no reporter had been left on duty, but suavely praised Sullivan as the man who had dealt with the call. After Beaverbrook rang off, Sullivan was immediately promoted to the role of reporter. The incident said much about the source of power exercised directly within Express newspapers by its proprietor right up to his death in 1964.

His Editors strove to please Beaverbrook at all times; even the frosty Charles Wintour was not immune. He sent me early one morning to a London railway station to meet Lord Beaverbrook who had returned by sea from Canada in a liner, disembarked at Liverpool, and then travelled to London in a private railway coach hitched to the back of an express train.

Wintour instructed me to approach the proprietor and say: 'Good morning, Lord Beaverbrook. The Editor of the *Evening Standard* presents his compliments and asks if you have any instruction for him.'

Wintour also advised me to check before the press baron's arrival whether his train was late, and if so why; this information was to be given to the great man on arrival. Having read my Evelyn Waugh I was tempted to counter any questions with the answer: 'Up to a point, Lord Copper.'

Feeling like a medieval courtier I duly performed the pantomime of a stiff bow, introducing myself, gravely telling the little old man in a black hat and coat sitting in a wheelchair, that his important arrival had been delayed four minutes by a slight signals failure in Hertfordshire.

He wheezed his thanks, said he had no immediate message for his Editor, but would 'see him later'.

On my return to Shoe Lane I went to Wintour's office and somehow maintained a straight face as I gave him a detailed account of this trivial nonsense. Wintour did not smile or even wink, but asked anxiously: 'How did he look?'

His grey face seemed to go even paler when I said Beaverbrook looked 'reasonably well', and had promised an early meeting. I went back to the News Desk to give a dramatised account of my morning to Ronnie Hyde who was tremendously amused, especially relishing Wintour's anxiety.

I do not know exactly what Beaverbrook did to inspire terror into his senior executives, except hold over them the threat of instant sacking, but I recall Wintour cross-examining me again after my only lunch meeting with the proprietor.

When I said after my return that Beaverbrook had treated me kindly, Hyde responded: 'You're alright. He doesn't pay you enough to treat you roughly.'

As the Beaver grew older, stories about virile, active elderly men became more common in his newspapers. The two world wars were always referred to in Beaverbrook papers as 'the first German war' or the 'second German war'. This recognised the Beaver's annoyance that Hitler had overturned his support for appeasement policies in the 1930s and his infamous prediction in 1938 that 'there would be no war this year, or next'.

Ronnie Hyde firmly reserved the right to admonish his reporters himself. He hated any attempt at such communication directly from the Editor, and at conferences I never heard him apportion blame to individual reporters for any failure in 'getting a story'.

Hyde was virtually unknown to *Evening Standard* readers, but he was the man behind thousands of news stories, including many scoops, through his news sense, his own contacts, and his ability to galvanise his staff to meet tight evening paper deadlines.

One of his favourite orders to reporters was: 'Don't tell me the story, write it!'

He would say: 'I appear to be strict with them only because on an evening paper we cannot waste time. They've got to respond immediately.

'I only blame staff when they do nothing......for God's sake do something, even if it's the wrong something!'

Unlike the *Evening News*, Hyde's reporters on the *Standard* took turns in an all-night shift in the office, which sometimes gave the paper huge momentum in getting to grips with a story which had hit the morning papers late, and needed speedy following up for the evening paper first editions.

He had invented the *Standard's* 'Late Night Reporting Corps' which covered fashionable parties in the West End, and were also charged with providing the News Editor with tips about impending scandals which might emerge when leading politicians or businessmen had dropped their guard.

Three times married, but childless, Hyde was insatiably curious about people, and an inveterate gossip. Originally from middle-class Manchester, he had become a devoted Londoner: he dined frequently at Simpson's or the Savoy Grill, seldom missed West End first-nights, adored cricket at Lords, and was fascinated by political and high-life scandal.

His sybaritic lifestyle was latterly restricted by teetotalism, due to ulcers and a poisoned liver, said to be due to lengthy drinking sessions with his close friend Herbert Gunn, the *Standard's* previous Editor.

Many thought he should have succeeded Gunn as Editor, but News Editors seldom if ever make that leap. Hyde was the exception in having a far wider vision and sophistication than many 'hard news' men, and I suspected it was a source of disappointment that he remained entirely chained to the News Desk throughout his career.

He did not like Wintour, and would make acidly sarcastic remarks about the Editor's judgement after Wintour had returned late from a West End lunch to quiz the News Desk about the coverage of the day. Wintour, I am sure, was not fond of Hyde, but thoroughly understood his value to the paper.

Wintour had an intimidating habit of writing constant memos beginning with the question 'How could it happen that….?' These were received with the utmost distaste by Ronnie Hyde as if he was handling envelopes containing excrement. He would hold them between two fingers at arms length as he dropped them into the waste-paper basket.

I enjoyed large slices of luck reporting for Hyde, not least when I was despatched to interview Yorkshire housewife Viv Nicholson who had just won £152,000 in football pools, a massive sum then.

I appeared to be the only reporter at the London railway terminal, accosting her on the platform.

I asked her what she planned to do with the money, and Viv answered robustly: 'I'm going to spend it of course!'

'What, spend and spend?' I asked.

'Yeah,' she said with a cheeky grin, and hurried away with the pools representative to a London hotel to receive the cheque.

I phoned my story through immediately from the station, and I reported her as saying: 'I'm going to spend, spend, spend!'

This was head-lined over my story in the paper, even before she spoke to the press at the hotel, and it was used repeatedly during her well publicised life as a rags-to-riches-to-rags-again story as a pools winner. In 1998 her life was celebrated in a musical called 'Spend, Spend, Spend' which won an award for Best Musical of the Year.

I was utterly amazed to be involved in a second Epsom Derby drama. Twenty-six runners in the '62 Derby were galloping down to Tattenham Corner when seven horses fell in a dreadful melee, one of them fatally breaking a leg. I was standing at ground level at the rails by the finishing post as riderless horses galloped behind the leaders in a scene more reminiscent of the Grand National. The disaster enabled Larkspur, a 22-1 outsider, to romp home to produce trainer Vincent O'Brien's first Derby triumph.

Amid vast confusion and din I extracted quotes from shocked trainers of fallen horses, and crumpled jockeys. Thanks to Hyde's impeccable organisation I was able to use an exclusive land-line near the finish to phone my story for a major re-plate on the last edition, earning a joint by-line alongside the *Standard's* racing correspondent Peter Scott.

I was ahead with the story because the racing correspondents were prevented from leaving their press box by excited crowds surging down the stairs.

Next morning Hyde made a rare error in forgetting to send anyone to Epsom Hospital where three Derby jockeys were lying injured.

He sent me late, and I missed a hospital press conference, only to wander without permission into a ward where I found jockey Tommy Gosling sitting up in bed, being visited by his pretty fiancée. He chatted away about the disastrous race, and it made a nice exclusive for the *Standard*, magisterially acknowledged by Mr Hyde.

I was increasingly assigned to the better stories, and was frequently by-lined over a widely varied diet of news. I should have realised 'the best of times is now', because there was a quota of disasters and disappointments awaiting later in my reporting career.

I covered Prince Charles's departure from London Airport for his first day at school at Gordonstoun, noting the Prince 'looked a little lonely...' With his hands permanently clasped behind his back Charles looked like a small prisoner in the custody of Prince Philip who personally piloted a Heron aircraft of the Queen's Flight to take his son up to the schooldays in Scotland which Charles has since said he absolutely hated.

I was watching from the beach at Cowes when Prince Philip's racing dinghy *Coweslip* capsized with him just offshore. I managed to grab a holidaymaker with a camera; we waded out to get a lift on a launch, and circled Philip in the water clinging to his boat, while he greeted us with a stream of naval language.

A fuzzy wired picture and my somewhat florid account of the capsize enabled a *Standard* re-plate which scooped the opposition.

They were trivial stories, but they were fun, and a welcome change from the daily catalogue of London's train and tube mishaps, and sordid crime. It says something for Wintour's catholic view of news in his West End paper that I spent many days in east and north London reporting the growing problem of homeless families, and outbreaks of racial tension.

My reports were increasingly being published under my by-line and the period I spent as a general reporter for the *Standard* was among the most enjoyable parts of my reporting career.

In October 1961 I had a small taste of foreign reporting when I flew to the Canary Islands to join the liner Stirling Castle carrying 262 islanders evacuated from Tristan da Cunha after the eruption of its volcano.

The 'story' for the British press was the reaction of the islanders to the outside world, since most had never left their remote South Atlantic home, had not seen television, nor experienced other modern amenities. The tabloids called them the 'Rip Van Winkles' of the 20th century, but I found them rather more sane and balanced than some of my fellow Britons.

Thank heavens the *Standard* expected a more sophisticated treatment of the story, and I was able to explore the possibility that the islanders, with their close family structures intact, might not be deprived of life's real essentials.

The most significant element in the story came three years later when most of the refugees rejected life in England to return to Tristan da Cunha.

I began to feel, with the ignorant arrogance of youth, I had mastered evening paper reporting despite the occasional hiccup, and was enjoying myself, when this agreeable lifestyle ended abruptly overnight in mid-1963.

It was entirely my own fault: despite the darkest forebodings I could not resist Hyde's offer of 'promotion' to Deputy News Editor. I told myself I needed the pay increase, since we had bought our first house in Blackheath, and I was running a battered old car.

The new role meant working indoors permanently in the *Standard's* noisome news room, but worst of all I virtually ceased writing news stories.

Instead, I sat next to Ronnie Hyde at the news desk, attended by two male secretaries, the ever obliging Reg Smith and his mate, surrounded by shrill telephones and noisy tape machines. It was more like a factory, with bare floors and brick pillars painted a ghastly green. The grimy windows received little light from the narrow confines of Shoe Lane, virtually an alley between Fleet Street and Ludgate Circus.

At first I had no time to pine for reporting; I was in the hot seat, and frequently I struggled to maintain some credibility. I was much younger than most of Hyde's battle-hardened senior reporters, and somehow I had to achieve their respect and their cooperation in working against the clock.

Shamefully, I began to mimic some of Hyde's mannerisms, especially an air of calm languor cloaking an iron will, but I do not think it fooled anyone.

I would return from the Editor's conference, sometimes more than a little bothered, to dish out assignments at rapid speed.

Since the *Standard* had no foreign desk this meant communicating sometimes with our few staffers overseas, including the sardonic scribe Sam White in Paris and Jean Campbell in the US, both treated by Wintour and Hyde as superior beings.

On the whole, the reporting staff were remarkably helpful, but there were some colourful explosions of temperament. An exuberant lady reporter, June Baker, responded to my attempt at impersonating Hyde's sarcasm by throwing a milk bottle across the news desk, just missing me. I am afraid I pretended not to notice; June had a shapely figure and a heart of gold, and I liked her just as much as all the younger male reporters did.

One morning, in sole command on the news desk, I became deeply frustrated by lack of action on the part of the overnight reporter. I seized him by the lapels and dragged him across the desk to look into his eyes, accusing him of drug taking because his pupils were contracted. We sacked him on the spot, and years later when I met him in a more exalted capacity at the BBC he thanked me fervently; just as well because he was technically my superior by then.

I had to fire instantly another reporter for fighting the front door commissionaires in the downstairs lobby whilst drunk. It was a stark contrast to the political correctness of modern employment regulations, but I do not think we committed injustice, and alternative jobs were far more plentiful then.

My friendship with Hyde grew apace, and he revealed considerable charm and a certain vulnerability. We exchanged cordial visits to each other's homes, and I accompanied him on his surprisingly nervous attempts to drive a new car through London's traffic.

All-day conversation with Hyde was a redeeming factor on the news desk, and I learned something of the dark art of news editing. Twice I was despatched at speed from the office with a briefcase full of banknotes which were to be paid to someone with a dangerous libel claim, in return for a signed waiver against legal action.

Hyde suffered bouts of bad health, and I was in sole charge for long periods early in my new role. Each day started with the daunting challenge of presenting my agenda for the day's coverage at Charles Wintour's 8.30 a.m. daily conference attended by the heads of all editorial departments. Wintour would sit, hunched and white faced, frowning as my list of intended assignments was revealed.

Then he would express incisive instructions on his own priorities for news coverage, and explain precisely how he wanted these stories treated. He hated devoting space to the racing fixtures, and would groan with rage when the Sports Editor informed him there was a heavy race programme that day.

My respect for Chilly Charlie grew as I experienced at close quarters his talent in producing a superb combination of swift news coverage with high quality features enhancing the news, as well as a strong accent on entertainment and the arts.

My lunch with Beaverbrook occurred without warning one Saturday morning early in 1964 when a curt telephone call summoned me to hasten down to Lord Beaverbrook's country residence, Cherkley Court, near Leatherhead.

Derek Marks, our rotund Deputy Editor who had been an astute political correspondent for the *Express,* said nervously: 'You'd better take the Editor's car. For God's sake get down there quickly.'

I was in sole charge of the News Desk but for once was allowed to delegate to a reporter.

I waited in Cherkley's hall, equipped with a ticker tape machine, until a black metal cage lift creaked down to deliver Max Aitken, first Baron Beaverbrook, and undoubtedly the premier Baron of Fleet Street. At 84 he exactly resembled the cartoonists' caricatures: small, gnome-like, with a wide mouth, and wispy hair.

I had grave reservations about him; I did not share his politics, I had read about his mistakes over pre-war appeasement of the Nazis, and I did not approve of his views on Europe or the Empire.

None of this mattered. The old man charmed me, and won me over completely, displaying with ease a gift which many others had recognised, that in his company he could make you feel you were fleetingly the most important person in his life. He had used it as one of his ploys in gaining great riches, and much power.

He courteously introduced me to Lady Beaverbrook, widow of his friend Sir James Dunn, who he had only married the previous year. He hobbled ahead into a dining room where I joined him and Lady Beaverbrook for a geriatric lunch of shepherd's pie and small portions of bread and butter pudding. I was encouraged to take wine, but the old man was only drinking water.

The Beaver solicitously checked my current salary, asked about my married state, my hopes, my fears, my ambitions in journalism, and my opinion of the *Evening Standard*.

He talked about current news stories, and the state of Fleet Street papers with the intimacy and knowledge I would have expected from a practising journalist. I was eased into the sort of conversation I enjoyed with Ronnie Hyde.

Beaverbrook suddenly turned from the table to seize a recording instrument of ancient vintage from a wheeled desk, barking a memo into its black Bakelite mouthpiece for transmission to some editorial minion whose name I missed. I sincerely hoped it was not aimed at Wintour, based on my burbling about the paper.

We bade goodbye like old friends, and I returned to London wondering if I was about to receive a massive pay increase, or instant promotion – or perhaps the sack? Surely Hyde was not going?

None of these exciting possibilities occurred. It seemed it was part of the Beaver's policy of keeping tabs on 'bright young men' who could be useful one day.

Whole careers had projected from such meetings – the Beaver had once appointed Michael Foot as Acting Editor of the *Evening Standard* – so I surmised it was just possible I could be on the way up in the Beaverbrook empire, although I doubted I could break out of the prison of 'hard news'. Was this a good idea? Would I enjoy jumping through hoops to keep the Beaver and his heirs happy for the rest of my working life? Was an indoor life at Shoe Lane, or within the menacing jungle of the Express building my ultimate ambition?

Although I paid lip-service to it, I was sick of paternalism, whether it was from newspaper proprietors or politicians. Did

Beaverbrook know I was not only a fully paid up member of the Labour Party, but Secretary of the Blackheath party? I had formed a friendship with a rising star, the Greenwich MP Dick Marsh. Certainly Charles Wintour knew of my politics; he remarked curtly in his farewell speech when I left his employment that 'Clayton is a serious journalist, although he is a Socialist...'

I acquired a Labour card after reporting Harold Wilson addressing election meetings with great wit and verve, and I had admired his performance as opposition leader in the Commons. Hyde and I had visited the press gallery during the dramatic Profumo debate, and we agreed that Wilson's performance was impeccable.

I, and many others of my generation, were enthusiastic about Wilson's prospect of a achieving his 'white heat of a second industrial revolution'. We wanted no more of Macmillan's or Douglas-Home's grouse moor government.

My Labour party membership only lasted three years. I would eventually become disappointed in Wilson as Prime Minister, although recognising his struggle in controlling the Labour Left. I became disillusioned by trade union misuse of power, and disgusted by Labour's adherence to old class-war in its dealings with the countryside, and foxhunting in particular.

During my stint as Deputy News Editor some of the greatest stories of the century washed across our desk: the Great Train Robbery, the Profumo Affair, Winston Churchill's funeral, and the climacteric of President Kennedy's assassination.

Ronnie Hyde was superb during the Profumo affair; its mixture of high-life, politics and sex suited his tastes exactly, and he had a remarkable number of West End contacts who helped us move the story forward to provide numerous scoops.

I was shocked by Fleet Street's failure to refute John Profumo's public denials of his affair with Christine Keeler, until he admitted all in a Commons statement. We all had masses of evidence, including signed affidavits, of his dangerous liaison, but even the tabloids declined to go over the top first. So much for 'publish and be damned' I reflected with some disgust at the Establishment's caution.

Wintour and Hyde were both out on the town in different plush restaurants the night Kennedy was shot. They each phoned me repeatedly for a relay of the Kennedy story as I watched it breaking on my TV screen at home.

We were all too busy at the time to recognise the major significance for newspapers that it was television which brought first news of the biggest story of the decade, and secured the nation's attention thereafter in reporting each stage of the tragedy on their screens.

It was the first indication that television would be the overwhelming rival to print as the prime source of news information and background.

I was utterly frustrated during the run of major stories to be consigned to organising others to write them. I was allowed 'out' on May 25, 1964, to report a special edition of 'In London Last Night', when Fleet Street paid tribute to Lord Beaverbrook on his 85th birthday at a dinner at the Dorchester Hotel given by his fellow Canadian, Lord Thomson of Fleet, proprietor of the *Sunday Times* and later *The Times*.

He astonished everyone by the robustness of his speech in a booming trans-Atlantic accent at a Dorchester Hotel dinner. There was wry humour at his own expense, tart comments on contemporary journalism, and tantalising references to his war-time cabinet role in which he had interviewed the mad Nazi Rudolph Hess, and had been Churchill's emissary to Stalin.

He claimed to have persuaded Stalin that Churchill was not going to make peace with Germany, leaving Russia to fight alone.

The Beaver disarmed Fleet Street's finest with his remark about their black trade: '....the curious and interesting thing about journalism is that everybody always knows far more about it than the journalist knows himself. You are subject to criticism – you receive some praise, I admit – but that praise is sometimes suspect.

'You are not entirely free from the influence of the sycophant – he is about you everywhere and always. But there is an extraordinary notion in the mind of mankind, a universal idea – that each and every one of us could run a newspaper, if we only l had the chance, far better than the journalist could do it himself.

'Well, I got the chance – I soon learned that I was a know-nothing. And after years of anxiety and much misery our papers began the slow but steady upward climb...'

This was riveting stuff from a man who had raised the *Daily Express* from 300,000 to four million sales.

All I had to do was provide comments from the guests on Beaverbrook's speech, and they were full of praise and surprise that the old man could stand up and speak at all. It was easy to garner their genuine praise, although they were a hard-boiled bunch, described by Thomson as the 'greatest gathering of newspapermen ever brought together at a dinner in this country'.

I was not entrusted with reporting Beaverbrook's actual words; they were delivered in transcript to the Editor.

The well wined guests were right to marvel, for clearly the speech had been a huge physical achievement; the Beaver went home to bed, and never left it again. He died only a fortnight later on 9 June, and others far higher up our *Standard* food chain were selected to write the fulsome tributes in his newspapers.

I reflected that my chance of a sudden promotion had virtually disappeared with the demise of the proprietor. I could see ahead only a working life tied to the News Desk, with a reasonable chance of one day succeeding Ronnie Hyde or returning to the ranks of hard news foot soldiers, since I would have had no chance to specialise. I wished I had the courage and the money to leave newspapers and seek the higher education I lacked.

For the first time I yearned to live in the countryside again. My passion for foxhunting and country life expanded faster as I laboured on the news desk to meet inexorable evening paper deadlines. I feared I was losing my own ability to compose a news story or a feature at speed. The prospect of becoming simply an organiser of other people's talents for the rest of my life was appalling. I was extremely unhappy in my work.

In the trade press I read an advertisement for a News Editor for Southern Television, based in their Southampton headquarters. It hardly seemed a possibility, since I had no television experience, but without hesitation I sent a brief letter of application, with a cursory CV, and was stunned to receive a swift reply, inviting me to an interview at their London offices.

After one meeting with a group including their Head of Programmes, Berkeley Smith, a charming ex-BBC man, I was offered the job, and heard myself accept it for a salary barely higher than my present £3,000 a year, but with accommodation allowances. The combination of Fleet Street experience and my south coast background appealed to Southern TV despite my total ignorance of television.

Everyone at the *Evening Standard* appeared to accept my resignation with regret, but I had not cloaked my frustration as well as I thought. No colleague seemed surprised I wished to escape from the inexorable routines of the News Desk, although I greatly valued Ronnie Hyde's training in news management and handling staff.

He bade me a warm farewell, and we kept in contact as friends for the rest of his life. He was awarded an OBE, barely adequate I felt, a year before his death in October 1955. I learned from his wife Joan that he wanted me to make the address of tribute at his funeral at St Bride's, Fleet Street, and I was honoured and touched to comply, however inadequately.

When I left the *Standard* I was looking forward fervently to resuming foxhunting in Dorset, to the pleasures of my native south coast, and to opening the door on a new career in the exciting world of television. I was rash enough to feel I had skills in public speaking and acting which had yet to be used.

However, as I drove through leafy Hampshire to Southampton for my latest reinvention I was suffering severe doubts about going back to the sticks. This was my fifth job change, and it threatened to be an impulsive leap into oblivion.

After one week in a cramped office in the converted cinema which Southern TV used as a studio I was convinced this time I had impulsively jumped a big hedge straight into a heap of fertiliser....it seemed a dreadful, crass mistake I would regret forever.

Chapter Eight

TAKING TO THE AIR

I became deeply indebted to Charles Wintour – for *refusing* my plea for help.

Stupidly, I panicked soon after joining Southern TV.

The shock was profound in being reduced from my *Evening Standard* seat of illusory power, however minor, to the status of a floundering beginner.

After only a couple of months I telephoned Ronnie Hyde, ignominiously confessing that I had joined a Mickey Mouse news outfit which I hated, and asking if I could rejoin the *Evening Standard*.

Within a few days Hyde arranged lunch at Simpson's-in-the-Strand with Charles Wintour. The Editor was courteous, and charming, but heard my tale of woe with a slight frown, and made no comment on my wish to return to the *Standard*. We bade farewell, and I heard no more. Wintour never explained his motive in ignoring my plea, but I could hardly blame him for not taking on board someone who had jumped ship once, and might well do so again.

It was an excellent decision; if I had returned to the *Standard* I would have missed a decade in television with far wider horizons than I could have achieved in evening paper journalism. The *Standard* Editor's rejection was a powerful rejuvenator.

Right, I thought, I'll show you. Somehow, I vowed, Charles Wintour would be watching me on national TV before long.

Back in dreary Southampton it seemed a tough challenge. My problem was to learn quickly the grammar of television which is entirely different to that of the printed word. The sheer mechanics of television were a damnable mystery to me, but there were no instructional courses at Southern TV available to me.

I thought I was flexible enough to make the change, but for the first couple of months it was agonising. I was living in depressing digs in Southampton during a five-day week.

I changed my Southampton digs to a berth on a house-boat on the River Itchen where several other Southern staff had stayed, and that proved more interesting, although I kept cracking my head on low wooden ceilings. Incomparably the best happening during my 18 months with Southern TV was the birth of Maxine, who gained her early training on the *Maidenhead Advertiser* and rose to cover national and international news in the UK and New Zealand. Her brother Marcus was born two years later and became a highly effective TV producer and cameraman in New Zealand and Singapore. Much later I acquired a step-daughter Georgina, now a lawyer in London, who shared my love of horses and rides well.

I was making painfully slow progress in converting to television journalism at Southern TV. My newspaper reporting and news editing experience was of little help, but my previous sub-editing stint at the *Bournemouth Times* was useful. I had to sub-edit news items and film from stringers up and down the southern coastal area, from Dover to Somerset, to produce two five-minute news slots used in the magazine programme.

The biggest challenge was that Southern expected the News Editor to act additionally as a studio director operating in a tiny, cramped newsreader's studio attached to the subs' room.

I had to press the right buttons to bring up the film on to the screen, counting ten seconds to allow the film to roll before the pictures appeared.

It was a nightmare: for weeks Southern TV viewers were subjected to sudden blank screens during their local news, with pictures coming and going erratically while the news reader ploughed through the stodgy menu of local news in answer to my failed attempts at accurate cues on the studio mike.

In full size TV studios the director verbally calls the shots from whichever source he chooses, and one of his line-up of assistants, called a vision mixer, presses the buttons. Operating as a one-man producer/director was a sharp learning curve, and invaluable experience, but I expected the sack at anytime for sheer incompetence. Surprisingly no-one upstairs at Southern seemed to notice, and I never heard of complaints from viewers. Terry Johnson, Editor of *Day by Day*, occasionally grunted 'get it right for God's sake,' but he was absorbed in producing a bright, entertaining magazine programme, and seemed to care little about the news slot. It was certainly true that viewers much preferred the affable local weather man Trevor Baker, and I do not blame them.

'There's bugger all news happening, and they go out to get a cup of tea while it's on,' said Johnson caustically. I suggested making the news more arresting by heralding it with some lively galloping music I found in the sound department.

'Old fashioned crap,' said Johnson, and instead chose a low key modern jazz theme. It might be modern, but it would not detain anyone from making the tea I reflected bitterly.

Although I had the title News Editor, I sat ignominiously squeezed between several sub-editors in the small production staff of the early evening news magazine programme. There were two or three girls working as telephone copy-takers.

I was merely a cog in the small hot-house kingdom ruled by Terry Johnson. Even he did not rate the luxury of his own office, but operated from a desk in one corner, using a mixture of hard boiled humour laced with sarcasm to control his staff. He retained full control over the handful of staff reporters, since most of their work was in the magazine programme not in the news slot; I found myself completely frustrated as a News Editor.

An ex-*Brighton Evening Argus* sub-editor, Terry was a tough and talented features man, but he suffered the insecurity of many in television, and at first he was keen to ensure that the newcomer from Fleet Street was kept in his place.

After a few months he concluded I would be absolutely no threat, and we became amiable colleagues, often visiting local clubs and restaurants in the evenings.

I learned more about television and its ways from Johnson's conversations in the evenings than in the office. Like many TV production staff I was to encounter, he had something of a phobia about 'performers', anyone who actually appeared on the screen. He emphasised that real power in television lay in the hands of producers and directors, and rightly predicted this would increase further as the industry developed. Not for the last time I heard TV reporters described as mere 'microphone holders'. Television inevitably blends an element of show biz with journalism; this was resisted by many in the early days of TV news, but has now been embraced wholeheartedly in a world of glamorous presenters and reporters constantly talking live to camera. Personality now plays a dominant role in TV news and current affairs, just as it does in most other fare on our screens, but the personalities are strictly controlled by the gurus in production and direction.

As if waking from a nightmare, suddenly I felt far happier and confident in my new life.

The nightly TV news bulletins flowed with fewer glitches; I managed to punch the right buttons most of the time, and I felt I could improve further, but my private ambition was to become one of the 'performers'.

Southern's own output at that early stage was very limited; mostly it took feeds of national programming from the major ITV companies, but it forged its own reputation for some worthwhile children's programmes, and scored a hit with an unpretentious series called 'Out of Town,' written and fronted by Jack Hargreaves.

He was a bespectacled, bearded former agricultural journalist with a natural gift as a broadcaster. He was ahead of his time in explaining and exploring the English countryside, not only its flora and fauna, but as a place of work. The south coast strip covered by Southern offered a marvellous range of film subjects, and Jack would sit in a small studio rural garden set with a potting shed, chatting away to camera to link his modest film outings. He came over as a friendly uncle, and was deservedly so popular that 'Out of Town' became widely screened in other regions.

When he learned I was intensely interested in the countryside, and a keen foxhunter, he became a friendly companion perfectly willing to spare time for the newcomer.

At that time the regional TV companies contributed news inserts from their territories to ITN, which the regionals jointly owned. Launched in 1955 under Aiden Crawley as editor, ITN was breaking new ground in its coverage, and proving a formidable competitor to the BBC still inhibited by post-Reithian attitudes, whereby TV news was still read by full-time readers instead of journalists.

Southern could provide good outdoor picture stories from its long coastline, but national TV news rarely emanated from its towns and cities. It seemed to me there was far more scope for better news coverage, but we badly needed a team of reporters solely dedicated to news, with greatly increased length for local bulletins.

I learned much when I attended a conference in Aberdeen of all regional news editors. It was chaired by ITN's brilliant Editor, Geoffrey Cox, who was later knighted. Cox's analysis of TV news and his predictions of its future expansion and major importance, fired my enthusiasm for my new role more than anything I had heard since I left Fleet Street. I had admired his distinguished work as a correspondent at the *News Chronicle* and I was impressed by his transformation from newspaperman to superb television journalist. Perhaps I could go some way to following his example, I wondered?

Best of all I compared notes with other regional news editors, and was reminded that local news was a key requirement of commercial TV companies retaining their valuable licences.

Several urged me to me more bullish at Southern, emphasising that my job was not a luxury, but a necessity for the company.

At Southampton I began to insist on more 'interference' in news coverage by our reporters, and we increased our contributions to ITN, which were noted higher up because each regional company received a credit on screen over its items appearing in the national news.

Southern used large scale entertainment among its efforts to sell itself to the communities of the south coast. They formed such a diverse group that Southern was frequently chosen for lucrative test-marketing for national TV advertising campaigns. Johnson and I attended frequent dinners for civic leaders and business people. They were pleasant occasions, but I wished the company would spend the money on local programmes, especially news. I believed the local BBC news coverage was generally better than ours, although Johnson's magazine programme was more innovative than the local BBC output at that time.

The infamous phrase 'a licence to print' money, injudiciously ascribed to commercial television by Lord Thomson, applied already to the young south coast company.

Southern was launched in1958, owned mainly by the *Daily Mail* owner, Associated Newspapers, and the Rank Organisation whose tough chairman Sir John Davis was rumoured among the staff to strike terror into Southern's executives when he visited the studios.

A policy of running too much of its local programming on tight budgeting when the company was reaping a harvest from its lucrative 'sunset strip' franchise contributed to its undoing. If Southern had showed any sign of investing in news as a means of gaining viewers, I might well have decided to stay with the company.

I was not as shocked as Southern's executive appeared to be 20 years later when the Independent Broadcasting Authority finally put it out of business by refusing to renew its franchise, awarding it instead to another bidder, TVS.

In the mid-1960s the BBC was expanding its national news service which was being made to look stolid and dull in comparison with Geoffrey Cox's team of bright young reporters and interesting presenters, starting with Chris Chataway, Robin Day and Reggie Bosanquet.

BBC News decided to import far more talent from established news reporters in Fleet Street and elsewhere, with the intention of converting them to the new medium.

This was only partially successful; the newcomers brought far more news sense and urgency to BBC bulletins, but few of them were good broadcasters as such, and some never appeared at all at home on the box.

I benefited from the policy because early in 1965 I responded to an advertisement for a whole intake of national TV and radio reporters. Later I was told there were well over a thousand applications, so I was fortunate to be selected for the short list; my mixture of newspapers and regional TV experience was a great asset.

The next obstacle was a broadcasting test in which I was required to research and write a report from a genuine current news story of my choice, and then read it to camera.

I selected the problem of young hospital doctors working horrendous hours for a pittance in the National Health Service. It was instructive to note that mention of the BBC easily secured interviews with young doctors in a busy Kent hospital.

I knocked together a script in TV news style, and queued with other anxious applicants in a basement studio of Broadcasting House in Portland Place to deliver my piece to camera. At least I knew how to look at the camera, and speak confidently with flow, not burying my head in the script, although there was at that time no help from a telly prompter.

As a child of radio's wartime era of glory it was thrill enough just to enter Lord Reith's famous headquarters based on the design of a ship, but I had little confidence I would pass the scrutiny of the BBC's executive class, some of whom seemed all too similar to the RAF officer recruiting board who had consigned me to other ranks.

Several weeks passed, and I had given up hope, when suddenly a buff envelope arrived, offering me an 'appointment' as a BBC staff reporter at a salary just over £3,000 per year, slightly less than my

Southern salary, but offering London weighted expenses and a staff car in due course.

I would have grasped the job at any price, and I rushed an affirmative reply and broke the news to Berkeley Smith at Southern, who expressed polite regret at my departure. My leaving seemed to cause little surprise in Southern's newsroom.

Broadcasting House in Portland Place, known to the broadcasting tribe as BH, became my workplace, a remarkable building entwined in Britain's history throughout my life: to be a full staff member of the BBC seemed the peak of any ambition I ever had, and with hindsight I should have stayed much longer in radio, before plunging into the deep waters of BBC TV news at one of its most stressful times of development.

My first year with the BBC, in radio news and current affairs, was the happiest period of my working life to date. Tom Maltby was an affable head of administrative head of reporting, more like a civil servant than a journalist. He issued me with a Uher tape recorder, a heavy burden compared with today's lightweight equipment, and best of all, a Ford Cortina staff car.

More impressively, the Director General, Hugh Carleton-Greene, found time to give recruits to the reporting room a personal welcome and briefing. He had been Head of News and Current Affairs for a couple of years up to 1960, and was a distinguished former newspaper journalist. He was full of encouragement for our future in a brave new world of broadcasting news gathering. What a charming man, I thought. If he represented BBC management's attitude to journalists all would well. How little I knew!

I was full of optimism for my new life, unaware that I was to be gravely disappointed by the BBC's inability to manage working journalists effectively during the period of massive changes occurring during my eight years with the Corporation.

The BBC was, in 1966, starting major shifts in its tectonic plates which would take decades to resolve. There were already internal power battles of which I was unaware, but which would severely afflict myself and my fellow recruits to BBC news.

As I was to find out, the Corporation exhibited the worst management of working journalists I encountered anywhere during 47 years on the staffs of newspapers, broadcasters and magazines.

On the credit side, 1966 was a wonderful time to join the BBC: huge advances in technology and broadcasting techniques were underway. The News Division was trying to cope with expanding bulletins at a time when news at home and abroad was offering massive opportunities. Our budgets were small, and our London based staff of reporters was too small to cope with the editors' growing demands. We were called firemen by some; others called us 'performing fleas', always hopping about the globe.

I soon found myself in a relentless cycle of TV reporting overseas war and disaster, but first I enjoyed an idyllic spell solely on radio.

The Home Service and Light Programme had been so influential in my self-education, and awareness of the wider world, that I loved the medium.

I suffered none of the early pangs I had endured at Southern TV. I felt instantly at home in Broadcasting House's dusty offices, in its dark, radio studios, and most of all in speaking to the familiar shape of the huge beige microphones, much the same design as those used by Churchill for his great wartime speeches, or Tommy Handley in Itma.

I warmed to the in-house legends, such as a story illustrating a higher level of job security than any I had encountered. A male BBC producer was said to have been discovered having sex on his office desk with a lady colleague. At first the administrative bosses decided to sack them both. They heard lengthy pleas from colleagues of both parties, praising their integrity and professional brilliance, urging that neither should be dismissed. After much deliberation the admin department announced its decision: 'We will sell the desk.'

Another story popular in the reporters' room was probably true: a senior admin officer was showing a visitor around Broadcasting House when the visitor remarked there seemed to be far more offices than broadcasting studios.

The BBC executive replied tartly: 'We do a lot of other things than just make programmes, you know.'

In the early 1960s BBC radio staff at BH were the most civilised group of colleagues I had encountered. They exuded self-assurance; they were remarkably courteous, and they gave each other time and room to become great individualists, even eccentrics. Most people in news and current affairs were low paid in comparison with the middle to upper ranks of Fleet Street, neither did the radio staff enjoy generous expenses, but at the time there was a general belief that working in BBC radio conferred distinction and job satisfaction, despite the ever increasing drift of power and money to television.

In radio production you could dress as casually as you liked, wear sandals and a beard, and carry your sandwiches into the studio provided you did not rustle the wrapping paper too loudly.

What surprised me most was the vast amounts of alcohol BBC staff consumed during working hours. This was much encouraged by the Corporation's benevolence in installing drinks bars open long hours within its staff clubs. Old BH hands also dived regularly into their favourite pubs adjoining Portland Place. In news and current affairs this wrecked some careers, and spoiled others; like drink-drivers, broadcasters and studio managers do not perform better 'under the influence', especially during live transmissions.

Jack de Manio, a famous imbiber, was perhaps an exception because he fulfilled the British love of amateurism, becoming famous and popular for his inability to get the time right in his role as presenter of the *Today* programme, launched in 1957 as a far lighter diet of early morning chit-chat than it is to-day.

Jack was just as inaccurate on names as he was on time-keeping as I discovered. One of my first radio reporting jobs was to cover a West End art gallery raid, not more than a mile from Broadcasting House.

I was followed to the scene by a radio outside broadcast vehicle, a modest saloon car driven by a BBC engineer. He cranked up a telescopic aerial through a hole cut in the boot, all part of the home-made equipment for which the engineering department was famous, or infamous, depending on your latest experience of it. For years the engineers annoyed news producers by banning live telephone interviews because they were not of 'broadcast quality', no matter how vital the story. This veto was overturned by a new breed of producers and reporters.

I crammed my long legs into the back seats, and found myself broadcasting live on a lip-mike for the first time, in a two-way chat with Jack de Manio.

'Hello Michael Charlton,' he chirped, and then asked me who had carried out the raid, a question worth a prize for sheer incompetence.

'It's Michael Clayton actually,' I replied frostily, since any dunderhead knew Michael Charlton worked for *Panorama*.

Before another stupid question could emerge from Britain's most popular radio presenter, I quickly reported which pictures had been stolen, and gabbled that *of course* no-one knew yet who had done the deed. The police had only just begun inquiries.

'Well thank you,' said Jack genially. 'Goodbye Michael Charlton.'

I enjoyed most of all working on the lunch-time radio programme, the *World at One*, launched in 1965 and brilliantly edited by Andrew Boyle, the most accomplished and ground-breaking editor in BBC radio of his time.

Although softly spoken, and somewhat academic in aspect, Andrew was a forceful editor, determined to push the frontiers of radio journalism much further. He encouraged his small team to re-jig the programme content perilously while on air to update stories. His programme set the standards which *Today* emulated when it moved on from its fluffier diet of light feature material presented by Jack de Manio up to 1970. Andrew Boyle encouraged sparky live political encounters with the best performers in the Commons, and ensured his programme, affectionately known to us as What-Ho, was soon required listening for Fleet Street and the House of Commons. Boyle was great fun to work with, remarkably independent for his time, and willing to shake up the BBC hierarchy.

After his retirement from the BBC, Boyle scored a tremendous scoop with his book *The Climate of Treason* which unmasked Sir William

Blunt, the Queen's personal art advisor, as a Soviet double-agent.

Boyle made an inspired decision in appointing as presenter of *The World at One* William Hardcastle, former Editor of the *Daily Mail* and the *Sunday Dispatch*. A large, balding man with a keen sense of humour, Hardcastle was a journalist's journalist. He was among the first to develop further a style of non-deferential interviewing of leading politicians, and even heads of foreign countries. The purpose was revolutionary for BBC radio: it sought to extract a story from the interview which could be used later in the bulletins as a BBC exclusive. Nowadays it is standard practice, but whether it produces news stories of any weight or lasting importance is highly debatable. I was amazed when I heard Hardcastle grilling in live telephone interviews such formidable politicians as Northern Ireland's Protestant firebrand Ian Paisley, and Israel's female prime minister Golda Meir. I doubt if even the acerbic John Humphreys would take greater liberties with such giants today.

Hardcastle's style was far removed from the old non-confrontational BBC interviewing practice which allowed the subject to air his views with virtually no risk of embarrassment, and was much prized by senior politicians seeking a 'fire-side chat' with the voters.

Harold Wilson was good at such chats in his early days as Prime Minister, but he was furious when 'on the hoof' interrogation appeared.

'Which company are you from, son?' he grunted one day when I advanced towards him with a microphone on a London railway platform. He firmly refused to say a word, and stalked off with his aides. Another BBC reporter said Wilson jabbed him in the ribs with a fist when he made the same refusal to speak.

We learned that Number Ten conveyed to the BBC the Prime Minister's dislike of such approaches, but under Carleton-Greene changes on a much wider front towards 'modern' broadcasting practice continued unabated.

Wilson retaliated by ensuring the appointment of Lord Hill, former 'Radio Doctor' Dr Charles Hill, as chairman of BBC governors in 1967, with the task of curbing the BBC's disrespectful adventures, such as the superb satire 'That Was the Week That Was'.

Wilson's paranoia, and his row with the BBC over its increasingly liberal attitude to broadcasting news 'inconvenient' to government, under Carleton-Greene as Director General, have been well documented.

Bill Hardcastle could not quite escape his Fleet Street background: 'And is this a new dimension of terror?' he demanded in a radio two-wayer to Belfast where I was reporting an explosion early in the Troubles.

'Only if someone was sitting in the target area – it was a bomb in an empty lavatory' I reported.

Live broadcasting is by far the best way of entrapping the interviewee, even today when politicians routinely receive 'media training'. In a recorded radio interview you may attempt to trap the prey more subtly, by engaging in some easy, friendly questions before dropping the bombshell which really matters. Radio reporters could conduct a recorded interview at great length to extract the vital section needed, but in television news in the BBC's impecunious 1960s, the TV news reporter was discouraged from 'wasting' film; this privilege was reserved for *Panorama* and other current affairs reporters who at that time were nearer the front-line of controversial broadcasting.

Lord Hailsham, the ebullient Tory grandee, was a frequent interviewee for Radio Newsreel, and he well understood the medium.

'You can have two and a half minutes, and that's all,' he declared firmly as I unpacked my recorder.

'I've promised a major piece for the *Sunday Express* and I am not going to waste everything I have to say on radio first,' said Hailsham firmly.

Our payments for such interviews were paltry or non-existent compared with Beaverbrook's largess which was clearly a factor for some of our regular cast list of commentators.

One who well understood this was the left-of-centre historian and regular *Express* writer, A.J.P. Taylor. I interviewed him frequently, and he would always put his watch on the table to limit the length of the session. After several disasters I soon learned to check carefully after every interview whether the recorder had actually worked. It was not pleasant asking the likes of Hailsham or Taylor to repeat their performance.

By far the most odious politician I experienced in an interview was Richard Crossman, then Labour's Minister of Health and Social Security. Arrogantly granting me a joint radio and TV interview on a new government initiative, he kept demanding: 'Stop the camera!'

Then he engaged in a deep discussion with his civil servant aides, before ordering me to resume the interview at his whim.

I remembered the example of Leslie Lowe back in New Milton, and quietly pointed out to the Minister that I was not his servant, but a reporter for an independent public service broadcaster.

'Nonsense!' snapped Crossman. 'If I do this as an exclusive interview to ITN you'll be in real trouble with your editor.'

I swallowed my annoyance, but afterwards I urged the film editor to cut the Minister's interview to the bare minimum.

Radio Newsreel, the time-hallowed BBC early evening vehicle for news and current affairs, was given a new format similar to that widely used today. I was one of the first reporters used to present the new programme, and I was overawed and somewhat embarrassed to find myself introducing the Six O'clock News read by Alvar Liddell, one of the legendary golden-tongued announcers I had listened to as a schoolboy throughout the war.

He was graciously charming, but he could not have been pleased when a bunch of crass young reporters from Fleet Street intruded into the studio, and inserted voice pieces in a variety of non-establishment accents into the hallowed bulletins. One of my colleagues introducing *Newsreel* got Alvar's name wrong on air one day and received a magisterial correction from the famous voice.

I was thrilled to detect many other famous voices among the broadcasters who gathered at the bars of the BBC Club in Langham House, on the opposite side of Portland Place. We reporters in the new intake from newspapers were astonished by the BBC's practice of allowing virtually unlimited drinking in its staff clubs, within or close to its studios.

The gravelly voice of an elderly man ordering a round of drinks next to me at the bar, produced a stab of childhood nostalgia:

'Excuse me, but weren't you the Mayor of Toytown?' I asked.

'I certainly was, dear boy,' replied the actor Felix Felton.

'And weren't you Dennis the Dachsund as well?'

'Clever of you to spot it, yes I was,' he replied with a beaming smile.

'Sorry to bother you.'

'Not at all...' said Felton in the Children's Hour voice which evoked memories of my infancy.

As he collected his round he said: 'Radio gets into your head, doesn't it.'

WELSH TRAGEDY

For me the subtle pleasures of radio reporting from Broadcasting House were disrupted on 21 October in 1966 when I was despatched to the hell of Aberfan in South Wales. A coal mining waste tip had slid down a mountainside into Pantglas Junior School at 9.15 am.

I learned much about the BBC's greatness, and its huge faults, at Aberfan.

BBC Wales had all day been covering the tragedy which robbed the South Wales mining village of 116 school children among a total of 144 killed by the stifling tide of slurry.

The Cardiff BBC news staff worked magnificently covering the immense disaster in their territory, and they were not especially pleased to see me arrive in late afternoon from London to join the reporting of a tragedy which was deeply Welsh.

I was the first of a large influx of BBC national reporters, completed by a large, unwieldy outside broadcast television unit used that night for live transmissions by *Panorama*. There developed noticeable tensions between the national and regional teams, especially when the latter were confined to their own regional programmes. It was my first experience of the wasteful regional rivalry which beset the BBC, and too often robbed it of the extra strength which combined effort by national and local teams would have provided. Duplication, muddle and competition for local technical resources too often resulted when a major story erupted in one of the regions.

'Just find your own way up there,' was the only advice I received from Cardiff news editor Alan Prothero. It was just as well I did not argue; he did a good job covering Aberfan, and was later promoted to become a TV News supremo in London.

I found the valley road up to Aberfan completely jammed by chaotic traffic in darkness, and I abandoned my car to hitch a lift on the back of a local man's motor-bike.

Radio, with its wonderful economy of technology, was telling the world the story from a portable aerial linked to a Land Rover parked under a lamp post in the narrow main street.

Welsh reporter Arfan Roberts had manned the microphone all day, and unlike some of his compatriots, he cooperated with me fully, and we settled down to a gruelling all-night reporting stint.

The depth and size of the tragedy, the cruelty of blind chance in selecting so many children as victims, and the dreadful local background of guilt and ignorance which allowed the tip to become a killer, all combined into a nightmare in which anyone from outside Aberfan risked adding to the pain through insensitive intrusion.

I had no briefing from London or Cardiff of the sort I would have received from a Fleet Street news editor such as Ronnie Hyde, and I made my own firm decision not even to approach, nor seek an interview from a parent or close relative of one of the dead, who were constantly being carried into the village hall for identification.

I scribbled short scripts, carefully keeping them as a cool and detached as possible, which were inserted in the national radio bulletins, and updated every hour or so.

The bald facts of the mounting death toll, and the dreadful circumstances in which children were choked to death and buried in their classrooms, were horrific enough, without any attempt at emotional reporting.

Panorama's coverage that night fell into a trap which was awaiting at a time when TV viewers were far less accustomed to live broadcasting of disaster. One of their reporters was, at the behest of the programme's producer on the spot, interviewing Aberfan schoolchildren who had survived.

Through his earpiece he was instructed to ask them what they thought about the demise of their schoolmates. He blurted out the question, and next day in the press there was public uproar at a question condemned as gross intrusion.

In the climate of the 1960s perhaps it was intrusion, although nowadays one sees and hears far more crass and embarrassing questioning on air. Fleet Street tabloids somewhat hypocritically used the incident as a means of criticising the BBC, but some of us felt it was retaliation by an old fashioned press of the new medium which was fast taking over as the public's means of experiencing major stories as they happened.

I saw a recording of *Panorama's* Aberfan programme later, and thoroughly admired its achievement in conveying the depths of a hellish tragedy in grainy ill-lit monochrome pictures when night-sight cameras and other refinements were not available. *Panorama's* excellent reporter, David Sexton, was unfairly criticised, but overcame the setback to remain a leading current affairs reporter for a long and distinguished career.

As well as national bulletin inserts, I contributed recorded interviews with eyewitnesses and rescuers for Radio Newsreel, and the excellent regional programme 'Good Morning, Wales' which covered the disaster superbly.

Whatever professional detachment I had summoned up on air, I was more shattered by the sights and sounds of Aberfan than any disaster I ever covered until I reported from the children's burns ward in a Vietnam hospital.

I was given a post-Aberfan dressing down by a Radio Newsreel sub-editor for 'poor recording quality' on my portable tape machine, and no doubt he was right. I expected a lengthy de-brief from a London news editor after the worst UK disaster story since the war, but it never happened.

SCOTTISH DISASTER

I encountered regional prejudice within the BBC later, but never worse than on 2 January 1971, when I flew on a foggy night to Glasgow to report disaster during the Rangers-Celtic football match at Ibrox Park. Sixty-six supporters died when steel barriers collapsed on a stairway as the crowd surged out at the end of the match.

Scottish nationalism was rampant in the Glasgow newsroom when I arrived, minus a London film crew who had just missed the plane.

'We're no' having a Scottish tragedy covered by a London reporter,' said the Glasgow news editor emphatically.

I agreed amiably without argument, begged him for some cash from his office safe, and retired for the night to the best hotel I could find in a dank, dismal Glasgow. I was awoken at dawn by frantic calls from London producers.

The BBC's news coverage had been severely trounced by ITN who had sent a film crew to the stadium immediately, and achieved harrowing pictures and interviews.

The match itself had been covered live by the BBC, but their outside broadcast unit crew stolidly dismantled their cameras while the disaster was taking place around them. They were 'Sport' not 'News', and there was insufficient flexibility and news sense within the BBC at that time for anyone to insist they divert their cameras to covering a major story, throwing away a huge advantage. It emphasised to me that, unlike a newspaper, news was simply a department sandwiched between many other powerful interests such as entertainment and drama.

At that time current affairs at Lime Grove was a separate department from news at TV Centre. The golden age of BBC current affairs produced wonderful results, but its correspondents could be somewhat patronising about mere news bulletins.

'Just here for news are you?' asked a Panorama correspondent when he had just arrived in Saigon where I had been slaving to provide almost daily reports for several months.

'Yes, only the news,' I replied with a degree of sarcasm.

I expected BBC Scotland to give way in the ensuing internal row, but I soon learned that north of the border they were impregnable. The only 'solution' available to national TV news was to transport from London to Glasgow not only a camera team, but a film editing machine and a film editor, who set up a separate unit in the Glasgow studio to deal with my reports of the tragedy's aftermath. No-one worried about such commercial issues as duplication of resources.

I reported the Ibrox disaster's mass funerals, and the opening of an inquiry, endeavouring to avoid sentiment in the scripts, since the pictures of Glasgow in mourning were enough to indicate the city's trauma.

Afterwards I was not surprised to read Letters to the Editor in Scottish newspapers echoing the view of BBC Scotland in asking why an English reporter had been reporting a Scottish disaster, and criticising my temerity in asking the Rangers' manager Willie Waddell pointed questions about the safety measures at Ibrox Park.

Scottish nationalism in its most demented and inward-looking format was alive and well in the early 1970s, even during a disaster.

BBC Scotland's attitude to London 'interference' was matched by other internal rivalries I encountered throughout my eight years with the Corporation. The shining exception was BBC Belfast's staff who were splendidly cooperative with invading hordes of national reporters and producers, but there was more than enough news for everyone when Ulster was blowing itself to bits.

By far the worst example of territorial rivalry was a stern instruction given to me verbally by Derek Amoore when he was Editor of TV News. He demanded I should not allow BBC radio access to interviews I conducted during war reporting for TV. Amoore, often 'tired and emotional' in the office, was incensed when I retorted that I thought I was employed by the BBC to report news for the public, not for departmental glory. I pointed out that a radio interview was a good way of promoting a later report on TV.

It was ironic that after he left national television news Amoore became manager of BBC Radio London.

NORTHERN IRELAND – MUCH TO LEARN

I must confess that at first I regarded the task of reporting for BBC TV and radio the outbreak of the Northern Ireland Troubles in 1968 as something of a bore. Perhaps I reflected the mistaken view of more than a few of our mainland British viewers and listeners who were to be subjected to years of Ulster's passionate sectarian argument, and sporadic violence.

Of course, I was immensely mistaken: the conflict was to cause much misery and heartache, and to claim about 3,500 lives overall while grinding on relentlessly until the Good Friday Agreement brought a cease-fire from 1998.

Any sense of tediousness when Northern Ireland came up yet again on the new bulletins was shattered when the violence spread to mainland Britain, killing innocent victims, and nearly assassinating Margaret Thatcher when her Brighton hotel was bombed.

My presence in Belfast, Londonderry and other hotspots was intermittent. It often occurred between much longer stints in Vietnam, Cambodia, the Indian sub-Continent and the Middle East, all the scenes of wars and disasters which seemed far more dramatic than the intensely local Ulster punch-up.

Later I came to appreciate that Northern Ireland's violence mirrored so many of the world's conflicts caused by a lethal mix of tribalism and religion in the aftermath of partition.

Like most other London based reporters, I was woefully ignorant of the complex political history of Ulster when I travelled there with a TV crew to cover the Civil Rights March in Londonderry in 1968. I recall feverishly reading a handful of newspaper cuttings while we flew to Belfast where we would pick up a hire car to drive to Londonderry.

We were one of several BBC crews covering the march. Our colleagues from BBC Belfast were cooperative and friendly with the London incomers, contrasting with local pride and angst in some other BBC regional studios when we were 'parachuted' in from London to report for the national bulletins in the years before a 24 hour news service arrived.

My first attempt at coverage in Northern Ireland TV was an inglorious failure. We stood among applauding crowds as Catholic Civil Rights protesters marched through Derry led by Bernadette Devlin. Then we noticed a crowd of young men booing at the procession while they waved union jack flags.

'Let's get some of that, ' I said to the cameraman. To our horror the flag waving young men rushed towards us, punched the cameraman in the ribs, attempted to seize his camera, and chased him into a shop.

'Ah, so you've met the Loyalists,' said a local man with a grin when I followed into the shop.

Alas, we had no usable film of the Protestant 'Tartan Gang' who had attacked us, although some of our earlier footage was used in a corporate piece. The real story was further down the street when the march, which had been banned by the Government, was stopped by RUC officers who allegedly beat some of the protesters indiscriminately, causing injuries, and further sectarian uproar.

It was my first direct experience of the rough stuff which could so suddenly erupt in Northern Ireland, all too easily engulfing an observer. In Belfast I became used to seeing youths overturn and burn buses as if they had been practising for years. In Londonderry's Catholic Bogside housing estate I stood behind British soldiers using shields against barrages of stone throwing. If only those young men hurling the stones so accurately had taken up professional cricket.

Northern Ireland's Troubles never failed to come up with shock surprises. BBC and other visiting news crews usually stayed at the multi-storey Europa Hotel in Belfast, dining on the top floor in the evenings with food served by shapely local girls in brown leotards, an Ulster version of the Bunny Club.

I was about to dine with other correspondents on the top storey on the night when a Provisional IRA man delivered a bomb into the downstairs lobby in a box with IRA scrawled on it. All hotel occupants were immediately evacuated to the street. I recall standing outside in the dark, chilly and still hungry (I had been about to tackle an excellent steak) while cameramen tried to film from the street a heroic Army bomb disposal officer rendering the explosive object safe. With so many journalists as guests, attacks on the hotel gained the huge levels of publicity which the IRA so much desired. During 1970 to 1994 the Europa was damaged by explosives 33 times, earning it the title of 'the most bombed hotel in the world'. I retained my brown and gold Europa tie as a memento for many years.

During the day we would rush to yet another IRA bombing, or covered other aspects of the Troubles. The Protestant back-lash to the Republican violence emphasised that we were in the middle of two warring parties. This was conveyed to me when we reported a Loyalist rally addressed by the Rev. Ian Paisley, on the dockside at Bangor.

'I see the lying BBC is here today,' he thundered from his soap box, gesturing at my crew and myself. In a few minutes a group of Paisley's acolytes appeared in front of us with a bucket, and fiercely demanded we throw money into it. I replied that we couldn't contribute to either side. They responded by kicking my shins, and those of the cameraman. Thereafter, while Paisley hurled invective through his microphone, a bunch of men pushed us nearer and nearer to the edge of the dock. I decided on a time-honoured journalistic response: we made our excuses and left.

I was having a weekend off in Bournemouth when BBC TV news desk phoned to rush me to Ulster by private aircraft from Hurn Airport. Bloody Sunday was erupting into history in Londonderry on 30 January 1972.

I arrived too late to cover the shooting of 28 local protesters by soldiers of the Parachute regiment. Whether they were responding to IRA snipers has been a major issue ever since.

After producing an aftermath piece I was requested to go immediately to Dublin where there was trouble brewing. I found the Irish capital aflame with anger after the Derry shootings. The management of one of my favourite hotels, the Shelbourne, discreetly advised I should stay in an annexe at the back because feeling against the British was mounting, enflamed by events in Derry.

Almost anything overtly British seemed to be a target in Dublin. We filmed Thomas Cook's smashed show windows, protective boarding around BEA's offices (they were refused landing facilities at Dublin airport too), and most dramatically of all, the burning of the British Embassy.

I was amazed to see about 200 Irish policemen standing by while protesters hurled petrol bombs at the Embassy building in Merrion Square, already evacuated by the diplomatic staff. Men I could only describe at the time as 'supporters of the IRA' calmly walked through the police lines to pour on more petrol. A gelignite bomb had blown open the steel lined main doors, and the building was soon gutted.

My crew and I were working out of the Dublin news room of RTE, Ireland's national TV and radio company with whom we had excellent relations. When we rushed back at dusk to the studio with our precious film to be transmitted to London, I was amazed to find the RTE editors in a state of anxiety because their own crews had not yet returned with any film; they claimed to be held up by a road block which somehow I must have avoided.

We made our BBC film available to RTE, and they broadcast it in Ireland with an intro, but no eyewitness reporter's voice over film (which avoided identifying the arsonists). Meanwhile my film report dominated the main BBC bulletins that night, and was also seen by those Irish viewers who could pick up mainland British TV.

I have always been extremely fond of Ireland and its people, but I had seen stark evidence of the baleful influence of the IRA in the heart of the Irish Republic and was sure that worse was to come.

The assassinations of Christopher Ewart-Briggs, the British Ambassador in Dublin, by the Provisional IRA in 1973, and of Lord Mountbatten in County Sligo three years later, were surely confirmation enough.

I was less than popular with local Republicans when I filmed an interview with a girl in Londonderry's Bogside who had been tarred and feathered by older women under the supervision of an IRA man, and roped to a lamp-post, because she was accused of dating a British soldier. We did not give her name, and did not show her face, but in the street afterwards I was surrounded by a group of women shouting 'go away; we know who you are; go back to Vietnam!'. When I told them I would be glad to do so, the volume of shouting rose even higher and I swiftly made my exit.

I have made many friends north and south of the border, but my reporting visits during the Troubles always left me depressed; such a beautiful country, so many splendid people, but such a sad history, and so many pockets of underlying tribalism. I have seen the development of far better and wealthier communities in Ulster and the Republic since the Troubles. Long may the Good Friday agreement bringing peace to the province, survive and prosper.

*****

I hope the BBC's 24-hour rolling news operation has ironed out territorial nonsense nowadays, with radio and TV often sharing excerpts from interviews, and thereby promoting each other.

Without the need to gauge their success in mere profit, in the 1960s and 70s too many of the BBC's paper tiger executives indulged in endless internal war games, often at huge cost to the licence payers.

Meanwhile there was too little money for news priorities. Soon after I was despatched to TV news I discovered that decisions on the BBC sending a crew to cover a major foreign story were frequently made not on news values, but on whether there was enough cash in the current TV budget. After ITN had trounced us with exclusive coverage, there was a hasty scrabble for extra funding, and a BBC team would be sent belatedly to 'catch up'.

This was one of many realities lurking behind the 'glamour' of television which I was about to discover when for the first time I entered the headquarters of BBC TV news, then quaintly housed within the florid Victorian glass and wrought iron of Alexandra Palace.

Chapter Nine

CAMBODIA: MY FIRST
WAR – AND THE WORST

In the spring of 1970 I covered the most important war story on the planet – by sheer accident.

In early April I was dispatched with a film crew on a freebie flight offered by the War Office, to Singapore. We were to cover Operation Bersatu Padu, an attempt by the Heath government to assure the Malaysian and Singapore regimes that Britain would retain a British military force in South East Asia 'for as long as required'. The escalating Vietnam War was causing jitters throughout the region.

My film crew were cameraman Jim Taylor and sound recordist Dick Hill. Slim and wiry, Jim was an experienced TV News man, well thought of at the Spur (BBC TV News HQ). His sound recordist, Dick Hill, a fresh faced young northerner, was a hard working partner.

Soon after arrival in Singapore we made a short film report on the British Army's Jungle Training Course at Johore Baru in southern Malaysia. In tropical heat I trudged through some appropriate jungle and tried to make it sound significant, but it was not going to dominate the main bulletins at home. We tried one or two other local stories, but they were dwarfed by fast moving events in the Vietnam conflict.

The world's major news story was brewing in a country which would become infamous for brutal warfare and genocide. Cambodia had just plunged catastrophically into the Vietnam War. It was making alarming headlines in the world's press, including the *Singapore Straits Times* which I read with tremors in the stomach.

The North Vietnamese Army (NVA) was smashing up Cambodia's inept national Army formed by General Lon Nol, head of the new regime. With the aid of America's CIA, Lon Nol had staged a coup to snatch power from the hereditary ruler, Prince Sihanouk, an eccentric personality who played a jazz clarinet and made films. The Prince had performed wonders in walking a diplomatic tightrope to keep Cambodia out of the war, granting favours to eastern and western countries. He allowed the NVA and the Viet Cong, the communist guerrillas in South Vietnam, to use parts of his country as sanctuary in their campaign against the South Vietnamese regime over the border.

At the same time Sihanouk covertly allowed the US to bomb NVA bases in Cambodia. Inevitably Sihanouk fell off the tightrope. The Nixon administration wanted a ruler totally committed to the West.

The US encouraged General Lon Nol to declare war on the North Vietnamese, thereby tipping his small country into the Vietnam conflict. The Americans backed Lon Nol with more B52 bombing raids on NVA positions in Cambodia which allegedly killed over 100,000 Cambodians, fuelling the rapid growth of their own communist force, the murderous Khmer Rouge.

Even the most profound Indochina experts failed to predict the Khmer Rouge would become one or the world's most fearsome killing machines, murdering up to three million fellow Cambodians after they took power in 1975.

In 1970 it was soon clear this was to be an exceptionally brutal extension of the Vietnam War. It was to be my first war – and the worst. One of the Cambodian Army's first ploys was the use of local Vietnamese born residents as human shields. There were reports of whole families from small ethnic Vietnamese communities driven in front of the Cambodian Army in battle, only to be slaughtered by the North Vietnamese troops.

The Straits Times also carried a highly disquieting story of an American news crew having just been killed by the NVA in Cambodia. Brian Barron, then the BBC World Service correspondent in Singapore, and a knowledgeable guide to the pleasures of the City State, warned: 'I should enjoy yourself while you can. You'll be off to Cambodia very soon.'

Sure enough the BBC Foreign desk sent a brief cable 'requesting' me to fly with the crew to Phnom Penh on 24 April.

Our elderly Air Cambodge Caravelle from Singapore was manned by exotic Cambodian air hostesses attired in flowing pink and blue silk costumes. They smiled and giggled as they fluttered up and down the aisle, giving us the closest attention since we were the only passengers apart from a few beefy men in civilian dress who were closely studying weapons catalogues, presumably arms dealers scenting business.

The beautiful chief stewardess kept smiling when she advised us that as the plane landed at Phnom Penh there might be 'just a risk' of gunfire on the ground. I was not reassured when she added that we were not to worry; the gunfire was not aimed at us.

Although conflict had moved to only 15 miles south of the capital, Pochentong airport betrayed no air of crisis, exhibiting a pleasant tourist atmosphere when we arrived at dusk. A passport official gave us a routine Cambodian smile and wished us a 'pleasant stay'.

Grinning porters shouldered our huge stack of luggage, including the crew's awkward wooden tripod, and the shiny steel box carrying their cumbersome 16 mm film camera. In South East Asia's high temperatures and humidity the camera's metal shoulder brace would prove cumbersome and uncomfortable for the cameramen in battle zones. We noted enviously that some Japanese and US crews were already using much smaller cameras with radio links to the sound box, giving cameramen and sound men far more freedom of movement.

A wonderful stroke of luck occurred when a smooth young Cambodian man in spotlessly clean white shirt and grey slacks invited us in good English to make use of his white Peugeot estate car, and his services as guide and chauffeur. We accepted immediately, and I have been profoundly grateful to our guide ever since. I owed him my life on many occasions.

He handed us his card: 'Sok Nguorn – Guide, Bayon Travel Agency'. Mr Sok, as I always called him, had transferred his tourist role to guiding journalists flocking to Phnom Penh to report the start of the war which would destroy his country, and Mr Sok himself.

I engaged him throughout my stay as interpreter and guide. He was my salvation as well as guide on every trip we made with him to the battle areas. There was some amusement at TV Centre when they saw film of Mr Sok following me round a battle scene with an umbrella and a box of sandwiches, legacies of his days in tourist work.

We called first at Phnom Penh's leading hotel, Le Royal, set amid trees and lawns, but it was already packed full of journalists and TV men from many countries. They lounged around the swimming pool or exchanged news and rumours in the bars and restaurants.

Mr Sok ushered us next to the modest Hotel Khemara on the Monivong boulevard, one of the delightful, tree-lined streets created by the former French colonists. Despite the emergency, the city known as the 'Pearl of Asia' was still beguiling with its sleepy charm, elements of French chic, and oriental exoticism. There were charming squares reminiscent of Provence, contrasting with the glamour of the Royal Palace and Pagodas.

Although it claimed to have air conditioning, my Khemara bedroom relied on a large fan revolving from the ceiling where dozens of geckoes, were clinging upside down by their toe pads, occasionally darting with alarming speed to snap up insects.

From my bed I gazed up at the lizards and their prey, mosquitoes and other flying insects swirling round one dingy light bulb. I lay awake in the tropical heat for several hours, reflecting that my vocation to be an international journalist was about to be severely tested. Beware of what you wish for, I thought, before I dropped into a deep sleep.

The surreal Cambodian war we were to attempt to convey in monochrome film to millions of people watching the telly thousands of miles away, was fascinating and at times horrific. The story needed analysis in depth to make any sense to a western audience, and I yearned to write newspaper articles on the full story of the unfolding Cambodian disaster.

As a BBC staff man I could not write such articles, and after hectic days with the TV crew I was too tired to attempt extra work. The best I could manage was to send radio commentary to the BBC's venerable current affairs programme we called 'Fooc' (From Our Own Correspondent). I was delighted when it was re-printed in *The Listener*. It said more about the reasons for Cambodia's war than I was ever able to communicate in film reports where the relentless priority for TV news was battle footage.

Not even the most profound students of Indochina foretold the horrors which would engulf Cambodia when the Khmer Rouge finally marched into Phnom Penh five years later. I was appalled but not entirely surprised when the fully story of the Khmer Rouge's appalling cruelty and genocide emerged. From the beginning of my tour of the country I became disquietingly aware that underneath Cambodia's smiling facade there was a dark underside of brutality and contempt for human life. It was born of centuries of feudal repression and savage revolutions.

The Phnom Penh I awoke to on my first morning was ravishing. Despite the dire emergency, Phnom Penh could still captivate the visitor. I drank coffee in charming flower-decked squares. At night we ate delicious French-Indochinese food on the boat restaurants moored on the Mekong River, returning to our hotel in cycloes pedalled through the exotically scented flower market.

The City had billed itself to tourists as a gateway to a lush green country inhabited by seven million 'friendly people'. Despite the growing threat from the Communist forces there were still French rubber planters living in Phnom Penh with their Cambodian wives or mistresses. In 1970 they seemed to have a certain immunity from attack.

I grew quite fond of the Khemara Hotel, where bowls of delicious steaming noodles were delivered to my room as a dawn breakfast from the restaurant downstairs. The few staff were courteous and helpful, seemingly unworried about the war lapping so close to their city. I never attempted to move to the journalistic hothouse of the Hotel Phnom.

Soon we fell into the daily routine of television crews driving crazily up and down the long narrow highways from the capital to each small, chaotic scene of conflict between the effective North Vietnamese Army and the tragic-comic troops of Lon Nol. Motor transport was scarce, and Cambodian Army soldiers often travelled in Pepsi-Cola trucks. They were mainly teenage soldiers wearing trainers and parts of uniforms. Many had been unpaid for months because officers were purloining the cash.

On our first morning the crew and I reported to the Cambodian Army's 'Departement de L'Information' where the charming chief information officer, much to the delight of the western press, rejoiced in the name of Colonel Am Rong. Just how wrong were his optimistic reports on the 'progress' of Lon Nol's army, we discovered that very day.

I was issued with my 'Carte Speciale de Presse', and then it proved all too easy to get some battle footage. Without any briefing Mr Sok knew exactly where to take a TV crew to film the latest fire-fight. He remained extraordinarily calm throughout every foolhardy trip we took in his tourist limousine.

Perhaps from habit, Sok gave us a commentary on local tourist attractions as his driver took us south of Phnom Penh down the road towards Takeo. After only about 20 miles, we saw a small detachment of Cambodian troops firing French artillery of elderly vintage towards a belt of trees, beyond a plain of scrubland. When the artillery ceased, a detachment of about 50 Cambodian infantry troops walked towards the trees, occasionally firing their motley array of rifles, ranging from American M16's to Chinese-made weapons seized from the North Vietnamese by the Americans and passed on to Lon Nol.

Without let or hindrance we TV men followed close behind, Jim Taylor humping his huge camera amid stifling humidity, with Dick Hunt tethered to him by the sound wire. This was indeed a TV war; you were given every liberty to get killed or injured whenever you liked.

Suddenly there was a different sound, the inimitable chatter of the Soviet AK-47 assault rifle. It struck fear into me whenever I heard it thereafter. The AK-47 was copied by the Chinese, and supplied to the North Vietnamese and Viet Cong, so whenever I heard it, the bullets were likely to be incoming.

This was followed by a few mortar rounds and whoosh of a rocket from the NVA. The Cambodian troops immediately flung themselves to the ground, and so did we. The NVA troops ahead were well dug in, and they were now returning fire with professional skill, a sharp contrast to the performance of Lon Nol's ill-trained motley army.

After lying on the ground for an hour or so, it seemed a good time to get our film back to the BBC. At one point we thought we saw a group of men in black running through the trees ahead. It was the one and only time I saw the NVA in action. Later I would see scores of dead NVA and Viet Cong men stretched out by road-sides in Vietnam, an ineffectual warning to villagers not to support them.

Also in Vietnam I saw a captured NVA soldier tethered by a chain from a leg manacle. His head was bleeding, his black uniform torn and muddy, but he looked back at me defiantly; another brave young man prepared to suffer grievously for what he no doubt believed was a noble cause, the unification of Vietnam under a Communist government.

We crawled and then walked briskly back to our car. Well out of range of gunfire I performed a terse piece to camera, and we drove back to Phnom Penh as if from a tourist trip.

At our hotel I typed a film script on my battered Olivetti portable typewriter, not BBC issue but a 21st birthday present from my mother which survived all my overseas assignments. We retired to the comparative quiet of the bathroom where Dick

Hill recorded my voicing of the script on tape which the London editors would lay alongside appropriate film we had provided.

Film and tape were packed in metal cans, and Dick took a taxi to the airport to ship the film as airfreight to London whilst Jim Taylor and I tucked in to a delicious brunch. I had the gravest doubts the film would ever arrive at TV Centre, Wood Lane, but amazingly all the film we sent from Cambodia found its way there safely. It was a far better result than we achieved shipping film in Europe through the chaos of Rome Airport. The Cambodian film got through even when trips from the city to Pochentong airport became more hazardous as the road was raked with NVA rocket fire.

Two days later a Cable and Wireless message from the BBC foreign desk wired an encouraging herogram: 'Highly regarded first rate pix and story. Congratulations to you and crew. National (BBC1) and Newsroom (BBC2) used 3 mins 15 secs. Newscasts.' The ten hour time zone advantage in South East Asia meant that our film could usually be shown the day after we shipped it.

During the month of May, 18 of my film reports from Cambodia were transmitted on BBC news, all producing cordial response cables from the Spur.

Very soon we discovered the comparative ease of our battle excursion was desperately misleading. I was made sharply aware of the dark side of the Cambodian culture when we filmed the bodies of Vietnamese immigrants drifting past the city in the Mekong river, their hands lashed behind their backs with barbed wire. They were victims of the anti-Vietnam hysteria whipped-up by the Lon Nol regime.

An immigrant Chinese family, owners of a tourist shop I visited, went on their knees before me, weeping and pleading for help from Cambodia's wave of lethal racism against North Vietnam and its Chinese backers.

On 8 May we were crawling along in Mr Sok's limousine at the front of a convey of TV crew cars along Highway One towards the Neak Luong ferry. We were trailing two or three of the Cambodian Army's ancient tanks, and several truckloads of infantry troops along Highway One, built on an embankment above the plain of paddy fields and scrubland. Suddenly the chatter of AK-47 gunfire caused the trucks to brake sharply.

Well-aimed rifle fire poured from treetop positions into the Cambodian trucks ahead. The troops leapt out in panic, some of them bloodied with gunshot wounds. I caught sight of a bloody mess, which had been a man, on the turret of one of the Cambodian tanks, but we were in no position to film anything at that moment.

We flung open the doors of the Peugeot, and regardless of hands and knees cut on sharp thorns, we crawled rapidly through scrub down the embankment onto the sandy plain below. As I hit the road I heard a crash, tinkle, as bullets hit our windscreen. I had been sitting in the front passenger seat exactly in line with the incoming bullets.

It was my closest escape from incoming fire – the luckiest escape in a lifetime – and I was very shaken. Jim Taylor and Dick Hunt bravely carried their camera and sound kit as they crawled down the embankment. We were soon accompanied by Cambodian troops from the lorries, callow conscripts, who seemed particularly useless. One of them, a few feet from me, began to unscrew the cap on the end of a wooden handled grenade, grinning inanely as he did so. Most Cambodian troops continued to smile during the fire-fight, showing little awareness of personal danger.

'For God's sake, throw the thing,' I shouted. After what seemed all too many seconds, he lurched to his feet and threw it ahead. The grenade exploded well ahead, but did absolutely no damage to the enemy. By now the better organized element of the Cambodian Army were firing mortars and machine guns at the NVA positions. After exchanges of fire for about an hour the North Vietnamese had withdrawn efficiently through scrub and paddy fields. We had stark evidence that such ambushes were among the major risks whenever you followed the Cambodian Army.

'Try a piece to camera?' Jim Taylor croaked, clutching his camera while lying down, with Dick valiantly fiddling with his sound box. I collected something of my wits, and delivered a dishevelled 'under fire' piece. It was far short of the calm I had intended to portray in battle pieces to camera but my desperation was authentic.

I was lying in a trench among a group of Cambodian troops in floppy olive and green battle fatigues who looked completely nonplussed, and were doing very little to respond to the 'incoming'. They jabbered and peered fearfully over the edge of the trench, but were doing nothing to return fire. This was not much help in conveying the atmosphere of being in a fire fight, but I was not in a position to consider the finer points of TV war production.

So as I lay there, I gasped out the following words to Jim's bravely held camera:

> 'This is the worst position we have been in so far in this campaign. We are under live fire from Viet Cong troops only a few hundred yards ahead. One minute we were on the road; the next, we dived for cover and we are now at this moment among the Cambodian troops. Mortars and rifle fire are coming in overhead all the time – and the Cambodian Army seems to have run into quite a packet of trouble on its way to try to recapture the Neak Luong ferry position.'

After a while the incoming fire ceased as the opposing forces moved back. I referred to the Viet Cong in my report, as did most reports at that time. In fact, the Cambodians had come up against highly experienced North Vietnamese units who had crossed the border to their temporary bases in Cambodia, and were now pressing the inept national army since Prime Minister Lon Nol so disastrously led Cambodia into the war.

After we regained the road, I performed another short piece to camera by Mr Sok's white Peugeot estate which bore plenty of evidence that it had converted from tourist limousine to war-time camera car. Thank heavens it later stuttered its way back to Phnom Penh safely, and I paid a couple of hundred pounds or so for repairs; cheap at the price.

I walked from the back to the front, and put my fist through the gaping hole in the windscreen, saying:

'This is our camera car here. We just managed to escape from the ambush battle which is still going on further down this road. We got out of the car seconds before this happened (fist through window). Bullets came through the window here. We dived for it in the ditches either side of the road. Then more rounds came through the front of the car, with bullets hitting the radiator. Meanwhile the Cambodians are still trying to take the village of Koki Thom ahead.'

During the piece to camera in the ditch there was no doubt from occasional flinching that I was under fire, but the sound camera does not pick up 'incoming' noise. It's the outgoing boom of guns near you which sounds most impressive on the sound track. When under fire in later work in Vietnam, and in the Middle East, I strove to be as calm as possible, and perhaps overdid it. No doubt I could have done with coaching, which illustrates where television documentary work inevitably becomes theatre at times.

Perversely I received a cable from London on a later Vietnam trip asking me not to sound as calm as if I was 'commentating on show jumping'. I was performing a piece to camera while South Vietnamese Skyraider planes dive-bombed us all too closely. Both incidents were hazardous, but the Highway One ambush was the nearest miss I experienced, and I was soon to learn of its effect on my cameraman.

I heard later that my Highway One piece to camera was shown for some years on BBC TV reporters' courses. The students were given advice on 'how to do it', and I suspect that my piece was not shown as the ideal example of sang froid under fire.

However, I doubt many of them were ever in quite the situation of having leapt from a shot-up camera car – and nowadays, very sensibly, they often wear flak jackets and helmets in war zones. Each situation is different, and I admire today's TV reporters who work under fire in the Middle East. It sums up the futility of most TV war footage.

To the viewer most of the 'bang bang' coverage looks much the same; it is very difficult for the reporter to convey the true peril of broadcasting under fire, partly because you cannot film the deadly incoming stuff. This is where the medium is certainly the message: are you communicating news or a voyeuristic thrill for the TV viewer while he sips his cocoa before going to bed? Our Cambodia ambush was shown on a Saturday evening bulletin, truncated in those days. Someone on the News Desk had the wit to phone my wife Mary beforehand to advise her that: 'Michael is perfectly OK if you're worried when you see the news tonight.'

The London literary agent Bagenal Harvey who negotiated several horse book deals for my authorship, said he could not imagine the BBC could possibly afford the sort of money he would need to negotiate for my TV work if they paid the real 'going rate' compared with BBC show business payment scales. He indicated politely that in commercial terms my TV reporting role was beyond folly, and I should work freelance as soon as possible. The problem was that BBC News was still operating on entirely out-dated managerial concepts at that time – and I did not yet have the confidence to try my luck as a freelance with Panorama, or ITV's documentaries, who paid far more.

[As a salaried BBC correspondent I was receiving £3,792 per annum in the spring of 1970. After sending dozens of TV reports from Cambodia and Vietnam, all transmitted on the national bulletins and many sold to other companies abroad, my annual salary at the end of 1970 was increased to £3,960.]

Max Hastings in his book *Going to the Wars* recalls the Highway One ambush as his first experience of TV war reporting. He admitted performing eight re-takes of his own piece to camera under fire for BBC Panorama because he kept lapsing 'into a string of frightened curses....'

He reports 'the BBC News car took a bullet in the windscreen', and just before the ambush 'I chatted to Mike Clayton, mostly about his passion for foxhunting.'

Film editors protect the viewer from seeing the very worst close-ups film of the dead and injured, even though more graphic shots of battle corpses are transmitted nowadays than in the 1970s.

Surviving is more about luck than judgment, and I have never ceased to be thankful for returning from Cambodia in one piece. Twenty-six journalists and camera crew were killed, or taken prisoner never to return, in the areas we were filming during my 1970 tour in Cambodia. It was estimated over 80 visiting reporters and cameramen or photographers were killed in the Cambodian conflict overall before the Communist victory in 1975, compared with over 300 journalists and photographers killed during the 14 years of the Vietnam war.

Experienced TV crews who arrived in Cambodia from Vietnam often wore the military type uniforms they were accustomed to using in battle zones, and some carried guns in their cars. They were clearly visible as TV war reporting crews from the west. As such they were almost certain to be shot out of hand if detained by the NVA or Khmer Rouge units on those long highways out of Phnom Penh.

Coming from Singapore, my crew and I had stumbled on a marginally safer method of travel and dress in Cambodia. Travelling with Mr Sok in our tourist limousine, wearing civilian clothes, we could have been taken for French rubber planters, who were much less of a target. On one occasion we halted at a mysterious road block on a highway crossing the flood plains around Phnom Penh. A small boy riding a water buffalo suddenly emerged from scrubland by the road, and looked at us with wide-eyed alarm, but said nothing.

'How far away are the NVA, Mr Sok?' I asked.

'They in this bush right here,' he replied. 'We stay calm and go. They may be waiting ambush.'

I tried to think of something else, as we tried to look nonchalant, entered the blessed car, and drove back down the highway with immense relief. Later we learned there was an ambush fire fight at that roadblock between NVA and a Cambodian Army unit with heavy casualties on both sides.

Sok would stop the car in villages, talk to locals and sometimes order that we turn back quickly because the men in black were further down the road. On one occasion another TV crew car surged past us while we halted in a village. They were hit by rocket fire some miles further, and never came back.

I knew an Australian cameraman staying at the Khemara who was working with that North American crew. Later that evening I knocked on his door to speak to the pretty Chinese girl with whom he was living. She opened the door, and in the background I could hear a man shouting while having a shower. It was the Australian. He had objected to not being paid his freelance fees by the other crew, so he had not joined that day's sortie – and survived. Such stories of casual death or near-misses were the common currency of journalism in the Vietnam War.

Probably the most publicised missing pressmen in the Cambodian tragedy were Sean Flynn and his colleague and friend Dana Stone. The reason for the extra interest in their loss was that Sean was the son of the film star Errol Flynn. Sean and Dana travelled the roads of Cambodia on high powered motorcycles. They were captured in April 1970, while I was based in Phnom Penh, by unknown units near the village of Chi Phou in eastern Cambodia, just short of the border with Vietnam. It was believed they were trucked and marched about Cambodia for months as captives. Sean Flynn's name and parentage was well known and it is believed they were kept prisoner by Communist forces, as potential hostages to be exchanged with prisoners in the hands of the Americans in Vietnam. This never happened, and it was believed that both were finally executed.

Their disappearance was the talk of the press brigade in Phnom Penh when I was there. It certainly emphasised that rushing on into insurgent areas without extreme caution was not be recommended. I took due note.

Ever since that spring of 1970 I have been fatalistic about my own mortality, but after Highway One I was far more wary. Get in, get a picture story, and get out, seemed to be the best policy for TV news crews film at that time, still using film instead of video, and without satellite feeds for live reports. Although many confined themselves mainly to 'authoritative' reports from city press rooms, some reporters I met in Indo-China were 'war freaks', relishing the chance of getting into battle zones, retailing the 'thrill' of being under fire amid an alcoholic haze over dinner in the evening.

During the Vietnam and Cambodia filming, and the Jordan airplane hijacking story I felt extraordinarily alive and fit after surviving each new threat. Perhaps this was due to adrenaline surge, but no matter how bracing the experience of survival I fervently believed that adding a little war footage to the nine o'clock news seemed a futile way of dying. I wanted to live more than ever before, and the ordinary pleasures of life were heightened.

The morning after the Highway One ambush I heard news of a re-engagement between the Cambodians and the NVA on the same site. This time the Cambodians had prevailed, driving away the North Vietnamese, and killing more than 20.

It seemed highly necessary to go to the scene to film the aftermath, as Max Hastings' Panorama team did. But I had a severe shock when Jim Taylor came to my room early next morning to tell me he was going home immediately. Looking terribly white and strained, but maintaining his composure, he told me he was not prepared to take the level of risks involved in filming warfare Cambodian-style. It was more dangerous than anything he had experienced, and he was catching the next plane back to London.

I accepted Jim's decision without protest, but there was no phone line to London I could use to discuss the situation with the TV Newsroom. Much later I received a letter from the Editor of TV News informing me that Jim's decision had been entirely accepted, and emphasizing that TV reporters and crews always had the choice of declining war zone coverage.

I did not find this particularly reassuring, since the BBC would not take out insurance on our lives when reporting wars. I was assured by a personnel officer that instead they would make large 'ex gratia payments' to our next-of-kin. Foolishly I nodded and accepted this verbal promise.

I had applied for endowment policies on my life to benefit my children, but they were rejected by the insurance companies because of my occupation.

Within an hour of Jim's decision to quit I was in business again. At the early morning Cambodian army briefing session I explained to other reporters that I had no cameraman, and an American TV reporter immediately pointed in the direction of a tall lean Chinaman. 'Try him; he's free.'

With a broad smile the Chinaman shook my hand and gave me his card: 'Ronnie Lee ARPS, Cine cameraman, American broadcasting Companies, New York USA.' Ronnie was more than ready to film for the BBC. He said he had worked for us in Singapore, and he knew we paid our bills – eventually.

Ronnie had come from Singapore looking for business, and he proved a highly proficient stringer cameraman, and a cheerful companion. Dick Hill stayed for a few days, suffering a severe bout of gastro-enteritis, and I had more or less learned to operate his sound box previously one day while he was ill in bed. Somehow I would have to be reporter and sound man with Ronnie Lee.

Our first mission was a report of fresh fighting near Koki Thom, the village near Prey Veng, east of Phnom Penh which the Cambodians were seeking to re-take from the NVA. Mr Lee insisted we travelled on his Honda motorbike, and I agreed after some hesitation to mount pillion. We carried the camera box in a small trailer rattling behind. Lee insisted his motorbike was much safer than a TV crew car because it made us look less military or press. I did not argue although I had severe doubts which grew as the road towards Koki Thom degenerated into a narrow dirt track with dense growth either side. It seemed ideal for an ambush.

Ronnie suddenly halted, and pointed at the road ahead. Even with my limited experience I recognised a round anti-tank mine lying in a shallow trench in the middle of the road. It occurred to me that it should have been covered with dirt, and if the NVA had laid it they were not far away.

'We go round it, but we stay on the road,' said Ronnie. He wheeled his bike carefully along the edge of the road past the mine. Ronnie kick-started the Honda bike and set off blithely, while I slumped on the pillion again, remembering that we had grossly broken Mr Sok's safety procedures.

Ronnie slowed and then halted as we approached some Cambodian Army trucks halted on a more open stretch of the road. There was gunfire in the bush ahead in belts of trees. Ronnie chatted amiably with a Cambodian Army officer who waved us forward with the a beaming smile. With long strides Ronnie took us towards a group of Cambodian soldiers lying in dug-outs. We filmed them firing mortars, gathered some general shots, and I did a hasty piece to camera about how the war was hotting up, and the growing battle to re-take the Neak Luong ferry crossing. Eventually the Cambodians succeeded in this venture, but only because the NVA made strategic withdrawals, later handing over the Cambodian struggle to the growing might of the Khmer Rouge.

When we motor-biked back to Phnom Penh I was relieved to note that someone had removed the road mine, but I did not relax until I reached the safety of my Khemara Hotel bathroom to record the tape accompanying Ronnie's excellent film.

Either it was a slow news day in London, or my piece was better than I thought, but TV News cabled me that national news had used ten minutes five seconds. Ronnie's film was acceptable, but there was a plaintive message at the end of the cable: 'Why Chinese characters on film tin?'

At the end of the day Ronnie asked genially: 'You come to party with me tonight? We have nice orgy.' I made my excuses and left.

Despite the confusion over the Chinese script, someone at TV Centre acted promptly to send the best possible replacement crew to Cambodia. A few days later I gave a warm airport welcome to cameraman Bill Hanford and sound recordist Bob Poole. Always cheerful, seldom showing signs of strain, they were a highly efficient, experienced crew, and good company. They proved to be a credit to BBC TV News during some of the hottest battle scenes its own men had so far covered in the Vietnam war.

I felt immensely buoyed up as soon as we shook hands at the airport. Bill, a stocky man who sported a beard for much of his career, earned plaudits for distinguished work in war zones long after I had left the BBC.

We sent a news film most days from Cambodia throughout May, not only covering a variety of fire-fights, but covering the wounded, and signs of crisis in Phnom Penh.

President Nixon had made his controversial, some said infamous, decision to send American and South Vietnamese Troops over the border into Cambodia throughout May. The NVA made the classic guerrilla decision to fade away to the west, but they were still prepared to engage with the weak Cambodian Army in the provinces close to the capital.

We grew used to the sight, and smell, of dead bodies from both sides littering the ground after their clashes. Because of the American incursion, Cambodian President Lon Nol and his officers were bullish at this time, cheerfully promising a victory over the Communists. The reality was that his Army remained inept and ill-equipped. One severely injured senior officer sought a lift with us in Mr Sok's car back to hospital in Phnom Penh because no military transport was available. I held a drip above his head as he lay on the back seats, oozing blood all over the smart interior.

We filmed incoming Americans once, when a reconnaissance unit of the 1st Air Cavalry landed briefly in their helicopters at Svay Rieng. Their CO seemed surprised when an English crew greeted him, but he gave a gungho interview with the usual American fluency. We did not know it at the time, but major damage was being done by Nixon's horrific B52 bomber raids further west and north in Cambodia in an unsuccessful attempt to smash the NVA's secret headquarters.

Bill and Bob were up for anything, and during the next four weeks we risked car trips much further from Phnom Penh. I was thrilled when we filmed at Angkor Wat, the famed temple complex to the north at Siem Reap where the tourist trade was wrecked by the war. I stood alone in one temple watching swarms of monkeys run up and down the wonderful carved arches.

Suddenly I felt a nudge in the ribs and whipped round in alarm to find an old man shoving a cross-bow at me. To my relief he grinned and held out a hand; he wanted to sell me the bow.

We narrowly avoided extinction one afternoon in mid-May when a unit of Cambodian troops we were following was bombed by South Vietnamese Sky Raider aircraft. These propeller-driven American attack planes, with bombs loaded under the wings, were spectacular dive-bombers, piloted by dare-devil South Vietnamese. The surrealism of Cambodian warfare was heightened for us by Mr Sok finding BBC World Service on his car radio. I was getting home-sick listening to the sedate tones of 'Mrs Dale's Diary' when the bombs fell.

A couple of truckloads of Cambodian soldiers were hit several hundred yards ahead. It was spectacular news film, with bodies and debris all over the road. The whine of the SkyRaiders continued, and more bombs exploded. Bill valiantly snatched some shots of the chaos after we leapt from the car to roll into a ditch. The Cambodians had no means of ground to air radio contact with their supposed allies, the South Vietnamese. Cambodian soldiers waved their national flag, shouting and screaming at the sky. After a while the South Vietnamese pilots seemed to understand their lethal error, waggled their wings and flew off, leaving a horrible scene of death and destruction among the Cambodians.

A fierce tropical thunderstorm hit us, and we lay in warm water rapidly filling our ditch for some time before struggling out to report the aftermath. Our report received 8.52 minutes on the main news bulletin, and a herogram.

There was cause for amusement for the news viewing theatre at TV Centre when we sent footage of the Cambodian Army's re-taking of the provincial city of Kampong Cham from the NVA. We had crossed the Mekong river in a motor boat, lying on the bottom because sporadic rounds of incoming fire were coming from the opposite bank.

Fortunately the NVA unit withdrew before we reached the other side. Bill Hanford filmed some shots of me stalking about during a rain shower on the battle area, with Mr Sok holding an umbrella over my head while he carried my water bottle and a packet of sandwiches. This added fuel to my Newsroom nickname of 'Squire Clayton', earned by my penchant for foxhunting. It demonstrates the superficiality of television that this image was long remembered by my colleagues when the serious war reporting was forgotten. Michael Buerk, my successor in TV news, referred to the umbrella incident derisively in his own memoir, but totally incorrectly stating that I had 'insisted' on carrying a 'gaily coloured' umbrella in Vietnam. Trivial images survive all too long in TV journalism. The medium is indeed the message.

Nixon's incursion into Cambodia produced one achievement for the US and South Vietnam through the discovery and removal of huge caches of enemy weapons and other war materials. They had been carried down from North Vietnam on the Ho Chi Minh Trail to be used by the NVA and the Viet Cong in their battles inside South Vietnam. It was a major setback for the communists and helped to bolster the South Vietnamese regime of President Thieu.

TV News cabled us to fly to Saigon to follow up this story. On 31 May I said farewell to Cambodia, not with reluctance, but with the impression I had been privileged to explore a uniquely beautiful country before it was devastated. Cambodia and its capital city would become a tragic shell of the country I reported from in 1970.

As our Air Vietnam plane landed at Saigon's Ton Son Nhut airbase we gazed down at vast rows of US and South Vietnamese military aircraft and helicopters. This was warfare on a massive scale, different in the complex of weapons to anything seen in the second world war.

When we walked down the steps from the airplane into Indochina's humidity and stifling heat I saw scores of green canvas objects lying on the tarmac by a transport plane. American soldiers were going home – in body bags.

We had been reporting a brutal side-show in Cambodia. In Vietnam we were to be in the front row of the main event: the largest conflict since World War Two.

We were to film war on a far greater scale, but in Vietnam I never felt so imperilled as on those long straight highways of Cambodia.

Chapter Ten

THE VIETNAM
EXPERIENCE

Vietnam was the greatest TV war of our time, and perhaps the last on such a scale. No army has since embraced television news as the Americans did throughout the 14 years of the Vietnam War. In the bitter inquest after defeat by North Vietnam in 1975 it was recognised in the US that intense TV coverage of the war on American screens had been a major factor in producing a tide of anti-war sentiment inside America. From 1970 it caused politicians to withdraw American troops before ensuring the South Vietnamese army could reliably withstand the forces of the North.

In 1970 the United States Military Assistance Command in Vietnam (MACV) was still giving many war correspondents remarkable help. The BBC was in the top category of trusted broadcasters, and my crew and I went through MACV's amazingly generous accreditation process.

My pack of four press cards issued on 1 June 1970 in Saigon allowed me to 'cover the operational, advisory and support activities of the Free World Military Assistance Forces, Vietnam'. Should I fall into enemy hands I had one identity card in Vietnamese proclaiming that I was 'Bao Chi', the press, and asking my captors to treat me as if

I had the rank of major. It was well meant, but having just come from Cambodia I was under no illusions about the treatment of press by Communist forces.

Most important were the cards enabling us to seek transport on American helicopters to war zones when space permitted, and to gain accommodation on US bases. This was the invaluable key to the huge TV coverage the Vietnam war received. We were not usually accompanied by minders, and it was left to the discretion of local commanders as to whether we accompanied soldiers on assault missions. It was vastly different to the Middle East and Indo-Pakistan conflicts I was to cover later, where correspondents were virtually barred from getting anywhere near the battle zone.

The difference between reporting in Cambodia and Vietnam was rammed home when the crew and I were kitted out in olive-drab battle fatigues, jungle boots and floppy hat, with the compliments of MACV in Saigon. A grinning American soldier explained as he handed me my kit: 'We ain't just looking after you, buddy. We don't want you guys wearing coloured shirts to attract in-coming fire when you're standing next to our guys.'

President Nixon was scaling down the US presence in Vietnam in 1970, but it was still immense. Saigon's charming French colonial character was by now largely submerged by the war. American and South Vietnamese military vehicles shouldered through flocks of Vietnamese families perched on scooters. At night young American soldiers thronged garishly lit girly bars lining narrow streets. Sex was not the only commodity abundantly on offer: there were street markets selling everything from kitchen goods to US Army uniforms, and even weapons.

We stayed at the mercifully air conditioned Caravelle Hotel opposite the colonial-style Continental Palace hotel described by Graham Greene. In the evenings when we were in Saigon we joined others of the large international press contingent, drinking at tables under the green awnings of the Continental. William Shawcross, who had arrived with a BBC Panorama crew, met us there one evening. He was to write 'Side-Show', the much praised indictment of the Nixon administration's bombing of Cambodia, and its actions to drag the country into the war.

'Just here for News?' asked Shawcross. 'Yes, just the News,' I affirmed. He said kind words about our film reports from Cambodia, and we genially discussed the proposition that in television terms 'coverage in-depth' is simply coverage 'at length'. Panorama would give a full hour to a report from Vietnam, but the sum total of our regular contributions in the news bulletins was far longer, and had its own long-term impact on the TV audience.

MACV was keen to show TV crews the successes it was having in uncovering the North Vietnamese arms caches just discovered over the border in Cambodia. We took a battered taxi ride to the main US helicopter port at Saigon. After checking in and waiting we clambered aboard a Huey helicopter heavily loaded with sandbags.

It was an incredibly exciting experience. Both side doors were open, with a machine gunner stationed at each. I stood facing the door, barely in the helicopter, with a foot of floor space on which to stand. The sandbags pressed against my back, and shifted alarmingly at times, while I clung with upraised arms to the inside roof. Despite the discomfort and danger I was thrilled by the remarkable feeling of speed you experience in a helicopter skimming just above miles of lush green jungle. Sometimes the jungle gave way to open spaces pitted with some of the many bomb craters littering South Vietnam.

Bill Hanford flew with his precious camera on his shoulder, taking marvellous aerial shots. Then our helicopter descended in a hill-top clearing. It did not quite land, but remained hovering a few feet above earth. The aircrew shouted: 'Jump!'

It was only a few feet and I landed easily, but just as Bill was jumping the helicopter lifted, and he had to drop well over six feet down. Somehow he kept on his feet, but the camera jarred heavily on his shoulder. He was in much pain for the rest of the day, but carried on filming regardless. All the good TV News cameramen were incredibly tough.

We were shown huge stores of guns and ammunition painstakingly brought down from North Vietnam by the Communist troops, some of the smaller items carried on bicycles. Most of the weapons were from China or elsewhere in the Eastern bloc. An officer gave me a gleeful interview on their haul. Some of these caches were handed over by the US to Lon Nol's pathetic army in Cambodia, but it did them little good.

During the next four weeks we travelled by helicopter from the DMZ, the line between North and South Vietnam, down to the Mekong Delta in the South.

We soon learned the hazards of helicopter travel. After one organized press sortie we experienced with a US Air Cavalry unit, we returned to base and drank coffee in a hut with other journalists, waiting in stifling heat for a de-briefing from the senior officer. Then an officer appeared and said: 'Gentlemen. The helicopter of the commanding officer was brought down during the mission on which you have flown. You are going back to Saigon, and we will inform you more later.'

I heard nothing more, but the incident illustrated the increasing hazards to US helicopters from the ground. NVA and Viet Cong troops were using shoulder-launched ground-to-air missiles to make helicopter transport even more dangerous.

When we flew by helicopter to the top of the infamous Hamburger Hill, where many Americans had lost their lives only 12 months ago, I asked an officer if it was now held securely by the US.

'We hold the top of the hill, and we hold the bottom. But Charlie holds the middle,' was his less than reassuring reply. There were many signs, even in 1970, that the Vietnam campaign was grinding down. My confidence was not increased when we stayed on American bases where some of the infantry were amazingly insubordinate. As a callow National Service airman I would have been immediately consigned to the Guard House, or worse, if I had appeared with the unkempt uniforms, and reluctance to salute, that was common on US bases I visited.

I was shocked to see some soldiers wearing peace badges on their uniforms, the same symbols worn by students on US campuses demonstrating against the Vietnam war. I did not see positive evidence, but judging by their giggling or spaced-out behaviour I could well believe more than a few US soldiers were on drugs, already fully reported by the American media. I saw enough to conclude that morale and discipline were far from ideal.

The bases on which we stayed were bleak. American officers' messes were dry of alcohol. In the other ranks' mess there were mountains of steak, hash and ice-cream. When we flew to Da Nang, which the 1st Marine Division was vacating as part of Nixon's much vaunted Vietnamisation programme, I was offered the bed of a sergeant who was said to be on night duty. The bedding and the sleeping quarters were filthy, but I was too tired to care. I got up at first light when a soldier slumped into one of the other beds. He said the sergeant wasn't on night duty; he was in the sick bay with hepatitis. I banished this unwelcome information from my mind as quickly as possible.

Night times in fire bases were rent with the sound of 'harassing and interdiction fire' (H and I). They fired artillery at intervals throughout the night at huge cost per shell to keep 'Charlie Kong' at bay. There had been night-time raids by suicide squads of Viet Cong who had cut their way through rows of barbed wire to storm inside US bases with blazing guns, scoring heavy casualties.

When 'H and I fire' was used, the Viet Cong kept well out of the way, going about their business in the countryside largely unmolested at night. US military strategy, as I experienced it, was to go out by day on Search and Destroy missions, kill as many NVA or Viet Cong as possible in ambushes, and then return to base. The US did not command large areas of the ground terrain with infantry. This strategy, designed to keep US losses low, was hopeless against the most committed guerrilla force in the world.

We had a taste of war with the ARVN, the South Vietnamese forces, when we flew back into Cambodia in their helicopters. At Kampong Trach not far inside the border above the Parrots Beak area we landed as IV Corps troops were re-taking the town from NVA forces. We walked behind ARVN soldiers with M16 rifles and bayonets, as they combed wooden houses and pot-holed streets. The

NVA had just withdrawn, leaving behind terrible evidence of their prowess in dealing with the local Cambodian Army unit attempting to defend the town. The unmistakable smell of death led us to heaps of corpses of Cambodian government soldiers. Then we filmed a small unit of injured South Vietnamese troops being carried back to Medi-Vac helicopters. They had been in a brief fire-fight with NVA making a tactical withdrawal.

With the sound of the South Vietnamese pouring gunfire into the jungle areas beyond the town it produced graphic war footage.

'Here's one for the viewing theatre, but they won't use it, ' said Bill Hanford as he filmed a close-up of an especially mangled Cambodian body.

When it was time to return, an ARVN officer directed me to fly back in the Medi-Vac chopper while the crew were in another helicopter carrying ARVN troops. I lay on the floor of the Medi-Vac among desperately injured soldiers, some groaning, but most stretched out stoically with expressionless faces and blank eyes.

It was a hellish journey, typical of many during the Vietnam war. I did not notice until afterwards that blood stains saturated my new boots and trouser bottoms. One poor man, for whom I held a drip, died quietly before we reached Vietnam.

Overall the South Vietnamese were considered by MACV to have performed well during the major incursion into Cambodia during 1970. They provided a major boost to Nixon's plan to hand over the war to them. Alas, early in 1971 the South Vietnamese Army's attempt to seize major NVA bases in Laos was a major disaster. The ARVN troops suffered nearly 8,000 casualties in battles with the NVA. The Communists performed remarkably despite being bombed by the hugely effective US B52 planes, and losing many men.

Spring-time was battle-time in Vietnam, because the monsoons arriving in summer made the flood plains impassable for military vehicles. General Giap, the North's commander-in-chief, launched a massive three-prong attack on the South in the spring of 1972.

The Foreign Editor of TV News, said: 'We think you are the man for the job. Would you be happy to go to Vietnam again with Bill Hanford?'

Happy was not the most appropriate word, but by then I had a great deal more experience of reporting overseas strife in the past two years, and I accepted. We spent three days of idleness in Bangkok waiting to get a visa from the South Vietnamese embassy, but I would much rather have got on with the challenge ahead. The atmosphere in Saigon when we arrived was far more tense than my previous visit. North Vietnamese troops were fighting three infantry divisions of South Vietnamese in desperate battles only about 50 miles to the north of the city. The NVA also fielded three infantry divisions, many of the troops former Viet Cong and highly experienced. They were supported by a tank regiment and several artillery regiments.

The key support for the South Vietnamese was still American air power, and South Vietnam aircraft and helicopters supplied by the US. American ground troops were no longer fighting, although US Rangers were often with South Vietnam troops as 'advisors', crucial in calling in air strikes whenever necessary.

Somewhat aged taxis queued early every morning outside the Caravelle hotel to take TV crews and correspondents on increasingly lethal trips up Highway 13 towards An Loc which the NVA were attempting to capture.

As usual it was all too easy to get extremely close to the action. The offensive in the South had been raging about a week when we arrived on 10 April. On our first sortie, made in a rickety old Buick convertible with the top down, we soon encountered ARVN troops firing mortars and small artillery at an NVA position.

'How far away are the NVA?' I asked the American advisor.

'About 500 yards. So keep your heads down. We're waiting for air support,' he grinned. I was always impressed by the professionalism and cool of the Rangers.

Suddenly the air attack arrived to provide the most exciting close-up war spectacle I had seen in Vietnam. With screaming engines,

Skyraider fighter-bombers began dive-bombing scrubland all too close ahead. These US-made piston-engined fighters carried bombs under their wings, and after screaming earthwards they ejected them before swooping up again. Their South Vietnamese pilots were highly impressive, but the North Vietnamese simply made one of their discreet withdrawals and sustained no casualties in this clash.

I performed a commentary on the sound-track while Bill filmed, and we received warm responses from TV Newsroom, although I was wryly amused by a footnote asking whether I could make my commentary sound 'a bit more exciting than a show jumping commentary.' I had been striving to be utterly cool in all war coverage since my Cambodian ambush piece under fire. This is where TV News edges into show business: when it comes to style there are pressures in the studio pushing you into the direction of hamming it up.

We were taking a step forward in BBC TV history: for the first time Vietnam war coverage was beamed back to London by satellite. Unfortunately this was an extra burden for the TV crew; indeed it increased our pressure enormously. We were not able to send satellite film from Saigon, so the film still had to be shipped in cans to Hong Kong where a BBC film editor was awaiting to transmit the footage via a local satellite link.

Technically, because of the ten hour time zone, we could show Vietnam TV reports in UK the same day it was filmed in Vietnam. I do not think it made the slightest difference to the viewer, but for ourselves it meant a hectic rush from a battle scene back to the airport to ship cans of film to Hong Kong on much earlier flights than we had used on our previous trip.

For a fortnight we sent battle footage every day, simply driving up Highway 13 in our battered taxi. The Vietnamese driver was usually as cheerful as any London cabby, even when his aged vehicle suffered tyre punctures, causing frantic wheel changes. On one occasion a fractured clutch link stopped the car, and we called at a war-damaged hut where a Vietnamese mechanic in oily overalls calmly carried out a hasty repair.

Missing the plane meant that ITN would beat us with that night's film report, and although I do not claim we were producing masterpieces, at least we never missed our slot from Highway 13. We stopped the taxi on the return drive so that I could hastily type a film-script. We recorded on tape my reading of the script at the side of the road, then packed the film tins into their bag with the tape, so that Bob Poole could drive straight to Ton Son Nhut airport to ship it to Hong Kong.

We usually arose at 5 am and set off an hour later, up the increasingly perilous Highway. There was no 'front line' in Vietnam; elements of NVA and Viet Cong ranged far and wide, and from about ten miles out of Saigon the road was insecure, with daily sniping or rocket propelled grenade attacks suddenly erupting on ARVN vehicles or any civilian cars nearby.

At Lai Khe helicopter base, the tarmac road gave way to dirt and rubble. We rumbled on slowly, checking with soldiers or villagers whether the road ahead was 'OK'. Soon we were slowed down by South Vietnamese troops, and we carried the camera gear and water bottle a mile or so up the road to where the ARVN were engaging their enemy, who were sometimes worryingly close ahead.

Helicopters, Hueys and the Chinook transport craft, and jet assault aircraft, roared overhead. The pressure was mounting because An Loc was now besieged by the 5th Viet Cong Division which had cut Highway 13 and captured the airfield. Only helicopters could take troops and supplies into An Loc and bring out the wounded. I made one or two tentative enquiries at an ARVN helicopter base as to whether we could get a lift on a flight to An Loc, and was mightily relieved when they firmly refused.

Alan Hart, a forthright personality, arrived for BBC Panorama at the same base, and after an hour or so, a chopper pilot agreed to take a TV crew into An Loc. It occurred to me that if we also flew to An Loc, our own daily service to BBC News would cease for days because the chance of returning quickly from the besieged town was remote. There was also an extremely high chance of being killed. So I was pleased to stand aside for Panorama whose heroic correspondent was prepared to stay in An Loc for days to produce a powerful piece.

We were wryly amused when, just as they were about to board the chopper, the Panorama cameraman said it was impossible because he had just his lost camera lens. Alan was incandescent with rage, threatening to send a detailed complaint back to Lime Grove. I sympathized with his disappointment and his valour, but Bill Hanford, Bob Poole and I agreed during our return drive that the Panorama cameraman had perhaps displayed more than a little commonsense. There are no medals for deceased war correspondents, just a lot of extra paper work in London.

It would have been a heroic mission. An Loc's north side was occupied in fierce fighting by the VC and NVA, but after a remarkable fight-back from the 5th ARVN Division and reinforcements, the Communists were beaten off. US air support bombing the NVA was the crucial element in the battle.

Don McCullin, the utterly intrepid press photographer who built a major reputation for taking huge risks, was also at the staging post. He took a lift in the helicopter trip to An Loc.

He recalled in his memoirs 'an appalling night under heavy shell fire' in a small hole in the ground. He photographed South Vietnamese paratroopers in full flight from the enemy, and concluded that 'for concentrated devastation those 24 hours were among the nastiest of my life'.

No doubt the Panorama crew, or mine, could have survived to capture amazing war footage in An Loc. But a TV crew at that time was far more encumbered with equipment than a stills photographer like McCullin, carrying one or two light cameras.

An Loc was one of the most devastating examples of the fighting prowess of the North Vietnamese, a signpost to the defeat to come five years later. But getting war footage was all too easy on many fronts in the 1970s and I shall never regret my own decision to forego the TV scoop awaiting in An Loc. I greatly admired dear Don McCullin, and the contribution his pictures have made to proving the well-known fact that war is hell.

In the summer of 2013 I saw a TV documentary on Don McCullin's war reporting career. I admired him for expressing grave doubts about the values and motivations of a war photographer's role. He regretted that many of those who indulged in this work regularly became 'war junkies', getting their kicks from the battlefield. He noted gloomily how TV audiences became de-sensitised to continual war footage on their screens in their comfortable homes. I used to return from Vietnam or some other war theatre, and would find myself having supper with people who said: 'You must tell us all about it.' But the conversation quickly became immersed in the problems of central heating or the local waste bin collection. I was once congratulated by a foxhunting friend on my recent work in Korea. When I explained that it was Vietnam, the answer was: 'Well somewhere out there anyway...'

Don McCullin confessed the toll his work had taken on his private life, as it did for many others, including myself.

It seemed significant to me that the McCullin documentary relied heavily on a great deal of television footage vividly illustrating the settings in which he worked. Television cameramen who risk their lives in battle are seldom, if ever, celebrated in the same way as ace press photographers. We owe an immense amount to the many nameless TV cameramen who showed the world the futility and horror of war in Vietnam for many more years than I spent in its special version of hell.

Whenever possible I attended the 'four o'clock follies', the daily MACV and ARVN news conference in Saigon. The briefings were packed with military jargon, and the daily recital of casualties and damage was a depressing picture of a grinding war in which neither side was gaining much.

'Collateral damage', or 'damage to friendlies' meant that a South Vietnamese village ostensibly loyal to the Thieu regime had been inadvertently shelled or bombed.

Compared with the Cambodian side-show this was modern war on a huge scale, now raging from north to south. I wrote radio summaries from the briefing and broadcast them to London. They gave me an opportunity to report on the whole Vietnam war scene, instead of 'bang bang' film required for a television report if it was to get much screen time. Late at night I would walk to the Reuters office in Saigon to read the latest news tapes. It was delightfully cool and quiet. I understood what a paradise the city must have been for wealthy French colonials in better times.

I listened night and morning to surprisingly informative bulletins on the US forces' radio in Saigon. It is amazing how little sleep you need when you are reporting a war. I never really switched off, always ready for something dangerous, or at least uncomfortable, to erupt.

One morning the military radio channel produced something of a TV scoop. I learned that a Communist rocket attack had hit the outskirts of Saigon, probably for the first time. We caught a taxi to the wooden shacks in the suburb which had been struck, and found ourselves the only TV crew on site. There were several casualties and some injured among the Vietnamese householders who seemed to accept the raid with stoicism.

BBC Newsroom cabled that US and other networks had eagerly seized the film, and it had a prime slot on the main home news bulletins.

As well as the push near Saigon, Hanoi's legendary Commander-in-chief, General Giap, had launched simultaneous attacks in South Vietnam's central and northern regions.

After a fortnight on Highway 13 where the NVA had been repulsed with the help of US air power, we flew by helicopter to Pleiku air base in the central region. Three divisions of NVA, supported by tanks and artillery, were pushing from the north-west towards the provincial capital city of Kontum.

Things were not going well for the South Vietnamese. They fled in disorder from an NVA attack at Rocket Ridge to the north of Kontum. Kontum was open to enemy attack and with deepest misgivings I accepted a ride into the city on an ARVN chopper from the Pleiku base. I never took these trips in a spirit of glad anticipation. It was simply necessary to get the job done, and my plan was to 'get in and get out' as quickly as possible.

We walked behind groups of ARVN infantry trudging towards the northern perimeter of Kontum, only to halt abruptly when they heard enemy gunfire.

This was the first time in Vietnam we had filmed fighting inside a city. Bill got some dramatic footage as we crouched in doorways, while the South Vietnamese exchanged fire with NVA units seeking to take Kontum.

I could hardly believe it when we saw NVA tanks trundling towards us at the far end of a long boulevard. I had always thought of the enemy as shadowy figures staging ambushes. This was warfare nearer a European scale. The South Vietnamese troops began to move back hastily. In a city they could not rely on calling up an air attack to support them.

We retreated at a brisk trot to the helicopter pad, only to find a scene of chaos and panic developing. Groups of South Vietnamese troops were clamouring to board helicopters to get out of the city. Discipline and order had been abandoned. NVA gunfire seeming to be closer, but I was much more alarmed by the ARVN's craven behaviour. No senior officers seemed to be taking charge. It was all too reminiscent of Lon Nol's pathetic army in Cambodia.

An RPG rocket hit the far side of the chopper pad, and we took refuge under a lorry. It was not a good choice: when we crawled out we noted the lorry was full of explosives and ammunition.

We flashed our MACV press passes as we asked for a helicopter place, but we were among a throng of competing ARVN troops seeking to get places. I began to fear we were about to find out just how the NVA treated captured western TV crews – if we survived their take-over of the city. Even when the war was not close we had already become accustomed to waiting hours at chopper pads until there was room on a helicopter. Time was running out.

Then a co-pilot from a just-landed Huey beckoned us to get on board. The pilot and crew shouted angrily as South Vietnamese troops piled on with us. The maximum load was ten, but there were about 20 of us crushed closely on the deck with some perilously clinging to the stanchions by the wide open doors on either side.

Several ARVN officers were carrying television sets and bags of cameras. I yelled at Bill: 'Film what you can.'

His reply summed up the limits of TV war reporting at that time: ' 'Fraid not. We've run out of film.' Even if he had the film it would have been desperately difficult to gain enough room to operate the camera.

I reflected numbly on the futility of reporting when the pictures mattered so much. We were taking severe risks, but the damned mechanics of filming meant the most dramatic part of the story was lost to us.

The South Vietnamese chopper pilot turned round, drew a pistol and flourished it at the ARVN troops whose combined weight was threatening disaster. Several men reluctantly dropped off as the helicopter hovered a few feet off ground. Now we were shuddering and lifting, despite a load of about 15 men.

To my horror several soldiers were hanging on to the landing skids underneath. The chopper crew pointed guns at them and yelled, and they dropped down at least 20 feet as we rose higher. One of the side-gunners on the helicopter stamped a boot on the hands of one last soldier still clinging to the skids. He screamed and let go, falling at least 50 feet on to the hard surface of the chopper pad.

Within 20 minutes or so we were landing at the Pleiku base. In the usual surreal context of the Vietnam War, within another 20 minutes we were tucking into a hash and ice-cream supper. Afterwards we sat among US helicopter support troops in the tropical darkness. Amid whoops and cheers from the servicemen, half a dozen Vietnamese bar girl dancers appeared on a stage in hot pants and brief tops and gyrated to deafening disco music. We sipped coca-cola as the entertainment switched to a film show, but the screen suddenly went blank. The reality of war had returned. A strident siren warned of a rocket attack on the base. We slumped in a concrete shelter until all was clear, and next day hitched a ride on a C130 transport helicopter back to Saigon to ship the film. I did my best to convey in the script the panicky retreat by elements of the ARVN divisions in Kontum, but without supporting film it had low impact in a TV bulletin.

Conflict was still raging in the central area, so we flew back to Qui Nhon near the coast, intending to fly back to Pleiku. Somewhat to my relief this was not possible. The ARVN, with much-needed reinforcements, were putting up a stiffer battle to save Kontum. It was now besieged, with the NVA cutting the road to Pleiku. The siege was lifted after a fearsome American B-52 air attack smashed down on the NVA forces around Kontum, killing many and aborting their campaign. Thank heavens I was never on the ground when B-52's rained from their bombs from above.

After a brief return to Saigon we flew back to the central area, landing at the Qui Nonh base. Several US TV crews, and Michael Nicholson and his ITN crew were also there.

Suddenly the other crews seemed to have disappeared.

Nicholson and the Americans had managed to find space on an ARVN C 130 chopper flying up to Quang Tri. They were on their way to a major television story.

Quang Tri, capital of the province just below the DMZ border with North Vietnam, was being hammered by Giap's troops attacking from the north. His forces included the famous NVA 308th 'Iron' Division, plus infantry regiments, tanks and artillery.

On 1 May mass panic set in among the ARVN troops defending Quang Tri province and the city itself. The confusion we had filmed at Kontum was magnified into a terrible retreat from Quang Tri in which soldiers, their families and other refugees fled south. About 20,000 civilians were killed.

The taking of Quang Tri by the NVA was a major episode in the Vietnam war, and those TV crews who were there snatched some memorable film of the desperate retreat. There were film shots by cameraman in helicopters of refugees on the ground pleading to be taken on board. As a TV cameraman, and indeed as a reporter, it is useful to operate as if you are simply reporting a drama, not part of it. I could well understand a cameraman in a South American revolution who carried on filming as a soldier aimed a gun at him from close frame and fired. They found the whole sequence in the camera after the TV man had died.

I missed the Quang Tri film story, mainly because more transport north was not forthcoming for some hours, which meant we were likely to miss the story. In the field in Vietnam, TV news crews seldom had access to the wider picture of events, nor could we foretell how each fresh conflict would develop.

Also, I freely admit that having escaped the Kontum attack, I flinched at attempting to film yet another NVA triumph from the losing side. Mistakenly I believed there was a lot more mileage in the Kontum story if we waited awhile, but it proved impossible to return there while besieged.

BBC Newsroom never reproached me. They had excellent coverage from their US partner NBC, and the relentless tide of events in Vietnam soon focused on more developments in the tragedy of America's ambitions to prop up a weak and somewhat corrupt South Vietnamese regime.

We travelled back to Saigon in a US crewed transport helicopter. The pilot asked me: 'How long y'all here in Nam?'

I said we expected to return perhaps in a fortnight.

'If I only had a fortnight to do here I'd go to the nearest shelter and lock myself in until it was time to go home,' he retorted. 'This here is just a killing machine.'

We filmed various stories, including a memorable visit to a Korean unit allied to the South Vietnamese. They were a grim-faced bunch of well-trained troops who were reputedly highly successful in holding and containing the areas around their camp in the Central Highlands.

An officer told me they had hung a Viet Cong prisoner by his feet above a fire, just to give a warning to a village that it was unwise to cooperate with the enemy. No they hadn't burned him; it was just a demonstration, it was explained to me. There was no question of a BBC crew being invited to film this form of anti-insurgency. Compared with the indiscriminate killing of many 'friendlies' by US and ARVN bombing patterns, such activities on the ground, however barbaric they seemed, appeared far more effective, and cost far fewer lives. I felt safer in Korean-held territory than in most other war zones.

In Saigon we filmed what I thought was one of the most poignant stories we sent back, but it was not rated highly in London. Small crowds of severely wounded ex-ARVN soldiers, many in wheelchairs, others hobbling on crutches, staged a desperate protest in the city's streets against their lack of care and financial support by the corrupt elements of the South Vietnamese regime. One or two wheelchair protesters flourished weapons in a vain gesture. The trim, helmeted Saigon police fired tear gas among the demonstrators, and went for some of them with batons. Coughing and spluttering we filmed the story, and I voiced a sympathetic script. No battlefield bang-bangs on this one, and it received little reaction in London

Near Danang we filmed Vietnamese children, swathed in bandages in a burns ward. The smell and the sights were so appalling that we all took a while to recover when we left.

The story-line seemed to me vitally important: these children had been injured by Viet Cong troops who had punished their village for being cooperative with the US and South Vietnamese. VC soldiers ran through the village throwing satchel bombs into dug-out shelters where the children were hiding with their families. Many were killed, and many others were scarred for life, or died slowly from their hideous burns.

I received a cable acknowledging the story, which was shown in a highly edited down version. The message asked us to concentrate in future on battle film. Nowadays I think BBC TV news is much better at recording the attendant miseries of warfare, and I much admire the compassionate news reports I have seen on the dead and dying in the 21st century Middle East conflicts. In my day there was far too much obsession with 'bang bang' battle scenes. From the viewer's point of view one piece of war footage looks much like another. Of course the conflict needs to be covered, but so does the consequent suffering of civilian populations.

In 1975 after I had left the BBC staff, I watched at home the TV footage of the fall of Saigon. I did not feel the slightest regret that I was not sharing the valorous duties of intrepid TV crews covering these momentous events. I noted with approval that most western TV crews left by helicopter before the NVA tanks crashed through the gates of Saigon's Imperial Palace. Some journalists staunchly stayed on to report the final drama, and they deserve admiration. They had no guarantee that they would not suffer the deaths suffered by so many of their profession earlier in the futile tragedy of the Vietnam War. This time they were merely ushered out of the country by the victorious North Vietnamese.

Chapter Eleven

COD AND CHESS WARS

I came away from Cambodia and Vietnam with a deep distrust of helicopter travel. After reporting what should have been a far less hazardous story, the Cod War in Iceland in September 1972, I became equally wary of small aircraft.

Suffering from over-spending its budget as usual, BBC TV News sent me to Reykjavik twice that summer without a film crew. I was to work with an Icelandic stringer cameraman, Gisli Gestsson. He ran his own successful photographic and media business in Reykjavik, and clearly knew everyone of any importance.

Although the prospect of the partnership did not please me, the reality was splendid. We struck up a happy working relationship immediately – and it was entirely through Gisli that we achieved a world-wide scoop in a specialist area of which I was singularly ignorant. It proved to be one of the rare stories which evoked laughter rather than pain.

Apart from a near brush with disaster I enjoyed every minute of my trips to this strange volcanic island where there is 24 hour sun in the summer, and total darkness in winter, where there was a ban on drinking spirits in mid-week, and where extraordinarily beautiful blonde Icelandic girls were likely to invite you to dance with them, rather than waiting to be asked. Virtually no trees, no dogs, and steaming geysers all add to the unique Icelandic scene. Despite representing the media of their Cod War 'enemy' I was treated with great courtesy by the Icelanders. I still recall drinking vodka while sitting in delightful tubs of natural hot mineral water at two o'clock in the morning.

'Get some film of our trawlers at sea,' they said in the Newsroom.

'And while you're there we'd like you to do something about the result of the Fischer-Spassky chess match. We shan't want much on it. There's no need to get technical about the chess.'

This assessment of the story was far from accurate: the 1972 world championship contest between America's Bobby Fischer and Russia's Boris Spassky has since been hailed as the 'Match of the Century'.

I was a tyro chess player, having learned the rudiments of the game at Bournemouth Grammar from a splendid Czech emigre schoolmaster who could play ten boys at once – and win. So I was rather more interested in the Fischer-Spassky contest than the TV News Desk. When I refer to this news desk I do not mean the overall News Editor, or even the Editor of Television news. Unlike a newspaper where you deal directly with the boss, the BBC ran its news desk in my day on a strange system where contact with reporters was maintained by a series of rather faceless individuals who I do not recall meeting when I was actually in the News Room. Unfortunately they sometimes lacked continuity between shifts, so that the succeeding 'man on the desk' sometimes seemed to know very little about the story you had been working on abroad for the previous few days.

The second Cod War broke out that summer when Iceland suddenly expanded its off-shore fishing limits into areas where British trawlers operated. Clearly the seas were being over-fished, and trawling was Iceland's major industry.

Britain huffed and puffed, vowing to go to the International Court of Justice. Meanwhile an Icelandic patrol boat chased foreign trawlers out of the new exclusion zone, and cut the trawling lines of a British fishing vessel. A nice little 'confrontation at sea' story brewed up when the Royal Navy sent some small armed ships to protect our trawlers.

Also staying at the Saga Hotel was David Attenborough, working on a BBC wildlife programme on Iceland's prolific sea bird population. Less expected was Clement Freud, the Liberal MP, broadcasting wit, and gastronomic writer.

We had an entertaining dinner at the Saga, during which Clement was less than enthusiastic about the heavily braised fish on the menu. We shared a keen interest in horse racing on which he was a judicious gambler.

Next morning I accompanied him to Reykjavik's radio station where I sent to London a voice-piece to be used with Gisli's film shots of Iceland patrol boats going out to sea. Then Clement performed a live interview with BBC Radio Four's World at One, anchored by the wonderful Bill Hardcastle.

'So what's the food like?' asked Bill. 'You must be enjoying some wonderful fish meals in Iceland?'

Mr Freud grimaced into the microphone and replied: 'I haven't dared eat very much yet. I saw something dreadful being flambéed in surgical spirit at the next table last night, and I really couldn't face trying it myself. They have wonderful raw materials in fish here, but they haven't yet discovered how to cook it!'

With difficulty I suppressed hoots of laughter during Clement's acerbic interview. When we emerged from the studio we were met by a somewhat distraught Icelandic gentleman who had been despatched from the Tourist Office. They had listened to the interview with horror. Clement courteously persisted in his views on Icelandic cooking, and offered to give them some 'constructive advice'.

The offer did nothing to mend already frayed Icelandic-British relations.

I would have been quite happy to send pseudo learned analysis of Iceland's fishing problems down the line, but the dratted needs of television meant that we had to hire a light aircraft to film British trawlers and Royal Navy escorts far out at sea.

My task was to burble a live commentary to Gisli's film. We shared the cost of a charter with a keen American newspaperman who seemed to have an enormous budget.

The weather closed down as we passed the wild coastline on the far side of Iceland from Reykjavik, so the pilot obligingly flew as low as possible over the tossing waves, rather too low I felt. As a devout coward who firmly wished to return from every story in one piece I did not want any heroics over a story about the price of fish. There were several vessels below plunging about on the waves which Gisli assured me were British trawlers, and their escort, plus a watching Icelandic gunboat. I could see very little through the haze. We circled over the ships interminably as Gisli performed re-takes, and I chattered away into the microphone, hoping I was making some sense of a situation I could barely discern.

There seemed to be no confrontation between the two sides in the rather pathetic Cod War, and I was quite keen to fly back to test the Saga Hotel's dinner menu again.

Alas, the zealous Yank journalist kept requesting that we fly further out just to see if he could spot some sign of the Cod War in action.

At last the pilot turned towards land, and I was pleased to see the sandy coastline below. Suddenly everything went pear shaped.

'We are running out of fuel,' the pilot croaked on his intercom to us. 'There's no problem. I will put down on the beach, and we'll get some more fuel.'

No problem? I was seething with alarm. We were breaking the cardinal rule of good journalism: you should report the story, not *be* the story. Not for the first time I wondered how many minutes they would devote on the bulletin to my unfortunate demise.

We passengers stayed remarkably cool, although for me it was more a case of being stunned. I heard a nasty buzzing sound. Gisli calmly informed me it was the 'stalling buzzer', indicating the engine was in danger of stopping as we swung low over the beach.

'Oh really?' I said faintly.

The plane landed on the sand, rolled a remarkably short distance and then stopped abruptly. I leapt out of the tiny cabin to find myself surrounded by seals and large sea lions who flapped their flippers only a short distance away before gazing at us in wonderment, although they appeared totally relaxed about our arrival.

Ahead of the plane I saw a huge hole in the sand. If we had rolled forward just a few more yards the aircraft would have somersaulted into it. Fortunately I was not in a mood to analyse the situation, but overwhelmed with joy at having survived a ridiculous crash.

'Thank God, ' I shouted, hardy noticing that heavy rain was sheeting down, drenching my blazer and flannels. We trudged through the downpour over the sand to a narrow road bordering the beach.

After only a few minutes I heard the blissful sound of an approaching vehicle.

'Thank God! ' I shouted again. As a large van approached I thumbed it down confidently. Then I stood aghast as the van driver totally ignored me, drenching me in a cloud of spray as it swept past. Traditional Icelandic hospitality seemed scarce this side of the island.

Wet through, we trudged for about 40 minutes along the road, with no sign of another vehicle, until we entered a small village of modest wooden buildings, reminding me of the Yukon in Charlie Chaplin's 'Gold Rush'.

With relief we entered the village bar where a group of highly relaxed local workmen were smoking and drinking whiskies. Yes, there was a hire car in the village which could drive us back to Reykjavik.

How long would it take? About a 12 hour drive they said.

We tucked into a fish snack, and despite being wet through I slept through the long, wearisome drive back to the capital, arriving in the early hours.

From my hotel room next morning I phoned the News Desk at BBC TV Centre, where someone I did not know heard my breathless account, and merely responded: 'Is the film OK?'

I rang off, and waited for him to phone me back. This time he said they had been 'a bit worried' because there had been a report from Reykjavik that our plane had lost contact, and they were hoping for more news soon! I had been unable to get a call through to home, and the News Room genius promised to ring my wife 'just in case there was any worry'. You had to give him top marks for keeping calm in the face of a reporter's little problems out there in the real world.

My film was transmitted for about five minutes on the main bulletin without reference to the reporter having nearly been killed obtaining the story, all part of the stoic tradition of sub-editors everywhere.

*****

After the near drama of the Cod War, my reporting of the Fischer-Spassky chess match finale proved to be pure farce. Fischer had already created a legend through his eccentric antics during the earlier stages of the contest, beginning on 11 July. He complained about his seat, and failed to appear at various sessions, leaving Spassky to judge his next move while facing an empty seat.

There has been much debate as to whether Fischer was merely an unstable eccentric, or someone with an eye on the main chance. Before the match began he had failed to show up several times in Reykjavik, prompting a wealthy British chess fanatic to donate an extra $125,000 to the prize money, bringing the winner's share up to $156,250. This did produce the great man's appearance in Iceland, but he was still playing hard-to-get before he boarded a plane.

I was among the press and TV crews awaiting his arrival in Reykjavik.

Everyone else had walked down the steps from the aircraft, except Fischer. We waited impatiently, and then suddenly a tall young man hurtled down the steps, rushed past us and jumped into a large black saloon car which accelerated away immediately. Somehow Fischer had completed his passport facilities on the plane, to make his whirlwind arrival. It was a taste of things to come. Most reporters and cameramen were furious; some had failed to get a picture. I found it highly amusing. Good old Gisli had snatched a shot of Fischer in his whirlwind exit, and I added a somewhat sardonic voice commentary.

Fischer's erratic gamesmanship during the match was obviously meant to be a major problem for Spassky who seemed a far more balanced and attractive character.

The game was adjourned on 31 August after 40 moves, and Spassky resigned next day. The chess pundits began to write their intricate academic analysis of the match of the century. Fortunately I had not been required to provide running reports on the contest, which was far beyond my expertise.

After Fischer's victory was announced, the press and massed ranks of TV crews churned about like hungry cattle, seeking the all-important interview with the American winner. Fischer firmly adhered to his Greta Garbo 'I want to be alone' stance. There is no better way of heating up press interest to boiling point.

The great man stayed in his locked Reykjavik hotel room with a couple of local minders guarding the door. Someone in the frustrated press contingent suggested shoving some dollars under the door, which earned a wry laugh before they were shooed away from the bedroom area.

The combined media could only wait in the hotel lobby downstairs in the hope of nobbling the new world chess champion, although we feared he had already done a deal with some mega-media organisation. Perhaps he would shin down a drainpipe to avoid us.

Gisli wandered away from the mob for a while, and when he returned he indicated quietly that I should follow him. Rather nervously I left the stake-out, but in a side-room Gisli whispered: 'Just follow me. My cousin is one of Fischer's bodyguards. He's fixed it that we can get a two minute interview with Fischer in his room.'

Gisli led me up some back stairs to an upstairs corridor. He had a key which opened a bedroom door several rooms away from the chess player's door where the guards were standing.

To my increasing delight, Gisli had another key which unlocked the connecting doors into adjoining rooms. The last one gave us entry into the chess supremo's bedroom.

Tall and gangly, Fischer lurched to his feet from an armchair. His long bony face bore a distrustful frown.

'I give you guys just two minutes – and two minutes only, ' was his welcome in his New York Bronx accent.

'Absolutely. And may I congratulate you on your triumph, ' I beamed.

The Yank just scowled. So I proceeded to goad him by talking about money rather than chess. It worked like a charm.

The interview started thus:

CLAYTON: 'Do you think that in trying to get better facilities you've been instrumental in getting a record purse for this sort of thing? Has it purely been personal gain, or has it been to upgrade the whole game of chess as far as you're concerned?'

FISCHER blinked rapidly, and the words poured out: 'Basically to upgrade the game, you know.....and make it, you know. If I were interested in personal gain I wouldn't just be taking up chess.'

CLAYTON: 'You'd try your brain at something else would you?'

FISCHER: 'Yeah, I'd be in the stock market or something. That's where the personal gains at.'

CLAYTON: 'What are you going to do now?'

FISCHER: 'I'll keep playing a lot of chess.'

CLAYTON: ' Yes, quite...but what's your next target? Do you think there'll be a return game soon with Spassky for example?'

FISCHER: 'Definitely. I wanna play a return match. It's a question of money A, and B it's a question whether the Russians will let Spassky play; and C, I guess, does he want to play me?'

CLAYTON: 'The big addition to the purse...the fifty thousand pounds came from London, from an Englishman. Is it likely you'd consider playing the return match in England?'

FISCHER: Ah, it's a possibility. I mean, I wouldn't close the door to any place.'

CLAYTON: 'It doesn't worry you particularly where it is?'

FISCHER: 'I think the States would be a good place for the next match, because that's where they've got the facilities for TV, and you can do it right without creating a fuss.'

CLAYTON: 'How do you rate Spassky now? I mean what are your chances of holding on again in a return match with Spassky?'
FISCHER: 'Oh, I think I'd beat him much more easily. There's no question in my mind.'
CLAYTON: 'This is really because?'
FISCHER: 'I've broken him.'
CLAYTON: 'This is what you really set out to do isn't it?'
FISCHER: 'Yeah…yeah.'
CLAYTON: 'How would you rate him compared with other players you've played against?'
FISCHER: 'The best definitely. He gave me a real fight. All the other players I've played, they crumbled at a certain stage you know…and I never felt this with Spassky.'

Fischer was now warmed up, talking readily. The rest of the interview went like a dream. He talked compulsively, and even waited while Gisli changed rolls of film. I left with a warm handshake from the world champion – and about an hour of filmed interview.'
   We crept out of the hotel by the backstairs, leaving the world's press still waiting in the lobby. As an ignoble hack I felt extreme pleasure that the waiting throng included an ITN crew.
   We shipped the film by air safely to London where next day they used a great chunk on the news bulletins. The BBC's own late night TV chess programme played the whole thing. Although I was unqualified to ask technical questions, Fischer had given me a blow by blow account of his tactics throughout the match.
   They never told me how much money they raked in, but I believe the BBC made a killing on syndicating the full length interview worldwide, especially in the States.
   On our way to Reykjavik airport I suggested we called on Spassky who was living in a rented house en route. To my amazement Spassky answered the door himself, and courteously gave me a short TV interview on the doorstep, praising his opponent, and conceding defeat. What a nice man – but sadly a loser on this occasion who was treated disgracefully when he returned to Russia. There were reports

that he lost his State-provided flat, and his car, and had to queue up for a bus-ride into Moscow from the airport.

With breath-taking stupidity the BBC News Desk proceeded to snatch defeat from the jaws of victory. Next evening the Icelanders held a celebratory banquet, surprisingly attended by Fischer, and Spassky came too. It was a colourful occasion: the male waiters wore plastic helmets with horns in mythical Nordic style. The food was unremarkable as usual, but the hard drink flowed in torrents, poured by gorgeous Icelandic blondes.

After dinner the two great players produced a small chess board, placed it on the dining table, and chatted genially about their historic match, illustrating some of the moves. It was marvellous television – and ITN had it exclusively for the UK.

The organisers had asked for a paltry £200 fee from each TV crew filming the banquet. I relayed this to the News Desk, and some twerp said 'we' had already had a scoop, and it was decided we were not paying a penny. We had already gained an exclusive, and there were only a few crumbs left. I did not argue – some of my colleagues would have done – but I attended the banquet without Gisli and his cine-camera. He was now filming for a charming blonde Argentinian lady reporter who had turned up late, and needed a cameraman.

Years later I reminded Gisli of this, and he said wryly: 'The only trouble was the Argentinian TV company never paid me.'

A News Desk functionary back home apologised to me briefly on the phone after ITN transmitted a splendid news film of the chess banquet.

There were more developments pending in the Cod War story which needed my reluctant attention, but London phoned urgently to order me to fly immediately to Munich.

The Black September faction of the Palestine Liberation Organisation had taken hostage the Israeli team at the Munich Olympics on 5 September. I was about to miss one of the major stories of the 20th century: all aircraft flights into Munich were halted while the terrible drama unfolded in which hostages and terrorists were killed. There was no chance I could get to Munich from Iceland. The Olympic tragedy was more than adequately covered by sports reporters and camera teams already on the scene.

Meanwhile I was ordered to 'do nothing' until further instructions from London. I enjoyed an exceedingly pleasant short holiday during which I studied wildlife and inspected Iceland's unique breed of small horse which became the subject of several articles I wrote on returning home.

Perhaps I was not really so dedicated to reporting death and destruction news stories as I had been? I was enjoying being alive, with time to think.

Chapter Twelve

DEPORTED
FROM DACCA

Being a TV News 'fireman' seemed a wonderful way of seeing the world, but the major drawback was that you saw events at their worst. It was like visiting a wonderful city, but only inspecting the sewers. Most 'good news' stories can be safely left to the local staff reporters or stringers. But as catastrophe erupts in come the TV firemen.

When it came to suffering, the events I witnessed and attempted to report in the former East Pakistan in early 1971, reached the depths. Those in the Western nations who care about genocide in 'far off places' should have seen an in-depth film report. We failed to provide it, but we had a cast iron excuse.

As usual I was unaware of the full extent of horrors to come, as our crowded Pakistan Airlines plane trundled from Singapore down to Dacca (restyled as Dhaka since 1982).

I brooded that we were likely to experience something particularly dreadful as I read the press cuttings on East Pakistan's increasingly robust attempts to gain independence from the chains of West Pakistan, sited on the far side of India in accordance with the lunatic borders created by the British on giving independence to India and Pakistan after the war. I chewed mournfully on the very basic buffet then provided on this flight: an unpeeled orange, one roll and a soft drink of mysterious origins.

My fears were confirmed as soon as we landed at Dacca. Most of the airport staff was on strike in protest against the regime, and chaos reigned. We carried our own cases and camera kit from the runway to the third world arrivals building. The crew miraculously commandeered a small trolley for the heavy camera and its cumbersome wooden tripod.

Peter Mathews as cameraman, and Bill Norman as sound recordist, were assigned to work with me, which was an enormous relief. They were reassuring companions: exceedingly professional and calm.

A large impassive Pakistan Army officer from the West, equipped with a gun holster, checked our passports amid a deafening noise of shouts and chatter from hundreds of East Pakistanis. They were outside the arrivals building, pressed against the iron grilled gates of the arrivals building, thrusting arms through the gate and yelling at the arriving passengers.

Official airport transport was off the road in the strike. The shouting hordes were workers from Bihar or West Pakistan, urgently seeking to get out of the country before East Pakistan achieved independence, and old scores were settled against 'outsiders'. The rest of the crowd were drivers of taxis, decrepit cars and buggies, and rickshaws. They all desperately wanted our custom.

This was one of the poorest countries on the planet, and every coin that could be scrounged from people rich enough to travel by air was vital to the survival of somebody's family. A soldier eased the gates open a little, and we squeezed through into the midst of the scrum, a blend of noise and pungent smells.

Somehow we fell into the least awful taxi we could find, despite scores of beseeching hands pulling us towards other vehicles. We chugged off to Dacca's Intercontinental Hotel, a name which seemed a bad omen after my experiences in Amman and Belfast.

Michael Nicholson and his crew were at the hotel. Their presence was one of the main reasons we had been dispatched from London.

ITN had been transmitting excellent reports from Michael on the aftermath of the appalling cyclone which had hit the coastal areas of East Pakistan the previous November. Thousands had died, and many people were still dependent on the aid organisations for subsistence. The Pakistan government dominated by West Pakistan was accused of mishandling the relief programme, causing more unrest in Dacca.

'We've really done the flood story,' Nicholson told me confidently when we met in the bar. 'Today's strike is nothing much; they happen all the time. The Army has got things buttoned up here. It's all over.' For once the distinguished foreign correspondent for ITN had got it wrong.

Nicholson and his team pulled out next day, leaving Clayton and crew to film the 'left-overs' for BBC TV who once again appeared to have arrived 'too late'. I was not convinced about this, remembering ITN had pulled out of Amman just before the great aircraft hijack story 18 months previously. There was still a group of over 40 international press men in the hotel, including some old friends. They seemed to think the story was far from over. Continued unrest in Dacca still seemed worth reporting, and we sent daily film stories back to London. Poor Bill had his wallet stolen during a crowded street protest meeting, but otherwise it seemed reasonably safe compared with reporting in Vietnam.

Tyres were burnt by random groups of independence protesters in Dacca's streets; temporary road blocks were set up by the rebelling East Pakistanis. They waved black flags and shouted 'Bangla Desh', the State of Bengal, and 'Joi Bangla', victory for Bengal. They seemed to have persuaded themselves their battle for independence was virtually won. Opposition to the West Pakistan-dominated government was divided into complicated factions, but the most charismatic leader was Sheikh Mujib, President of the major opposition party, the Awami League.

A benign, likeable personality, dressed simply in the loose fitting collarless white shirt and trousers of his people, Sheik Mujib would stroll onto his front lawn in a Dacca suburb to chat with his followers and the world's press. He was a smiling, pipe-smoking man, much given to parrying hard questioning with disarming little jokes, or an offer of a cup of tea. He did not seem to me to be a hard-line revolutionary, and I never heard him preach a policy of violence – just non-cooperation and verbal protest. I doubt that he comprehended just how ruthless the Pakistan military regime was prepared to be in cracking down.

I reported symptoms of increasing violence by the Army when we drove into a forbidden area outside Dacca, where a curfew was in force. We filmed villagers mourning round the body of a man killed by bullets they alleged had been fired by the Army. They claimed over a dozen protesters had been killed by soldiers. Writing off the regime as having already conceded independence was a delusion. I was surprised that ITN did not wing its way back into Dacca after my reports of rising tension were transmitted in London, but apparently when Michael Nicholson got to Bangkok en route back to Dacca, he found all civilian flights were barred. PIA planes had been commandeered for large groups of Army reinforcements from West Pakistan who were flying to Dacca for the Operation Searchlight, the massacre about to be unleashed on a virtually defenceless civilian population.

Despite his air of calm, Mujib was taking huge risks with his own life, and many others, when he launched a campaign of non-cooperation with the government. It was making the province almost impossible to govern, and Dacca was becoming increasingly tense as people awaited reprisals from the West Pakistan-dominated regime.

The room maid in my hotel one evening came in to turn the bed, then sobbed and fell on her knees, clutched my legs and begged: 'Please sir, please take me away from here. Something very bad is coming. Very bad.'

She was unable to explain exactly what was on the way, but I patted her on the shoulder, gave her a tip, and explained that I couldn't even get myself away from this benighted country while trouble boiled up.

Nor was the relief story finished. We travelled in helicopters to far-flung areas where there was still suffering caused by the cyclone. We filmed villagers scrambling for bags of rice thrown from the helicopter. When we landed at small settlements I was amazed to see that many people near the coast were living in structures like small ridge tents, although instead of canvas, their shelter was palm leaves draped over the frame. Yet they were remarkably cheerful in adversity, and there was always someone who spoke English eloquently who would say something to camera.

I soon grew to like most East Pakistanis very much indeed. These slim wiry people have amazing vitality, and an ability to survive despite terrible pressures from their hazardous environment by the treacherous Bay of Bengal. In 1971 they were showing remarkable courage in resisting the repressive policies of the government headed by the hard-line Yahya Khan government based in West Pakistan. The West Pakistan military were usually large, moustachioed military men reared on wheat in the west of the country, while the smaller East Pakistanis rely on a staple rice diet. Most East Pakistanis were friendly, and especially welcoming to a BBC TV crew who could relay their country's travails to the world, thereby stimulating aid. They were accustomed to heavy flooding surging in from the Bay of Bengal, but the latest cyclone had been far worse than usual.

Many East Pakistanis were living in refugee camps on the Indian border where they had fled the flood devastated areas.

At the Intercontinental Hotel I met the ill-fated Pakistani politician, Zulfikar Ali Bhutto, a member of the country's elite, and chairman of the opposition Pakistan People's Party. He was attending talks between the Pakistan President, Yahya Khan and Sheikh Mujib.

I tried hard to achieve an interview with Yahya Khan but this was firmly refused. There was no problem in getting the charismatic Bhutto to talk. Educated in the US and at Oxford University, Bhutto was highly fluent and willing to talk endlessly to the media. He opposed the break-up of Pakistan, but he urged a conciliatory approach in dealings with the East Pakistanis.

He believed talks could be held indefinitely, and there was ample scope for easing military restraints on the eastern provinces. His policy was irrelevant to the tragedy unfolding.

Sheik Mujib demanded a complete transfer of power to East Pakistan. Yahya Khan and his military colleagues refused; talks broke down, and the President flew back to West Pakistan. More violent clashes were breaking out between East Pakistanis and the military. The government was losing control of many areas of the country. What would Yahya Khan do next?

The answer came in the evening of 26 March. We were among pressmen in the bar when we heard gunfire. Later as I flew out of Pakistan, I scribbled the following notes on the drama in the present tense, using a ballpoint pen on scrap paper. It was the only record I could achieve, for reasons I will explain below.

11pm First sounds of gunfire. Tanks rumble through the streets, also troops in jeeps. Soldiers increase the guard outside our hotel. From the lobby we see them burning the Bangla Desh flag, and a black protest flag which had been flying defiantly throughout Dacca. Front door of the hotel now barred by soldiers; guests refused permission to leave. We make our way to the top floor where Peter Mathews does his best to record the scene below on camera, and we record gunfire while I perform commentary.

Midnight-3am Firing increases; they're using recoilless rifles which make great thumps; plus automatic fire. Sheikh Mujib's press officer makes breathless statement to journalists, deploring the use of violence by the military regime.

2-3.30am: Awami League supporters are trying to erect protest road blocks, but the Army are firing at all these make-shift barriers. Outside the hotel in Minto Road two old cars are blocking the highway, and troops are pouring automatic fire into them. Troops are now firing at local people trying to take refuge in an alley by the hotel. Flashes reveal some huddled bodies in the alley.

Now the soldiers are shouting at people living behind a garage, shops and the offices of The People, an Awami League newspaper.

The soldiers are shouting: 'Come out and surrender – or we will shoot you down.' We cannot see anyone coming out in response. Now the soldiers are setting fire to the garage and offices; there are explosions and tongues of fire from fuel in the garage. Troops are deliberately setting fire to the paper storage shed and printing works by the newspaper office. Other soldiers are firing up and down to the road to make sure everyone takes cover indoors. Soldiers are shining torches at our windows in the hotel, but they have not opened fire on us.

3am We can see a very large fire in the University's Hall of Residence, some blocks away.

There's a rattle of small arms and thud of artillery or tank guns. Gunfire seems heavy in the residential area where Sheikh Mujib lives – and there is more gunfire in the Old City of Dacca. [Later it was reported that the Army was shooting students as they ran out of their burning rooms. The University was seen by the authorities as a hotbed of resistance to the regime, but there was no indication of students being able to mount an armed response to this night-time attack.]

4am Firing largely dying down, but troops on guard still outside the hotel. Tanks rumble past, with soldiers sitting on them, some shouting 'Allahu Akbar'! ('God is greater', a Moslem cry of victory.) Now jeeps are going past, some equipped with loudspeakers blaring warnings to the people.

8am Snatched a couple of hours sleep but I go to the front lobby with other journalists. We surge forward as Mr Bhutto, stony faced, leaves the hotel with an armed escort. For the first time he refuses to talk to us, and we are barred from following him.

9am-4pm Troops are now putting up the Pakistan national flag outside the hotel. No sign of any black flags in the street now. A spruce Army officer appears in the lobby to inform us: 'Everything is under control now', but says little else except that we are confined to the hotel as the city is now under martial law.

Several reporters who step outside the front doors are told by an Army officer: 'Go back. We can shoot our own people if they come on to the streets – and we can shoot you!'

No room service in the hotel for which the manager apologises profusely, but meals are being served in the restaurant. We can see two very large fires in the Old city where the poorest people live. There are palls of black smoke drifting over the buildings there. The local radio is announcing martial law, with a ban on meetings of more than five people. Government workers are ordered back to work immediately – or face dismissal and a court martial.

5.45pm All pressmen are summoned to the hotel lounge, where an officer announcing himself as Major Salek appears in a crisply ironed uniform. He smiles and announces: 'Gentlemen, in the current state of emergency in Dacca, you are all ordered to leave the country. Please pack immediately and be ready to board our transport at the front door at 6.15 promptly.'

To his everlasting credit Simon Dring of the *Daily Telegraph* disobeyed the military order. He went up to the roof of the hotel, and remained hidden there while the rest of us were herded into open Army trucks in the street outside. Simon's despatches some days later gave the first detailed eye-witness account of the extent of the massacre in Dacca. Wearing Pakistani native dress he toured the city after the shooting stopped, and the guard on the hotel had been lifted.

As a highly visible TV crew with cumbersome equipment we had no hope of remaining, and l looked forward to getting out of the country to tell the story to the world. It was a far bigger crackdown than we yet knew; it caused the death of up to three million civilians, many in the genocide wrought by the military, and many others among huge files of starving people trudging out of the country into India's neighbouring state of Bengal for months to come.

Armed troops escort us on to several open Army trucks, and sit on guard with their rifles pointing inwards at us. We are ordered not to leave the trucks as they speed briskly along the road to the airport.

We can see a big red glow and smoke over the Old City, and several near-demolished road blocks. Shanty houses and small shops are still burning, and more buildings are on fire on the perimeter of the airfield.

6.40pm At the airport a special search operation has been mounted for us in a hut. Military officers are sitting behind trestle tables. They call forward 'the BBC men' for special attention, demanding we hand over every can of exposed film, and sound tapes. Peter and Bill shuffle about, and hand over various tins, but retain some, claiming they are unexposed film.

When I protest, a Pakistan Airforce Squadron Leader shouts angrily in my face: 'We aren't having any more lies from the BBC!'

An Army officer is more courteous and says soothingly: 'It's all in the game. You would have done the same thing if you had the same problem in your country. We had no other choice. Things will be better soon.'

[I quoted this remark in a lengthy radio report I recorded later for 'From Our Own Correspondent' on BBC Radio 4, adding that this judgement was delivered on 'the solution of burning and killing which the military regime was at that moment applying in Dacca.']

As well as our film, the Army search party at the office confiscates my treasured portable typewriter (a 21st birthday present from my mother), also typewriters from correspondents representing AFP and a Japanese newspaper.

8pm We sit in the stifling heat of the airport lounge, still without a drink or anything to eat, listening to a radio broadcast by Pakistan's President Yahya Khan. It seems to be a tirade of threats against 'rebels' in East Pakistan.

4am We are herded on to a PIA plane bound for Karachi, accompanied by armed Army guards. The air crew are clearly embarrassed at having to carry out a mass deportation of correspondents from all over the world. At least we get something to eat and drink and some sleep.

7am The plane lands at Colombo, Ceylon, for re-fuelling. Several American correspondents, including Sid Shanberg for the *New York Times*, demand asylum in Ceylon. [Shanberg became world famous from 1975 after he was deported from Cambodia by the Khmer Rouge, leaving behind his Cambodian assistant. The story was recounted in the film 'The Killing Fields'] Shanberg is aggressively insistent (I don't blame him), and there is something of a diplomatic

186

incident. We are herded into a small, bare airport building by our Army guards. Several reporters seek to use a telephone on a wall at the back. Whether they actually make calls I do not know, but there is more shouting and pushing from the guards, and we are rushed back on to the aircraft. The aircraft captain apologises on the intercom for 'inconvenience' to passengers.

12.15pm We arrive in Karachi but are not allowed to disembark for one hour. They are setting up another special search process by the military. Our arrival has been much delayed by the protest in Colombo.

Senior immigration officials and Army officers are waiting for us in a reception hut. One officer barks at me: 'From the BBC? That's very unfortunate for you. We have been listening to more lies on BBC World Service!' He adds theatrically: 'Did you report that the Indians took Lahore in 1965? I think not!'

I shrug, which seems to annoy him even more.

[It was not the first time I had encountered anger from officials in various parts of the world because the good old World Service has been broadcasting the truth. It always made me proud to be representing Auntie BBC at her best.]

Reporters are asking to see their consuls in Karachi. I demand to see members of the British consulate – and remind the officials that Pakistan is a member of the Commonwealth, and therefore has signed up to codes of conduct with all other members. This sort of bluster cuts no ice at all. The Pakistan officers are becoming testier.

This time the searchers take all my note books and written documents, even an innocuous guide book to East Pakistan. Two officers actually smile when they note that I have amended the title of the book 'Living in Dacca' to 'Existing in Dacca'.

We are hustled by soldiers into small windowless rooms where security officers in starched uniforms sat behind desks. They are belligerent and forceful. All our film cans, including those with unused film, are confiscated despite my loud protests. I stress that Pakistan was violating its position as a Commonwealth partner in daring to interfere with the lawful activities of the British Broadcasting Corporation.

The above protest in my contemporaneous report sounded a bit pompous, but I thought it was worth a try. The security officers took absolutely no notice. When I demanded to see a member of the British High Commission they shrugged.

They went through my own case, and took away all written material, including a tourist booklet on East Pakistan. Then they ushered me to a cubicle where two soldiers told me strip. When I refused, they punched me quite hard in the ribs, and promised more.

Sure enough they soon found the tin of sound tape which I had taped to my chest in the hope that we would be able to broadcast an on-the-spot radio report, with gunfire background, I had recorded in Dacca.

'Never mind,' I told a mustachioed security officer wearing heavy horn-rimmed glasses, 'I still have it all in my head and through the BBC we shall tell the world what you have been up to in Dacca.'

He scowled and threatened: 'We can soon knock that out of your head.'

At that point I considered the prospect of indefinite detention in a Pakistani jail where I would be beaten up regularly. The best course now was sheer hypocrisy: I apologized deeply for making such a fuss. After all, you chaps were only doing your job etc. etc...

Someone must have informed the British consular offices in Karachi, because a somewhat languid young Englishman in a smart panama hat arrived just as we were allowed to leave the search area.

'Can't you demand the return of our film?' I asked. He shrugged and said: 'They've declared a state of emergency. There's nothing I can do at the moment. Where are you going to stay?'

I assured him my plan was to fly back to London on the next available plane to broadcast the story immediately.

'I should keep that quiet until you get away from here,' he advised.

Peter and Bob and I booked first-class tickets on a Scandinavian Airways plane to London, using the BBC's premise that crews directly leaving a war zone could upgrade for their journey home.

After nearly 48 hours without sleep and little food, we wallowed in luxury provided by beautiful blonde Swedish stewardesses.

I was picked up at London airport to be taken to TV Centre where I assembled a fairly dramatic eye-witness studio report of the Dacca atrocity, backed with maps and a few agency stills pictures. It went out on both main bulletins that night, and I sent a more expansive radio piece down the line to Broadcasting House for insertion in the home and overseas news services.

It was a huge disappointment not to have film to show, but I reflected that the dear old Beeb did have the muscle to ensure that my radio reports had worldwide currency, far beyond the circulation of any newspaper.

I wanted to write an in-depth report on my East Pakistan trip, and was able to do so for Radio 4's 'From Our Own Correspondent'. No-one at BBC Television Centre even mentioned my latest voluntary foray into good old sound radio.

Yet again, my first night's sleep at home was interrupted by a long distance call from the BBC's partner, NBC. I gave them a live interview on the situation in Dacca, and soon afterwards Mr Lester M. Crystal their European Producer for NBC Nightly News sent me an appreciative letter: 'Dear Michael, The feed of the Dacca material was very well received in New York. The show was especially pleased with the personal involvement you provided.

'Needless to say, it was a pleasure working with you. Thanks again.'

That was considerably better than any plaudits I received at BBC TV Centre on my return. Mild regret was expressed at the absence of our film, and I was given a week off before returning to the daily grind of domestic news – but not for long. Ali Bhutto became President of Pakistan in December 1971, after the collapse of the Yhaya Khan regime.

In the spring of the following year, the BBC was invited to send a correspondent to accompany Bhutto on a tour of the new Pakistan formed after the secession of East Pakistan to become Bangladesh. Bhutto at close quarters was just as impressive as he was in his public role, fully appreciating the value of good publicity worldwide. He was very cooperative with the media. He faced a mammoth task in seeking to reform Pakistan's history of dictatorial rule. Sadly there were dark forces in reactionary political circles, with the backing of the military, working against him from the start, and ill fate dogged his family after his own removal from power and execution in 1979 on trumped-up charges. His beautiful and talented daughter, Benazir Bhutto would serve as Pakistan's Prime Minister from 1988-90 and 1993-96, only to suffer assassination in 2007 when seeking to regain power. She was the first female head of a democratic Muslim country.

I was received most cordially at Karachi Airport by the same officials who had given me a rough send-off. Amazingly they had kept on file my notebooks and other documents, and these were returned intact. Bhutto himself was warmly cooperative, giving me an exclusive interview, and allowing me and my TV crew to travel on the presidential aircraft from Karachi to the capital, Islamabad, and then on to major centres, including Lahore near the border with India. We stayed with a Pakistan Army unit whose officers were mostly Sandhurst-trained. In their mess they invited me to sample a cup of tea, or 'special tea'. I opted for the latter: an amber liquid poured from a teapot, which proved to be neat whisky. It was reserved only for non-Muslim visitors, I was assured.

The level of affable cooperation from the Army fell short of giving me permission to visit the Indian border to see the aftermath of the conflict with India. This would have been the most newsworthy TV report during my visit, so the BBC in London advised me to come home.

MISERY IN CALCUTTA

I had already seen the devastating effect of the East Pakistan revolt, and the brutal response of Yhaya Khan's regime.

Thousands of refugees were flooding from East Pakistan across the border into West Bengal in India.

A large Indian army force was massing on the East Pakistan border, and ever-present hostilities on the West Pakistan border were hotting up between both countries. What a mess of misery Britain had bequeathed when she abandoned her Indian Empire. The lunacy of dividing Pakistan into two wings either side of India was never more stark than in the early 1970s.

The BBC had news and Panorama teams in Calcutta covering the growing crisis of refugees surging in from East Pakistan in the spring of 1972. Unfortunately the BBC TV News team had succumbed to a severe local eye infection and were unable to operate. ITN was running away with the story again.

At very short notice, as always, I was 'asked' to fly to Calcutta immediately. So urgent was my departure that someone in the News Room pulled a lot of strings to halt a British Airways plane while it was taxiing from its berth to the runway at Heathrow. Steps were hastily installed as your correspondent made a lone entry. Some passengers stood up in the aisles to get a view of this man who had delayed their take-off.

They returned to their seats, no doubt unimpressed, after being told by the stewardesses it was 'just someone from the BBC in a hurry'.

I was upgraded to first class and had the closest attention from the stewardesses. As we neared Calcutta the reason became clear. The Chief Steward came up to inform me that I would be the only passenger leaving the plane.

There was an outbreak of typhoid in the city, and no passengers would be taken on.

'Do take care,' cooed the stewardesses as, in shimmering heat, I made my lonely way down the front steps from the aircraft parked in an isolated bay well clear of Calcutta Airport's reception buildings, in those days an array of wooden huts. I could see other passengers chattering and pointing at me from the aircraft portholes.

Clutching a very small case and battered typewriter I entered an arrivals building empty of other incoming passengers, but there were several Indian women customs and immigration staff in gorgeous saris sitting behind desks. With flashing smiles and the good humour so typical of India, they gave me a warm welcome. Yes, they assured me, the BBC was always welcome in Calcutta, and they hoped I would enjoy my stay. Considering the misery I was about to report this was public relations of the highest order.

The reassurance of the welcome was somewhat blunted when one exotic lady official took me to one side and advised me to be 'very careful' travelling into the City. Groups of Naxalites, extreme left-wing agitators, were sometimes holding up airport buses on the airport road to rob the occupants, she advised.

'Make sure you take a really good fast taxi', she said cheerfully.

I slumped into a large battered American saloon from a huge range of taxis desperate for business outside the airport. It was driven blithely by a cheerful young man, and we arrived at the front door of the Grand Hotel in Calcutta without incident.

The Grand Hotel, by the Maiden, Calcutta's open grass parkland, was still an imposing reminder of Imperial India. I was given a spacious room off a balconied corridor looking down on to a central open courtyard which included a swimming pool and restaurants. Some of Fleet Street's finest were lying round the pool.

My needs in the room were served by a battery of staff, headed by a bearded and turbaned 'bearer'. Others performed the more menial tasks, with the lowest ranking cleaning the bathroom to gleaming cleanliness. Their keenness to serve, and their cheerful demeanor, was a delightful change from the somewhat drab London of the 1970s.

The caste system was officially banned, but the strict graduation of jobs in the service area reflected more than an echo of centuries old practice.

My window on the external side of the hotel looked down on a corrugated iron bicycle shed, manned by at least 20 men. Several slept inside the shed at nights; others slept on the roof, and all were engaged in a carefully graduated series of tasks from accepting tips from those leaving their bicycles under cover, to others who cleaned or repaired the bikes. In a city where hundreds of destitute families slept literally in the gutters each night, the possession of even the most meagre occupation that might produce a few rupees, was of desperate importance.

The contrast between the luxurious standard of living of the Grand Hotel's guests, and the teeming poor outside, was heavily reinforced as soon as you left the front door. On the pavement outside crowds of beggars clamoured for alms. The most distressing of all were children who had grotesquely misshapen limbs which they thrust at you while rattling tins waiting for your coins. It was routinely accepted that some of these crippled children had been deliberately maimed at an early age to ensure they would make effective beggars.

India had only been declared an independent republic 21 years earlier. Modern India of industrial growth, and a larger middle class, was still way ahead.

Calcutta, the hub of Eastern India, into which I was plunged was rightly described in my guide-book as a 'bustling, overcrowded but intensely vital city, India's largest.' Although I had seen plenty of poverty and degradation in the Middle East and South East Asia, the sheer size of the destitution in Calcutta was a severe shock. Sadly, it was amazing how quickly one joined the ranks of those who accepted the beggars as part of the inevitable Indian street scene, and pass it by with the same outward indifference of so many Indians higher up the scale. Many of those who visit India as tourists become remarkably inured to the endemic poverty and begging. It is one feature of a vast, remarkable country with a history and a diversity which I only tasted. One of my regrets is that I did not explore India thoroughly; I can well understand how many Britons have become so deeply attached to the country.

Despite the poverty all too easy to discern in Calcutta, I was soon engulfed in a far greater volume of misery and distress in the East Pakistan refugee story I had come to report. It was profoundly affecting, and has remained with me vividly ever since.

All was not well with the BBC contingent staying at the Grand. One reporter was still confined to his room, suffering from one of Calcutta's devastating dysentery bugs and an ugly eye infection. The eye infection had also been contracted by virtually the whole team of cameramen and soundmen, and some members of a BBC Panorama team who were assembling a feature on the tragedy unfolding from the East Pakistan border. As always they were terrified the news reporters would kill their angle, and they scurried off each day without letting us know where they were filming.

We had more than enough to occupy us in reporting the major refugee story coming in from East Pakistan. I soon became very familiar with the narrow, rutted roads from Calcutta up to the border to film the appalling exodus of men, women and children marching forlornly into India to escape the repression still being wrought by the Yahya Khan regime.

Migrant communities had long been seeping into West Bengal from East Pakistan, but now there was a surge which was overwhelming local sources of food and shelter.

I was deeply impressed by the attempts of the Indian government to provide relief on humanitarian grounds, and emphasized this as much as possible in our reports. The story told itself: we would film at the side of a road as columns of refugees staggered towards us, some dropping at the side of the road to die of hunger and thirst.

We filmed acres of tented refugee camps where people queued remarkably politely for small portions of rice. We ventured into desperately overcrowded hospitals where patients lay on the floor between the beds. Cases of cholera and gastro-enteritis were climbing.

As you neared Calcutta you could see refugees lying in large concrete pipes which were to be used for a local drainage project. I was especially impressed by the West Bengal Indians living in small villages who were giving up portions of their own meagre local food supplies to help the incoming refugees.

For once I felt our news film was of some real value, since the pictures of the crisis were spurring governments to send aid shipments. I was delighted when I found several friends from England among volunteers who had arrived to help. Among them were some foxhunting friends from the Whaddon Chase country, including Jim Cunningham, a keen hunting veterinary surgeon. He was a member of a Roman Catholic aid group. He had performed overseas voluntary work before, but had never mentioned it to anyone at home. Amid the misery it was relief to talk about foxhunting at home over vegetarian curry suppers in Calcutta. Even for Western visitors the crisis was producing some side-effects: restaurants in Calcutta were forced to observe several meat-less days on their menu each week.

After supper we would walk back through the silent streets, becoming all too accustomed to stepping over the sleeping bodies of the poor. Some were said to be paying pathetic sums of protection money to gangs who would otherwise attack them during the night.

One of the Grand Hotel porters said to me quietly one day: 'You reporters are telling the world that we have a cholera outbreak here. That is good, but you should realize that we get one every year anyway. It's not just the refugees that bring it in. It's part of the life here.'

So I sought a filmed interview with Calcutta's most famous inhabitant in the West: Mother Teresa, since sainted by the Catholic Church.

She seemed to be no taller than my waist, and I bent nearly double to hold the microphone, as we talked in her famous sanctuary where I had observed lepers among the needy arriving for attention from Mother Teresa and her team of nuns.

The interview did not go according to plan. The stocky Albanian-born nun spoke excellent English, but told me of her work in a matter-of-fact, unemotional manner.

Then I asked her, almost as an after-thought, whether she thought the huge families common in Calcutta were not a major cause of the poverty problem.

Mother Teresa bristled and said almost sharply: 'It may be so, but we do not kill unborn babies as so many people do in Britain. The use of abortion and birth control to limit families is wrong, and I would always oppose it here and everywhere else – including Britain.'

This was a news report, not an in-depth feature, and I did not pursue the point as far as I would have liked. Over a year later

Mother Teresa made a celebrated visit to London. I was assigned to interview her in a modest Catholic establishment in South London. She remembered me, and gave me a sweet smile, but stiffened when we dealt with the purposes of her visit. She spoke out emphatically against abortion in Britain and other Western countries, expressing the most orthodox of Roman Catholic dogma.

I kept my questions deadpan, and allowed her to expand on her strong beliefs on the 'sins of abortion'. I still fail to understand how anyone who daily witnessed the child beggars of Calcutta, and the poor sleeping in the streets, could preach anti-birth control as the word of a loving God. As a reporter of the world's dustbins of war and want, how could I not harbour serious doubts about religious dogma – even that expressed by a saintly nun whose example in serving the poor has inspired so many?

Chapter Thirteen

HARD TREKKING IN TANZANIA

It was seldom that I rather hoped the ultimate aim of an assignment would not actually be achieved, but this was the case when I was hastily dispatched to East Africa in the spring of 1971.

Idi Amin, an Ugandan army officer, had seized power from the country's ruler Milton Obote on 25 January, and the BBC foreign desk rather hoped that I might gain an interview with Amin or one of his henchmen. Amin had not yet achieved the murderous reputation he attained during his rule but even in these early days there was plenty of room for caution in dealing with him. With a sinking feeling I had read that several Western journalists and media men had been 'detained' by Amin's new regime and I was not keen to join them.

Our BOAC airliner touched down in an ominously quiet Entebbe International airport. The pilot informed us that he would not be taking passengers from Uganda and would be taking off again soon because of the 'emergency'.

Rashly I elected to walk across the runway to the reception hut area to see whether it was feasible for the crew to join me in entering Uganda.

'Be careful, very careful' cooed the plane's air hostesses as I descended on an emergency ladder and trudged across the airfield. There did not appear to be a soul in reception when I pushed open the door, but then a huge Ugandan army sergeant appeared. I did not like the look of the two pistols stuffed into the waistband of his capacious belly.

'Who you?' he demanded in a deep bass voice.

'I am from the BBC and I have been sent to interview the new ruler in Kampala,' I croaked.

'Best you go home,' he said menacingly.

It seemed best not to argue, and this was probably one of the best decisions of my life. I walked briskly back to the aircraft where we decided to disembark at the next destination, Dar Es Salaam, capital of Uganda's neighbour Tanzania.

Tanzania's President Julius Nyerere was recognised in the West as a far-seeing and moderate leader.

The crew and I booked into the best hotel we could find in Dar Es Salaam and I wired the office on the situation. Who should be in Dar Es Salaam than Michael Nicholson, my rival at the Jordan hijackings the previous autumn. He was in a similarly frustrated state, and we decided to explore the Ugandan border in a joint expedition. Much of Tanzania's tourist industry was suspended because of the emergency over the border. A local travel business was only too happy to provide Land Rovers, drivers and guides to a route they knew well, arranging accommodation on the way.

I had more than a few misgivings about the adventure but I could not let Nicholson go ahead on his own. It was my first experience of a joint venture with the highly competitive ITN. We set off on our safari across Tanzania's famous wildlife reserve, Serengeti, where some said they saw prides of lions in the distance, but the only wild creature I saw was a large snake wriggling off the road in front of the Land Rover. We saw Lake Victoria glistening in the African sun.

We decided to press on and spend the first night in the vehicles. It would be less than comfortable, but the guides warned us not to sleep in the open because of the danger from the plentiful snakes in that area. I was more than happy to stay in the Land Rover!

It was a few hours drive to the frontier with Uganda, but we were halted by a unit of the Tanzanian army on border patrol. There were about 30 armed soldiers with a young officer in charge. They made us alight from the vehicles and poked guns at us. Then they ordered us to sit down with our hands on our heads, a development I found somewhat alarming. Fortunately the officer in charge spoke English, albeit it with a strong accent and he demanded to see our passports. I remembered a veteran correspondent's advice on what to do in such situations, and I slipped a large dollar bill into my passport. This was received without comment, but at least the passports were handed back. I explained we were from the BBC and ITN and were merely seeking to tell the world about the revolution over the border in Uganda.

I did not like the fact that some of the younger soldiers were giggling as they were prodding us further with their gun, but I strove to maintain a smiling carefree air, although it was probably not very convincing. I had seen a lot of violence in Vietnam and Cambodia, but African violence seemed all too close-up and personal. After a conflab among the soldiers the officer demanded that we hand over any film that we had taken in the region and the cameramen duly handed over film that was entirely blank, one of the oldest ploys in a TV crew's response to such demands from foreign armies. They waved their arms emphatically and told us to return to Dar Es Salaam, a request I was only too happy to satisfy.

We trundled on for some miles on dusty tracks only to be met by scores of Tanzanians who had fled from their village. Our guides spoke to these people and told us they were running away because they had been bombed by Ugandan aircraft. We were very surprised that Uganda had aeroplanes capable of bombing, but it appeared that it was light aircraft from which someone had dropped by hand a small bomb, or grenade. Primitive stuff, but it was enough to cause alarm. The villagers had never experienced this form of attack, although it did little damage and caused few, if any, casualties. We understood from our guides that many of the villagers had slept in the open, and several had been killed by snake bites. We filmed the village and its panicking inhabitants. It seemed that Idi Amin was trying to spread alarm in neighbouring Tanzania because he believed that Milton Obote was seeking to gain sanctuary there. Obote later did indeed find refuge in Tanzania, followed by thousands of refugees fleeing Idi Amin's appallingly brutal regime in which many people were killed outright or 'disappeared'.

Following fighting along the border with Tanzania between Amin's troops and rebel Ugandans, the Tanzanian ruler Nyerere sent an army into Uganda in support of the rebels, driving Amin out of office and into exile in 1979.

I greatly admire the correspondents who cover conflicts in Africa, such as those in the Congo. They face extreme danger from the sort of close-up aggression which I encountered in only a minor form.

ITN's sound camera broke down when we were filming the bombing aftermath and, my crew gallantly lent them our spare camera which did not have a sound system but could be accompanied by a taped commentary. This was typical of the camaraderie which crews in trouble spots exhibit, and it is far more common in war zones than in many other walks of journalism. I enjoyed Michael Nicholson's company on this trip, and he thoroughly deserved the plaudits he received in his long and arduous career. Very sadly he died aged 79 in 2016.

On the way back to Dar Es Salaam we spent a night at an African village used to putting up tourists. Ah the bliss of a bucket and rope shower accompanied by the laughter of the maidens of the village, and a good night's sleep under mosquito nets, even though I found a menacing scorpion in my bed.

The cheerfulness and hospitality of the villagers was typical of many Africans I have met. The dry heat and the beautiful terrain emphasised why so many Europeans have been happy to make their homes in Africa for life, despite the risks of tribal war.

My Tanzanian footage was well used on the BBC 2 half-hour news channel but such is the way of TV news that I received a far warmer response from the BBC foreign desk for an interview I gained in Dar Es Salaam with a minister from war-torn Somalia who had fled into the Tanzanian capital. I learned of his presence from a small shortwave radio I carried everywhere to learn vital local news which was not otherwise available to a correspondent on the hoof.

London was disposed to keep me idly waiting in East Africa for the possibility of interviewing Milton Obote, but he never appeared while I was there. I must confess I spent the time in the casino in Nairobi before happily flying home.

If I did not appear in anything like a heroic mould in this episode, it was because my aim always was to get into dangerous spots only if necessary to obtain the story on film, and then get the crew out as swiftly and safely as possible. There were no medals for being a 'missing' foreign correspondent.

Sometimes senior executives would urge correspondents 'not to take risks', an entirely impossible request if the story was in a war theatre, but I could see that no-one in the studio would welcome the paperwork involved in the death of a reporter.

Chapter Fourteen

APPOINTMENT WITH GADDAFI

My last overseas assignment for the BBC, in February 1973, looked most unpromising, but went surprisingly well. On 21 February Libyan Arab Airlines flight 114 was making a routine trip from Tripoli to Cairo with 108 civilian passengers and five crew on board. It became lost over the Sinai Peninsular through a combination of bad luck and muddle. It was hit by a sandstorm which caused the crew to rely on instrument navigation before landing at Cairo, and the plane entered Israeli-controlled airspace..

The crew thought they were close to Cairo and started the descent, but they were intercepted by two Israeli Airforce Phantom jet fighters whose pilots reportedly tried to communicate with the Libyan crew visually by signalling with their hands, and dipping their wings, but the Libyan pilot continued his course – and disastrously, the Israeli fighters attacked with cannon bursts causing the airliner to crash to the desert below. Altogether 108 people died in the burning wreckage.

By any standard the Libyans had cause to be desperately shocked and angered by the tragedy which they saw as unprovoked brutal atrocity. It was a product of the appalling level of tension in the Middle East at that time. President Muammar Gaddafi, the eccentric ruler of Libya, vowed to attack Israel head on, but he was persuaded not to engage in war by the Egyptians who had their own plans for a combined strike which was to become the Yom Kippur War. Later the Israeli defence minister, Moshe Dayan, admitted the crash was an 'error of judgement' and Israel eventually paid some compensation to families of the bereaved. For now, tempers were boiling over in Libya to be expressed in fury by mobs in the streets.

For once the BBC Foreign Desk was immediately on the ball, assigning me to take a film crew to Libya to film the riots erupting in response to the aircrash, and the mourning of the bereaved. It was recognised that my chances of getting into the country were thin. Normally it took days to acquire a visa to visit Libya but we could not wait.

What a change from so many other BBC assignments where lack of funds caused us to wait too long before sending a crew, enabling ITN and others to get their first.

Someone in the Newsroom advised me to put 100 dollars in my passport when I presented it at Tripoli airport, but I was well used to this ploy, and recognised all too well that it could give a Libyan official a chance to charge me with attempted bribery. I could be assigned to one of the truly horrible Libyan jails which Gaddafi reserved for those he deemed to be out of order.

This time I thought I would try an appeal to the Libyans' sense of outrage by promising them to tell the world the terrible suffering perpetrated on their citizens.

All the way during the flight from London to Tripoli I rehearsed my little speech, but I had severe doubts about the outcome, and hoped the worst that would befall us would be a refusal to enter the country. I had suffered in Arab countries previously from the deep suspicions many had when a large cine camera was produced.

At Tripoli airport customs barrier I gave it all I had, histrionically, to stress my sincere concern about the loss of lives, and promised that no-one was better fitted than the BBC to make sure that the world knew of the disaster in the dramatic film reports we would send.

To my surprise we were ushered in cordially without the need to produce visas. Very soon we were lodged in a comfortable hotel normally used by VIPs, but now virtually empty. The most astonishing feature was the absence of the world's media. Where was ITN? I was sure Michael Nicholson would pop out of the woodwork any minute.

We hurried out to film flag-waving demonstrations by smallish crowds of protesters against Israel. Two security minders suddenly attached themselves to us, but they were merely holding a watching brief, and did not interfere. One of them spoke passable English and advised me a mass funeral was to be held in Tripoli next day.

I managed to get a phone call through to BBC London advising them that so far we seemed to have the story on our own, but I could not see this lasting long. I had left a few documents in a carefully arranged position on the dressing table in my hotel room. When I came back to the room after a tolerable supper in a virtually empty dining room, the papers were in a different position and someone had left my typewriter case unzipped, whereas I had left it done up. As I expected we were under some form of surveillance, however mild at this stage. It did not prepare me for what was to come.

In the dead of night I suddenly awoke to find four or five white robed and turbaned figures looming over me. A bearded face a few inches from mine said: 'Wake up Mr Clayton. We have something for you.' I sat bolt upright, but before I could protest, the intruders thrust under my face large grainy film prints of faces maimed with terrible injuries. They were lying in open coffins. A hideous sheaf of about 40 such prints was presented for my inspection. It was like a living nightmare.

'Send these immediately to the BBC, the spokesman demanded. 'We want everyone to see the faces of those who died in the aircraft shot down by the Israelis.

It seemed best not to point out that I had no electronic means of sending pictures instantly to the BBC, or anywhere else. We were not yet in the age of setting up satellite connections. Our film would only reach the TV screens of Britain after being transported manually across many miles with huge risk of being lost or damaged on the way.

Gathering what composure I could manage I urged the visiting spooks to leave the prints with me and said I would do my very best to see that they were broadcast.

I mentally crossed my fingers that we would be out of the country before lack of such pictures on TV was reported by the Libyan embassy in London. I did not press the point that these pictures were too horrific to broadcast in any circumstance.

The main streets of Tripoli were packed with mourners and angry protesters next morning. There was plenty to film as a build-up to the mass burial about to take place. A long line of open lorries began to appear. Plain wooden coffins were loaded onto each one.

We were not exactly welcome among the crowds, but no-one interfered with our filming. At this time of year Libya was quite chilly, but dust was being kicked up by the crowds. The mob probably regarded our presence as one more sign of the importance of the occasion. Suddenly the hubbub swelled into a roar of shouting.

'My God. It's Gaddafi. We'd better get to him quickly.' I shouted to the crew. Libya's ruler dressed in full Arab garb was escorted among the crowd by up to a dozen heavily-armed minders.

We pushed our way to the group as they stood on the pavement among throngs of people. The camera was rolling, and I pushed my mike towards Gaddafi who seemed not at all averse to say something. He was adept at capturing the world's attention with inflammatory words. Presumably he would launch into a tirade against the infidel Israelis.

Alas, some people in the crowd began firing guns into the air, worryingly near the Gaddafi group. He ducked to the ground, his escort closed around him and hurriedly ushered him from the scene. The risk of assassination was clearly an over-riding priority. Gaddafi was hustled from the scene by his guards, some of whom brandished rifle butts threateningly at me. I decided to apply for an interview later, and we gave our attention to the increasingly chaotic funeral scene.

Amid further gunshots the lorries began to roll forward, very slowly edging their way through the chanting crowds who now spilled across the road. There seemed to be no one in control, so the crew and I scrambled aboard the tail of one of the lorries.

We sat on some coffins, and took marvellous shots of the uproar all around us as the rough and ready cortege moved forward a little faster. We alighted when the lorries reached a large flat muddy area outside the city where rows of holes for the coffins had been dug. Our gamble had come off; no-one had taken the slightest notice of our position on a lorry. The graves were crisscrossed with loose planks to give the coffin-bearers access.

This seemed the best moment for me to try a piece to camera. To give it maximum effect I strode onto one of the planks across a grave, and turned to face the camera. Alas, my feet were muddy and I fell backwards into the grave on top of a coffin. There was a nasty splintering sound, but fortunately the lid did not break open. Amazingly my performance was totally ignored by the growing number of coffin bearers seething over the graveyard.

Unhurt but chastened I clambered out of the hole, and balanced on the plank again to perform a slightly distraught piece to camera. Then I repeated it in calmer fashion, to provide an alternative for the cutting room.

The cameraman assured me he was not actually filming when I fell, but I resolved to include a note with my script, warning the studio not to include my less than reverent antics over a grave. The morning had produced a highly impact-full film report.

We had another extraordinary piece of luck at Tripoli airport. The next scheduled flight to London was late, with the film changing flights at Rome Airport, a notorious spot for film consignments to get lost. We planned to let the sound man travel back to London carrying the precious film as hand luggage while the camera man and I remained in Tripoli in the hope of gaining the Gaddafi interview, with me acting as interviewer and sound man.

Good fortune erupted when we met an American crew also waiting at the airport to ship their film. We had missed seeing them at the funeral, perhaps because they did not travel on one of the lorries.

They advised us they were considering chartering a small private plane to go to Rome with their film and offered us a seat if we would share the cost. We did a deal whereby we paid our half the charter on my BBC-issued American Express card.

Back at the hotel I managed to call a Libyan government press officer who assured me there was no chance of the President giving me an interview. He was making statements to the world through the press office and had returned to a tented palace far out in the desert. By sheer good fortune our film arrived in London for the evening bulletins that very day. We received a glowing 'hero-gram' from London praising the film, and advising us they were offsetting the cost of the air charter from the numerous payments made by American and other TV stations across the world.

For once everything had gone incredibly well, a welcome contrast to the many occasions when a hasty dash abroad for a film story resulted in abject failure, through circumstances beyond the correspondent's control.

The Libyan story, quickly forgotten in a surge of world news, was my last overseas assignment before I handed in my notice to leave BBC News to accept an offer to start an entirely new life as the Editor of *Horse and Hound* magazine, the weekly bible of the horse world which I read avidly, and to which I often contributed.

It seemed time to try 'good news' journalism where the readers actually welcomed everything one published, as contrasted by the 'bad news' rewards of general news coverage which I had been engaged in since the age of 16, nearly 25 years.

Derek Amoore, Editor of BBC TV News, was most annoyed to receive my letter of notice. He told me he has just decided to appoint me as the BBC's Home Affairs Correspondent, a new post at the time.

I reflected that Amoore had not bothered to discuss the terms with me, nor to appreciate the huge change entailed in my working life by taking me off reporting abroad. I knew that a Home Affairs Correspondent would spend much of his time hanging about the press rooms of the Home Office and Scotland Yard. This did not appeal to me one whit. I had experience of both for short terms as a newspaper reporter and was glad to be relieved of these duties.

Amoore gruffly insisted I should work out my 3 months notice with a stint as a member of the BBC's Parliamentary team in the House of Commons. They were a most congenial group led by Peter Hardiman Scott, and I enjoyed my last few weeks as a BBC staff man.

Somewhat to my surprise, Amoore was warmly appreciative of my work as a TV correspondent in his words at my farewell party in the news room.

BBC producers still used me on occasion after I left the staff.

During my early years as Editor of *Horse and Hound*, I did regular stints as a presenter with John Timpson on the prestigious Today programme on Radio 4. There were big news stories running at the time: Edward Heath's disastrous battle with the miners, resulting in a dreadful 3 day week and fuel shortages for Britain; the Watergate affair which ended President Nixon's tenure in the White House; and quite a lot of mayhem on Britain's roads and airways, suffering from lack of investment and infrastructure.

It was arduous work, arriving at Broadcasting House in the early hours of the morning to pre-record some interviews and write the links one would voice in the live programme from 6.30 to 9 am. Then, after a dreadful cup of BBC coffee, I would start my day's work at *Horse and Hound* at our offices in High Holborn.

For each Today session I was paid the princely sum of £30, less a commission to my agent, Bagenal Harvey. It was a far cry from the huge sums paid to presenters on radio and TV today, even taking into account the inflationary years of the 1980s and 90s.

I was amused that none of my staff at *Horse and Hound* seemed to be aware of my other commitment for some months, until my Deputy Editor Hugh Condry asked casually one morning; 'Was that you I heard on my car radio the other morning?'

I assured him that it was, but my time on Today was about to end unceremoniously. The regular requests for my time 3 days a week on the programme simply dried up. I was puzzled by this and naively assumed that a producer would at least have advised me that they required my services no more and even perhaps expressed thanks.

My agent assured me it was much in line with the BBC's usual handling of freelancers. I have read accounts of well-known broadcasters being suddenly deprived of their regular slots without any warning. However, with the BBC, when one door closes another soon opens. I was invited to take part in Radio 4's Any Questions programme, one of the long-standing success stories of the airwaves.

In this role I appeared as the Editor of *Horse and Hound*, expected to express views on rural matters, and sometimes to defend foxhunting in noisy exchanges.

The chairman of the panel, David Jacobs, had made his name on Juke Box Jury. He was a smooth operator and was a pleasant companion on our trips to far-flung parts of the British Isles to dilate on the topics of the day in live broadcasts on a Friday evening. My appearances were noted with approbation by my new employers at *Horse and Hound*, the board of IPC Magazines, who regarded these sessions as welcome publicity for the magazine. On the Any Questions programme, I found myself arguing political and economic issues with some of the sharpest minds from the House of Commons. Fortunately my recent visits as a war correspondent to so many trouble spots added some weight to my pronouncements on international issues, even if I could not pretend to be a pundit of great renown.

I particularly enjoyed sparring with Richard Marsh, Labour's Transport Minister, and with the Labour MP who never quite made it to become Prime Minister Neil Kinnock. I much enjoyed the company of the urbane Roy Jenkins at the traditional suppers enjoyed by the panel before each programme.

The most exciting Any Questions experience erupted in Northern Ireland. The women of Londonderry's republican Bogside rushed onto the platform and seized the microphone to stop the broadcast after a series of especially outspoken attacks on the IRA by the tough-speaking journalist Woodrow Wyatt. BBC engineers cut us off the air and played bland music instead. Meanwhile, after police had restored order, we recorded a further session of further questions and answers which made a full programme to be broadcast as the repeat next day.

EPILOGUE

During my stint as Deputy News Editor of the *Evening Standard* in the early 1960s I sought solace from the gruelling indoor regime by resuming horse riding and hunting, the joys of my childhood and teens in Dorset and Hampshire.

From the age of eight I had gained valuable experience by working at weekends in local riding schools before saving up to buy an unbroken New Forest pony for £12, delivering newspapers before school to pay for his keep. I sold him to buy a larger pony which I broke in and rode for several years until I rapidly outgrew ponies.

Although chronically short of spare cash, I kept up my riding on hireling horses as often as possible during my early years in newspapers.

Whilst working on the *Evening Standard*, thanks to a legacy from a great-uncle who hunted in Essex, I bought my own horse, the first of many, to follow regularly the Old Surrey and Burstow Foxhounds whose country was within easy reach from my home in Blackheath. This friendly and welcoming Hunt, not yet hit by the M25 and other south east urbanization, fanned the flame of a passion which has remained for the rest of my life.

In order to pay for my horsemanship which became increasingly addictive, I began freelancing for *Horse and Hound* and *The Field*, and in 1967 I completed my first book, *A Hunting We Will Go*, followed since by over 20 more books on equestrianism and hunting.

I assumed it was to discuss future freelance articles that Walter Case, veteran Editor of *Horse and Hound*, invited me to lunch at the

Reform Club in late 1972. To my amazement he urged me to apply for his position, as he was being compulsorily retired the following year on reaching 65. I heard a voice say 'Yes', and somewhat to my horror realized it was mine. It was one of many impulsive decisions, but this was one I would never regret.

I discovered later that my name had been impressed on Walter Case as his successor, by Dorian Williams, the BBC's illustrious TV equestrian commentator, who had become a close friend and confidante since I hunted with him in his other role as Joint Master of the Whaddon Chase. Dorian was a main contributor to *Horse and Hound* as anonymous author of a weekly column called 'Off The Bit', until his untimely death aged 72 in 1985 robbed the horse world of one of its greatest talents as a broadcaster and writer. I was also warmly recommended by another friend, Capt. Ronnie Wallace, legendary leader of the foxhunting world as Chairman of the Masters of Foxhounds Association.

I spent the next 26 years as Editor, and later Editor-in-Chief, of *Horse and Hound*, and later *Country Life*, both owned by IPC, Europe's largest magazine publishers. In late 1973 I left the BBC to become Associated Editor of *Horse and Hound* before taking on the editorship at the end of the year.

I found myself transported back in time to *New Milton Advertiser* production, because *Horse and Hound* was at that time run economically as a weekly newspaper, in monochrome only on cheap paper. It was highly profitable, with a circulation of just below 70,000 per week. Walter Case had ensured it remained the 'must-have' weekly publication for everyone involved in riding, hunting and amateur race riding.

With a staff of only six, including my secretary, I soon found myself a hands-on Editor with a busy working week – and for nearly two years I was still engaged in freelance broadcasting, appearing two to three days per week as co-presenter of BBC Radio 4's morning news programme 'Today'.

I soon discovered that large publishing houses engaged entirely different printers to suit each of their publications. While the women's magazine group, and many other titles in specialist fields, were liberally illustrated in colour, and produced on shiny, coated paper, *Horse and Hound* was a 'cash cow' thriving on very plain fare in the production process.

Horse and Hound's production schedule was by no means easy to operate: from Monday to Wednesday the reports which made up most of the magazine, much of it hand-written and sent in by post from freelances of highly varied writing skills, were sub-edited in the office; many needed completely re-writing on a series of ancient typewriters. A messenger service transported the edited copy every day to a small printing works in far off Stratford, East London, where it was set in columns of lead type.

These were 'pulled up', printed in long columns on newsprint, and sent back to the office in High Holborn. The staff then cut and pasted these paper columns into page sheets, leaving spaces for pictures and headings, and they were sent back to the print works to be 'made up'. Page proofs came back from the printers each day, but late news pages still had to be made up on Thursday nights. Pictures had to be sent earlier in the week to a separate processor to be made into photographic 'blocks' which were sent to the printer. There was little opportunity for including a 'late' picture.

Every Thursday evening, at the end of a long day in the office, the editorial staff drove their own cars through heavy traffic to the small, noisy printing works in Stratford. Publishing conglomerates, such as IPC, appointed the printer they considered most suitable and economical for each of their large portfolios of magazines. *Horse and Hound* survived and flourished on a basic, frugal, printing system suitable for a weekly black and white newspaper, and thereby earned handsome profits, at that time making a surplus on its cover price, so that virtually all the revenue from advertising was sheer profit.

Walter Case had ceased to go to the printers regularly, but I resolved never to miss this onerous outing. It was the precious window in which as Editor I could make late adjustments to the magazine, see all the pages before the issue 'went away', and make late decisions. Visiting the Stratford printing works carried me back nostalgically to my start in journalism. There was the same somewhat sweaty atmosphere in the print room, the never-forgotten smell of printing ink and hot lead in the pots attached to the elderly type-setting machines.

As editorial staff on *Horse and Hound* we were strictly not allowed to touch anything on the 'stone', the bench on which the page make-up took place, but we stood next to the chief compositors as they placed the type in the metal forms, making up the pages. An ability to read metal type upside down became second nature to a 'stone sub-editor', one who worked with printers. The busy East London printing staff were cheerfully cooperative, but Horse and Hound was just one of their contracts, and they worked under inexorable deadlines.

This labour-intensive process of production worked remarkably well, but it was incredibly laborious compared with today's digital make-up in virtually noiseless offices. There were so many possibilities of interruptions in the lengthy chains of communication of the magazine's content, and yet the system rarely failed. Some correspondents used British Rail's quaint parcel service to send in their reports, which added to the risks of non-arrival. In dire circumstances my secretary took copy over the phone on a head-set, but in the main the dear old weekly, founded in 1884, relied on the devotion of its staff to cope with antiquated systems already overtaken by many overseas printers.

Even within the frugal editorial budget, it was obvious there would be ample room for updating the magazine's presentation and content, although from the start I was cautious about introducing abrupt changes. The readership was highly conservative; most horsemen had grown up with *Horse and Hound*, and would strongly resent a sudden new direction in their weekly bible. It seemed best to endeavour to do better the things which the readers already liked.

With such a small staff, I would have to be a hands-on working Editor at full throttle if we were to carry out the changes in the magazine I knew were needed. Founded in 1884, *Horse and Hound* still had a whiff of Victorian England, although it had in the early postwar years abandoned a *Times*-style front page of tomb-stone columns of advertisements, for a monochrome picture often with no heading referring to the magazine's content. Walter Case was a canny handler of the budget, keeping well within a very modest page rate. He had no ambition to be one of those editors who achieve success by increasing their staff and freelance contributions, even if it meant routinely under-spending the budget. He proudly showed me a dusty file in a cupboard, containing manuscripts of what he described as 'articles', which I took to mean 'features'.

'They're useful to slip into the magazine when you have spare space. You don't have to pay for them until you use them. Very good when the weather's bad, and there's no racing and hunting,' he told me.

'Really?' I replied, thinking of the planned layouts and schedules for the feature pages of the newspapers on which I had worked. One innovation I determined to achieve immediately was a weekly editorial meeting, when the staff and I would review the last edition, and decide on the next. Les Carpenter, chairman of IPC, had tentatively suggested during an inaugural interview that 'the title does need a bit of brushing up; we'd expect you to bring it up to date, but do be careful; no need to rush it. Remember the old magazine is profitable, and plenty seem to like it as it is.'

Walter Case commissioned very few pictures, except those needed to accompany horse show reports. Many useful pictures arrived non-commissioned, and would only be paid for if used to fill corners in the make-up. He was proud of never publishing a picture of any rider falling off the horse.

'They don't like to dwell on that too much,' he said. But I knew all too well that falls are an inevitable accompaniment to riding, and most riders are extremely interested to see how someone else became parted from the saddle. I vowed I would certainly be breaking this taboo, although I was well aware the riding fraternity would certainly not enjoy a fall picture in which the horse was injured.

I liked the first-floor High Holborn office where the magazine was housed when I first became Editor. It was somewhat dark, even dingy, but it had lofty ceilings, and large windows overlooking the busy London street. It was very handy for lunch in the West End or the Strand.

Editors each had a key to use a special washroom, and twice a day a homely lady in a pinafore arrived in my office with tea, coffee and cup cakes. There was a rumour that a major move was pending; all IPC magazines were to be shifted from offices scattered all over central London to King's Reach Tower, a huge tower block on the South Bank of the Thames near Blackfriars Bridge. I shrugged and took little notice, but the move when it came made a fundamental change to the rest of my life in full employment. There would be no more special washrooms for Editors, and vending machines on landings would soon replace the friendly ladies with my tray. Open plan offices became the rule, and eventually the building was wired up for a massive switch-over to digital publishing processes.

I had a firm conviction, however arrogant, that I could edit *Horse and Hound* better than anyone else available in the England of 1974, but I was soon to realise that there were magazine techniques which I badly needed to learn, and polish. I was much helped when I joined the British Society of Magazine Editors, attended seminars and lectures, and made friends with other Editors, eventually chairing the Society myself.

I continued to run *Horse and Hound* basically as a weekly newspaper, but by stages introduced more modern make-up, far more pictures and features, and eventually full colour production. The magazine achieved a circulation of 96,000 per week in the late 1970s, but increasing specialization in the horse world, served by new niche monthly magazines, had some adverse effect on *Horse and Hound*'s all-round appeal, and the circulation sank below 90,000 before I retired, although profitability increased through colour advertising, and it remains to this day Britain's premier equestrian magazine.

I decided from the start that the Editor's office would not be a prison: I badly needed to explore the equestrian and hunting world, to become far closer to my readership. Somehow I would have to be a bridge between the old equestrian establishment, dominated by the Army, and the growing numbers of newcomers to the riding and hunting world, some of them grammar school products like myself.

The great sporting Editors of the 19th century, Robert Smith Surtees, also a brilliant comic novelist, and Charles James Apperley, known as 'Nimrod', both travelled the British Isles as hunting correspondents, producing copy eagerly read in the journals they edited in London. Privately, I was sure I could do the same, and I shall never cease to be grateful to Francis King and his management colleagues that they did not become alarmed when the new Editor was regularly absent from the office to report from the hunting field for his new weekly column 'Foxford's Hunting Diary', named after my prized hunter.

However, I had carefully noted the remarks of Ron Phillips, a shrewd main board director of IPC Magazines, when he interviewed me for the Editor's job: 'We don't care whether you never come to the office at all, so long as you turn out the title on time, and it puts on circulation. You won't of course be able to do that without coming into the office a great deal. We had to dispense with a yachting magazine Editor who was always out of the office when it mattered; he blamed it on the tides which always seemed to be against him when he wanted to come into land.'

My passion for riding to hounds was the most pressing motive which made the Editor's seat at *Horse and Hound* the prize I could not resist, but I looked forward with warm enthusiasm to sharing my love of horses and horse sports with the readership. A successful specialist magazine editorship involves a close, warming dialogue with others who share your own pleasures. I had a lot of fun, and some shocks, through editing the readers' letters column personally for most of my years in the chair.

Improving and updating *Horse and Hound* was a challenge. We needed to attract more young readers, without offending the older generation of loyal subscribers, and the sheer slog of bringing the magazine out efficiently every week often put a brake on the joys of riding far away from London. However, I freely confess that I did manage to hunt with nearly every pack of foxhounds, plus staghounds, harriers and draghounds, throughout the British Isles. Over the next two decades I had a loyal long-serving staff I liked very much, who treated me with respect and gave full co-operation. I noted that some magazine editors were inclined to drink often with their staff in local pubs, but I had been warned by Ronnie Hyde at the *Evening Standard* not to engage in that form of socialising, if only because of its unfairness to those members of the staff who do not frequent bars.

Every young journalist should receive sound training as a general news reporter and/or sub-editor before specialising in the field which commands your genuine enthusiasm. A university or college degree in journalism is not enough; practical experience is essential. Only the fortunate few gain the Editor's chair in the publication of their choice.

Equestrianism and hunting are world-wide sports. This ensured that *Horse and Hound* offered ample opportunities for travel which I relished. My weekly hunting column, Foxford's Hunting Diary, ensured that I rode with Hunts throughout Ireland, and all down the eastern seaboard of North America, from Canada, where I hunted in a snow storm; down to Virginia, Georgia and Alabama. I judged a special hunter class at Canada's Royal Winter Fair in Toronto, and in the US I made great friends with the leaders of foxhunting, which led to my being asked twice to address the American Masters of Foxhounds Association in New York. American and Canadian hunting people were warm and generous hosts. I made particular friends with Ben Hardaway, the charismatic, and highly amusing Master and huntsman of the Midland Hunt in Georgia. I rode after his hounds in his extraordinary Alabama country of marshland and coarse grass, inhabited by poisonous snakes. We went night hunting for opossum in the trees above us, and I was a mounted judge of Ben's extraordinary hound competition: hounds wore numbers daubed on their sides, and as many as 50 couple pursued foxes under one huntsman. We judges were supposed to pick out the individual hounds performing best, a tall order. Hounds hunted coyotes as well as foxes, and the former produced especially long and arduous runs from which they invariably escaped.

In Florida I hunted in intense heat with the Live Oak pack owned and hunted by Marty and Daphne Wood in the Panhandle, an extraordinary area of tree plantations and swampland where alligators and snakes lurked.

I instituted readers' trips to major overseas equestrian events. This took us to world championships in Kentucky USA, to Gawler in Australia, and to European championships in Luhmuhlen, Germany, and to Pratoni in North Italy. These excursions helped promote overseas readerships and advertising, and gave the magazine much added prestige in the UK. They were all fully booked by our enthusiastic readership who enjoyed exotic holidays in addition, such as a remarkable visit to Bali on the way home from Australia.

On most of my overseas hunting trips I was accompanied by Jim Meads who was a life-long specialist in the sport, a photographer who followed on foot the mounted followers and hounds many miles across country to gain his pictures.

In the UK I was fortunate to work in support of the magazine industry. I served as Chairman of the British Society of Magazine Editors which held monthly luncheons where major figures in the industry, such as Rupert Murdoch and Robert Maxwell, were among our speakers. There was also a stint as the magazine industry's representative on the newly launched Press Complaints Commission. It was good to work with leading Fleet Street figures in dealing with such thorny issues as the accusations that the press invaded Princess Diana's privacy during and after her divorce from Prince Charles. We were able to point out to our lay chairman, Lord McGregor, that the Princess herself made approaches to certain pressmen to propagate her own version of her disastrous marriage.

Within IPC I was the first chairman of our Editorial Focus Group which liaised between the journalistic staff and the management on many issues. All this led to my eventual appointment to the IPC Board of Directors and I was also Editor-in-Chief of *Country Life* and *The Field* for the last three years of my 24 years with the company. I cannot pretend that I enjoyed this as much as the role of Editor, but it gave me a considerable insight into the magazine industry: highly competitive, prone to industrial problems at that time, and struggling with the opportunities and drawbacks of the new technology in printing which cut costs, but ultimately ensured that many young people did not read newspapers or magazines in print, but relied entirely on their on-line sources, giving rise to the highly dubious role of social media.

I feel extremely fortunate in working in print publications during the final years before the on-line revolution, and the aftermath of today's Covid pandemic where editors are forced to produce magazines with their staff working mainly online at home. I admire the work that is being produced under these conditions, but I bless my good fortune in being among the generation who worked with staff attending the office every day where they worked as teams under the eye of the Editor.

Since I retired from staff journalism in 1997 I served for five years as Chairman of the British Horse Society, as chairman of my local Hunt, the Cottesmore, and as a regional chairman of the Countryside Alliance, while at the same time continuing freelance writing and broadcasting. Somehow I wrote over 20 books on equestrian and hunting topics.

It may be politics, it may be golf, fretwork or gardening, but the journalist who has knowledge and experience in a specialist field they love is the one most likely to claim at the end of a long life: 'I never wanted to retire – and I never did.'

My career highlight is best summed up in the sporting verse which *Horse and Hound* carried with its front page masthead, and which I preserved throughout my Editorship. It is an excerpt, which gave the magazine its title, from a poem called *The Good Grey Mare* by the Victorian sporting writer G.J. Whyte-Melville: 'I freely admit that the best of my fun, I owe it horse and hound.'

Now in my eighties, the verse in full is appropriate to my entire career in journalism, a steed which has carried me through many joys and perils. Marilyn Clayton, my beautiful wife for the past 34 years, has ensured, through her love and support, the private happiness and peace of mind which sometimes eluded me in early years.

I have lived my life – I have nearly done –
I have played the game all round;
But I freely admit that the best of my fun
I owe it to horse and hound.
With a hopeful heart, and a conscience clear,
I can laugh in your face, Black Care;
Though you're hovering near, there's no room for you here,
On the back of my good grey mare.

Further Merlin Unwin Books publications
by Michael Clayton

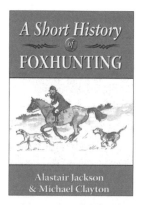

The Ride of My Life
Michael Clayton

A Short History of Foxhunting
Alastair Jackson & Michael Clayton

www.merlinunwin.co.uk